SOTHEBY'S

ART AT AUCTION

The Art Market Review 1994–95

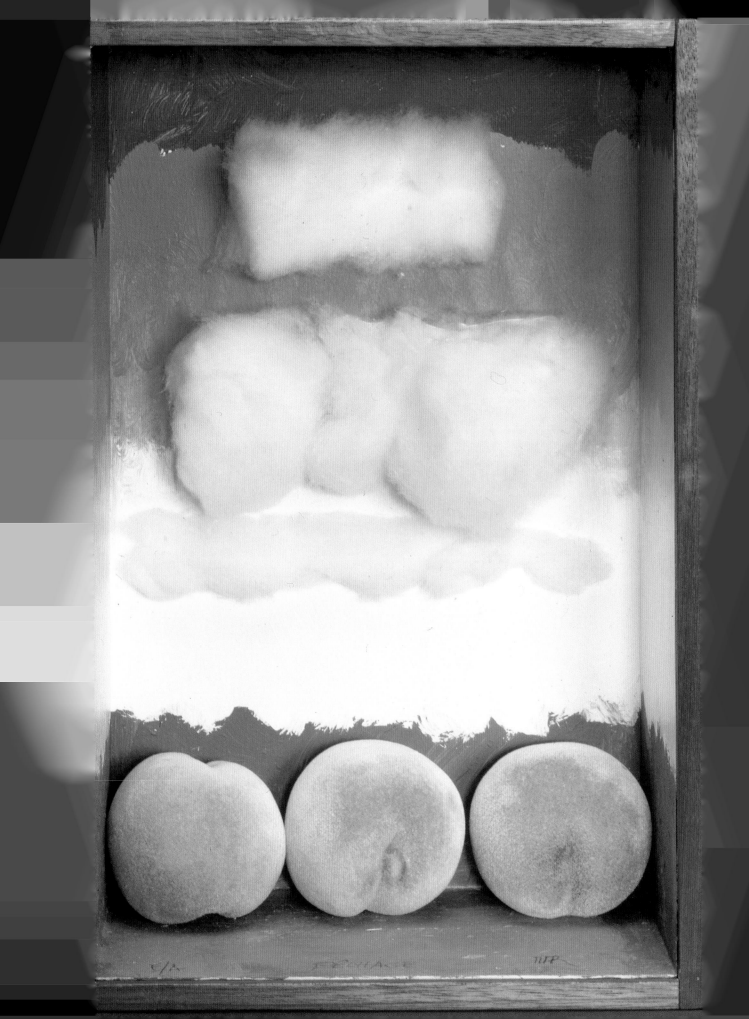

SOTHEBY'S

ART AT AUCTION

The Art Market Review 1994–95

CONRAN OCTOPUS

First published in 1995 by
Conran Octopus Limited
37 Shelton Street
London WC2H 9HN

British Library Cataloguing in Publication Data
A catalogue record for this book is available from the
British Library

ISBN 1 85029 7185

Printed in Germany by Mohndruck, Gütersloh

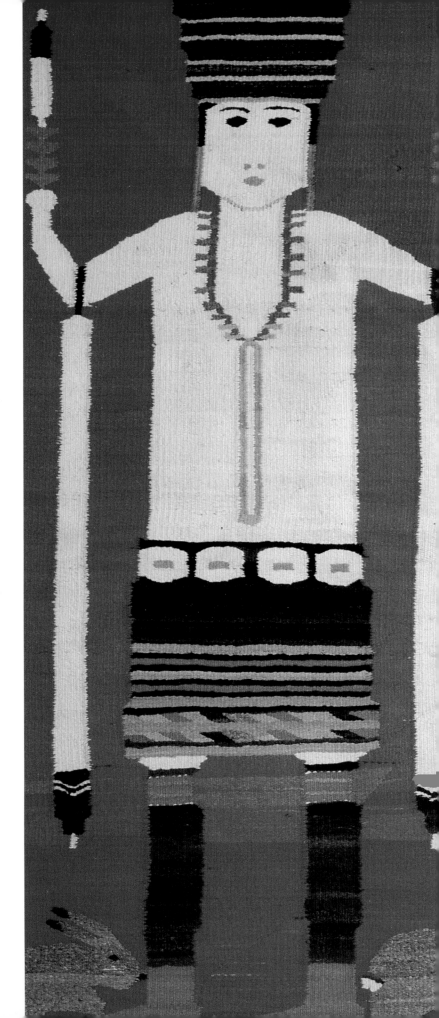

ENDPAPERS: AFTER JOOST HARTGERS AND AFTER
LAURENS BLOCK
New Amsterdam 1626 and New Amsterdam 1650: Two Paintings (detail)
c.1925–35, OIL ON CANVAS, the first: 50.8 x 76.2cm (20 x 30in),
the second: 25.4 x 76.2cm (10 x 30in)
New York $3,737 (£2,354). 29.I.95
From the Collection of The New-York Historical Society

PAGE 1: **An American parrot on latticinio ground weight**
NINETEENTH CENTURY, diameter 7.1cm (2¹³⁄₁₆in)
New York $34,500 (£22,080). 18.I.95
From the Collection of The New-York Historical Society

PAGE 2: MAN RAY
Pêchage
SIGNED WITH INITIALS, TITLED AND NUMBERED E/A,
36 x 24 x 11.6cm (14½ x 9½ x 4½in)
London £47,700 ($75,843). 23.III.95
From the Estate of Juliet Man Ray, the Man Ray Trust and
the Family of Juliet Man Ray

PAGES 4–5: **A Navajo pictorial rug (detail)**
273 x 188cm (107½ x 74in)
New York $13,800 (£8,418). 21.X.94
From the Estate of Sara Jean Christie

CONTENTS

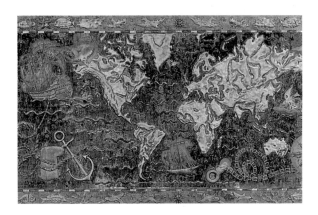

CONTRIBUTORS

FIONA BIDDULPH became a writer and television director specializing in the fine and decorative arts after studying at the Courtauld Institute. She has written numerous articles for newspapers and periodicals including the *Independent*, *The Art Newspaper*, the *Antique Collector* and *World of Interiors*. She has worked as a director on the Channel 4 television series *For Love or Money*. In 1994 Phaidon published her second book, *Metropolitain: A Portrait of Paris*, co-authored with the photographer Matthew Weinreb.

JOHN D. BLOCK is Executive Vice President and member of the Board of Directors of Sotheby's North and South America. In this role he oversees all sales of jewellery, clocks and watches, silver, Russian works of art and objects of vertu. He has supervised every Sotheby's jewellery auction since 1981, including the Collection of Annie-Laurie Aitken, as well as jewellery from the estates of Phyllis E. Dillon, Amelia Peabody, Mrs Benson Ford, Flora Whitney Miller, Clare Boothe Luce, Andy Warhol, Lydia Morrison, Ava Gardner, Paulette Goddard, Mrs Jack L. Warner, Thora Ronalds McElroy and Mrs Harry Winston. Mr Block is a graduate of Princeton University.

ISABEL BOUCHER started her career as a practising archaeologist and is now a freelance journalist writing on subjects as diverse as the latest technological advances in the art world and on archaeology. She has worked on the editorial staff of *The Burlington Magazine* and *Apollo* and, until recently, was Deputy Editor of *The Art Newspaper*.

DIANA D. BROOKS is President and Chief Executive Officer of Sotheby's Holdings, Inc., a position held since April 1994. She joined the firm in 1979 and in 1993 was appointed President and Chief Executive Officer of Sotheby's Worldwide Auction Operations. In both capacities she is closely involved with all major sales held by the company and has made a vital contribution to both the co-ordination and the integration of Sotheby's operations throughout the world.

DR BRUNA CARUSO CHERUBINI lives in Venice where she works as a licensed guide. A specialist in art history and the history of Venice, she has collaborated with the Superintendency of Art and the Municipality of Venice to catalogue works of art and lead thematic guided tours around the galleries and museums of Venice. She has contributed to the *Everyman Guide to Venice* (1993) and to *Churches of Venice* (1993), published by Electa.

RICHARD CORK is the Chief Art Critic of *The Times* and the Henry Moore Senior Research Fellow at the Courtauld Institute of Art. He has organized major exhibitions at the Hayward Gallery, the Royal Academy and the Tate. His books include *Vorticism* (1976) and *Art Beyond the Gallery* (1985), both prize-winning studies, and *David Bomberg* (1987), a monograph. From 1989–90 he was Slade Professor of Fine Art at Cambridge University. His latest book, *A Bitter Truth: Avant-Garde Art and the Great War* was published in 1994 and his exhibition on the same theme was held in Berlin and London the same year. In 1995 he was appointed Chair of the Visual Arts Panel at the Arts Council of England, and co-selected *The British Art Show 4*, touring Manchester, Edinburgh and Cardiff.

PHILIPPE GARNER joined Sotheby's in 1970 and rapidly achieved a specialization in Photography and Twentieth-Century Decorative Arts. He has remained one of the leading experts in both these fields and has published numerous books, including *The Contemporary Decorative Arts* (1980), *Eileen Gray: Architect and Designer* (1993) and studies of the work of Emile Gallé (1976) and Cecil Beaton (1994).

METTE DE HAMEL at Sotheby's Conservation Advisory Service will help you find the best solution for the safe-keeping and conservation of your tapestries. She is able to assess the condition of the tapestry, recommend treatment and help you find the most suitable conservators for your specific problem. A Fellow of the

International Institute of Conservation, she is also a well-known conservator of works of art on paper and was the former Director of the Textile Conservation Centre at Hampton Court Palace, London.

ROBERT HARBISON teaches at the Architectural Association and the University of North London where he is Professor of Architecture and Interior Design. He has lectured widely on art and architecture and is the author of many books which include *Eccentric Spaces: the Built, the Unbuilt and the Unbuildable*, and *The Shell Guide to English Parish Churches*. His book *Thirteen Ways: Theoretical Investigations in Architecture* will be published by Thames & Hudson in 1996.

PHILIP HOOK is a Senior Director of Sotheby's and appears regularly as picture expert on BBC TV's *Antiques Roadshow*. He has the unusual distinction of also having been a director of Christie's, which he joined in 1973 straight from Cambridge, where he read History of Art and won a soccer blue. In between the two auction houses, he founded London art dealers the St James's Art Group. He is the author of *Popular 19th-Century Painting* (1986), the comic novel, *Optical Illusions* (1993), and the art world thrillers *The Stonebreakers* (1994), which won the *Literary Review* Bad Sex prize, and *The Island of the Dead* (1995). He is married with two children.

HILARY KAY joined Sotheby's in 1977, later that year she became head of the Collectors' Department and the following year, aged 21, she became one of Britain's first female auctioneers. In 1981 she set up the first sale of rock 'n' roll memorabilia and in 1985 was made a Director of Sotheby's. Hilary is now a Senior Director and head of the Collectors' Division in London encompassing veteran and vintage cars, wine, stamps, musical instruments, clocks and watches, coins and collectibles. She regularly appears on BBC television's *Antiques Roadshow* and is the author of *Rock 'n' Roll Collectibles: An Illustrated History of Rock Memorabilia* (1992).

PAUL NEEDHAM is Senior Vice President and Director of Books and Manuscripts at Sotheby's, New York.

SIMON DE PURY is Chairman of Sotheby's Europe and Chairman of Sotheby's Switzerland. He is based in London and Geneva but devotes a large amount of his time to travelling. He is an auctioneer, conducting major sales in London, Geneva, New York, Monte Carlo, Milan, St Moritz and Zürich, and from 1979–86, prior to joining Sotheby's, he was curator of the Thyssen-Bornemisza Collection, Lugano.

JANA SEELY became a member of the curatorial staff at Hearst San Simeon State Historical Monument in 1991. Her background is in museum work and publishing, and she worked for many years as a freelance sculptor.

RONALD VARNEY joined Sotheby's in 1989 and is a Vice President of Sotheby's New York. He has written extensively on the arts for *Esquire*, *Smithsonian* and *Connoisseur* magazines, as well as *The New York Times*, *The Los Angeles Times*, *The Wall Street Journal* and numerous quarterlies. He is also a regular contributor to *Art at Auction*.

GLYNN WILLIAMS is a sculptor and Professor of Sculpture at the Royal College of Art, London. He has shown his work regularly since 1965 and has had 17 one-person exhibitions including a retrospective in Margam Park in 1992. He has been included in numerous mixed exhibitions and in 1984 represented Great Britain for the British Council in the Third Kotara Takamura Exhibition in Japan. He has work in public collections including the Tate Gallery, the Victoria & Albert Museum, the National Portrait Gallery and the Henry Moore Centre for the study of Sculpture in Leeds. He has written about sculpture for art magazines including *Modern Painters*, *Art Monthly*, *Art Review* and *Art & Architecture* and exhibits regularly at the Bernard Jacobson Gallery.

INTRODUCTION *by Diana D. Brooks*

The rhythm of a Sotheby's auction season is often exciting and hectic, with suspense and drama played out in the saleroom week after week as art works of amazing diversity are viewed by the public, bid for and taken away by new owners. From a relatively quiet, restrained stamp auction to a sale of Impressionist paintings involving large crowds and intense press coverage, the season is one of constant renewal and variety as each sale ends and another begins.

In this year's edition of Sotheby's Art at Auction, *we are featuring a short story, 'Portrait of an Incorrigible Collector', by the novelist and screenwriter Wolf Mankowitz. Originally published in an edition of* The Ivory Hammer *from the 1960s the story is here accompanied by specially commissioned illustrations.*

As in past years, we have tried to capture the sweep and colour of the season, its highlights and trends, while at the same time examining current issues and developments in the art world at large. In the first section of the book, Isabel Boucher discusses the advance of CD-ROM technology as it applies to the art world. CDs are revolutionizing the way museums make their collections available to visitors, and CD-ROM guides to major private collections are also being produced (as Sotheby's itself is doing for the upcoming sale of the Collection of Joseph H. Hazen in New York). The digital media revolution has clearly come to the art world. In this section, the reader will also find articles on interior design, exhibitions of the past season, a survey of new museum buildings around the world and an interview with Sir Eduardo Paolozzi, one of Britain's most regarded sculptors.

The season-end review of our sales worldwide appears in the second section of the book. The accompanying commentary by our senior specialists is complemented by photographic highlights and extensive information on sale results in every collecting category represented at Sotheby's. Our cover image for this year's book is Picasso's portrait Angel Fernandez de Soto, from the Collection of Donald and Jean Stralem. The extraordinary price this painting achieved, $29,152,500, was surely one of the most dramatic moments of the past season. Amid a packed saleroom buzzing with excitement the sale brought an astonishing $65.2 million.

HENRI MATISSE
La pose Hindoue
SIGNED, 1923, OIL ON CANVAS,
73 x 60cm (28¾ x 23⅝in)
New York $14,852,500
(£9,208,5500). 8.V.95
From the Donald and Jean
Stralem Collection
(LEFT)

A Tiffany favrile
glass and bronze
Wisteria lamp
1899–1920, IMPRESSED
*TIFFANY STUDIOS/NEW
YORK*, height 67.3cm (26½in)
New York $343,500
(£212,970). 22.IV.95
From the John W. Mecom, Jr.
Collection (ABOVE)

**Lucia di
Lammermoor,
Act III: The Mad
Scene gown**
DESIGNED BY FRANCO
ZEFFIRELLI AND WORN BY
JOAN SUTHERLAND IN
DONIZETTI'S *LUCIA DI
LAMMERMOOR* AT THE
ROYAL OPERA HOUSE,
COVENT GARDEN, 1959
London £5,750
($8,913). 9.I.95
From the Collection of
Dame Joan Sutherland, O.M.
and Richard Bonynge, C.B.E.
(ABOVE)

The auctioneer for the Stralem sale, Simon de Pury, discusses the year's activity in the Fine Arts, the highlights of which included outstanding sales of Impressionist and Modern art in London and New York, particularly in the spring, and a number of major single-owner sales, including Old Master paintings from the British Rail Pension Fund and The New-York Historical Society, and American and Latin American paintings from the IBM Collection. Remarkable results were also achieved in other sales of American, Latin American and nineteenth-century European paintings, in some cases yielding the highest totals since 1990.

But outstanding results were to be found in many other collecting areas as well. In the Decorative Arts there was the Mecom Collection, offering the most important group of Tiffany lamps ever to come to auction, the Jordt Collection of Korean art, the Carlo Monzino Collection of Netsuke, Inro and Lacquer, and strong sales of Americana, nineteenth-century furniture and pre-Columbian art. Jewellery sales were again impressive, with new world records set, including the SF19,858,500 paid in Geneva for a remarkable 100.10 carat diamond. In the Collectors' Categories there were excellent results for musical instruments, wine, stamps, coins and medals, sporting guns, cars, rock 'n' roll memorabilia and animation art, the latter area highlighted by the record sale of artwork from the Disney hit film, The Lion King. *Sales of Literary Property were also exceptional, with the Dr Otto Schäfer Collection of illustrated books the high point and a new world record established for the autograph manuscript of Schumann's Second Symphony.*

There were a number of firsts this season. In London we celebrated our twenty-fifth anniversary of wine auctions and in New York we inaugurated sales of fine and rare wine in association with the wine merchant Sherry-Lehmann. Also in New York we held our first ever auction of contemporary Indian art, from the Chester and Davida Herwitz Charitable Trust. The breadth and high quality of the collection brought a tremendous response from a group of international clients, many of whom had never participated before in an auction. In London we held our first sale devoted exclusively to Irish Art. The sale brought spirited participation by Irish private collectors and dealers as well as international buyers. On the continent we held our first ever sale in Denmark, which offered vintage automobiles from the Raben-Levetzau Collection and took place in October at the Aaholm Automobil Museum. Looking ahead, this autumn we will hold our inaugural auction of Western jewellery in Hong Kong, which comes in response to a growing demand throughout Asia.

The tradition of country house sales at Sotheby's is a long and distinguished one. House sales have traditionally attracted considerable publicity, sometimes internationally, and they have brought many new clients to Sotheby's. The past season witnessed several important house sales at Sotheby's, principally in Europe. In September and October we conducted a four-day sale

JEAN II PENICAUD
**A polychrome and
gilt circular Limoges
enamel plaque,
probably of
Marguerite
d'Angouleme,
Queen of Navarre**
FRANCE, FIRST HALF OF THE
SIXTEENTH CENTURY,
diameter 9.5cm (3¼in)
New York $140,000
(£89,600). 10.I.95
From the Collection of Cyril
Humphris (BELOW)

of more than 5,000 objects from Stokesay Court in Shropshire, one of Britain's grandest nineteenth-century mansions. With the help of old photographs as well as an 1898 inventory, Sotheby's reassembled the rooms of Stokesay Court as closely as possible to their original furnishing and decoration. Enormous crowds attended the viewing and auction, with the sale bringing a total of £4.2 million. On the continent, we conducted a three-day auction of 1,600 lots from the Palazzo Corsini, the greatest Baroque palace in Florence. The sale was held at the request of the Prince and Princess Corsini and comprised decorative furniture, ceramics, glass, carpets, textiles, books and prints from many of the storage rooms in the palace. The viewing and sale offered collectors rare access to the rooms of the palace. This auction was an outstanding success, with the total of L68 million

The library at the Palazzo Corsini, Florence: site of just one of the season's successful house sales, 26–28 September 1994. (ABOVE)

more than doubling the pre-sale estimate. In the United States, we sold the remarkable Collection of Dr and Mrs Henry P. Deyerle; one of the finest and largest collections of Americana in existence was auctioned.

In keeping with Sotheby's pre-eminent role in hosting major house sales in continental Europe, we are pleased to announce this autumn that we will be conducting a fifteen-day auction of property from the Grand Ducal Collections of Baden at Neues Schloss in Baden-Baden, Germany. The auction takes place at the request of HRH The Margrave of Baden and will consist of more than 6,000 lots, making it one of the largest and most important sales this century.

In the third section of the book, Art at Large, we conclude with an essay on some of the most outstanding single-owner collections that were offered during the past season as well as articles on preserving tapestries, auction discoveries, the maverick collector William Randolph Hearst and a Grand Tour of Venice.

The 1994–95 season at Sotheby's drew to a close with a very special charity auction in New York, Bid For Life. The event was held in honour of Robert Woolley, our long-time Director of Decorative Arts in New York and a celebrated auctioneer. Over the years Robert has made tremendous contributions not only to Sotheby's but also to numerous charitable organizations through benefit auctions particularly in support of those with AIDS. The Bid For Life auction drew many of Robert's friends, colleagues, acquaintances and admirers, and it was one of the most memorable charity events ever held at Sotheby's. It made $1.3 million, which will help carry on the good work of four important organizations that Robert has long supported himself, and holds dear to his heart. We were delighted to host this event.

PORTRAIT OF AN INCORRIGIBLE COLLECTOR

by Wolf Mankowitz

Felix Brodie was surprised that the loss of his fortune should make him so happy. Not that the first weeks after the collapse of the small Byzantium of textile interests which Brodie had put together through two decades did not bring its depressing moments. But the discovery that most friendship is fallible and that all loving is mostly expensive folly did not altogether surprise him.

Brodie in his moments of greatest success had felt the imminence of failure as a cold breath upon his neck. In the time of power he had experienced the unease of impotence. He had held a half-million of paper in his hand and felt the weightlessness of ashes. He had turned his head to look upon the sweet, sad profile of a woman he loved and found a cold dent upon the pillow. He had known in the moment of possession the inevitability of loss. Brodie understood, as a millionaire should not, the loneliness which distinguishes man from the soulless animals. The mutability of his fortunes was easy for him to accept, for he had that ultimate disqualification for continuous success in business, a sense of mortality.

Yet happiness, at the very second when the telex told him that his calculations had proved wrong and his present gamble was his last loss, he had not expected. Not the immediate uprush of relief, the surge of tears and laughter, the moments of intense, hoped-for hysteria in the cream silken office over Bond Street, in which the silk was the new Brodie synthetic which would never be marketed.

Brodie looked around the office scanning the Mayan, Aztec and Toltec objects which he had expensively looted from the galleries of Sotheby's, so conveniently near to his office. His attack as a dangerous underbidder had won him at specialized sales the status of a senior dealer or museum-buyer, and his seat was assured at the green baize table known as the 'inner ring'. Now he studied with seriousness and sadness each of the cruel and comic heads of stone and ceramic recently remounted against backgrounds of his new synthetic silk. The synthetic was lost but the frightening realities against it remained his. The small empire of Brodie was gone like the great buried ones with whose gravestones he had surrounded himself, the skulls at the feast, the runic writing on the wall of the ballroom, the truth about the shattered nothingness out of which men crawl and into which they must all again be precipitated.

So Brodie passed a year of disillusion, of liquidating his assets, of paying out his creditors, of junking his unique but now useless machinery. The Sotheby's sale of the Brodie Collection of Pre-Columbian *objets* will not be forgotten for many years – especially by Mrs Brodie for whom it provided a substantial settlement and a chalet in Switzerland and a convenient ski-ing slope with convenient ski-ing instructors. His daughter loved and needed him deeply and was irresistibly drawn by contrast to a helpless, useless, wanly handsome actor who needed her. Women always go to the man who needs them most, Brodie observed. His last mistress had left him heartbrokenly because he was too rich and too powerful to make her feel essential to him. Perhaps, he thought whimsically, if he sent her the balance sheets she would leave whoever she was with now and return. But she had left no forwarding address, and anyway her suspicions that she was inessential to him were justified. So then, he was free finally from needing all who had needed him to need them. It was a relief like happiness.

By the time Brodie had settled his affairs and found (as the truly rich always do in crisis) that he still had enough money left for all practical purposes, such as living, he was beginning to understand the truth about himself.

Because of his poor background and the inability of his studious and shy father to venture among strangers and wrest a living for his family from them, Brodie had early felt, out of love and respect for the old man, a need to compensate for his inadequacies. A need, really, to prove that what his father had not been able to do well, was not truly worth doing. He had wanted to make money in order to demonstrate the ease and the indignity of the process. He needed to show that the poor and beautiful old beggar in a Rembrandt painting is priceless and that his sweetness is as unpurchasable as the genius with which it is seen and recorded. And he wanted, too, to own the Rembrandt.

The rest of his paintings Brodie sold. Then, a few months later, when the sensational collapse of his group of companies was already forgotten in the excitement over the rise or fall of some other miniature empire, with a packing-case of books, the Rembrandt, and a photograph frame which showed his father in the year of his death on one side and his daughter in the year of her birth on the other, Felix Brodie disappeared.

Metropolitans feel that any of their number who leaves them suffers a symbolical death, and, of course, there is a deal of truth in the suggestion that to tire of London is to tire of life. But then, on the other hand, life is very tiring. Felix Brodie was under no illusions as to his indispensability even to his own executives and workers. They had all been taken over with his factory and the office typewriters. The looms were weaving away now, quite impartially, some other synthetic, not a better one, but one which, being a product of the giant who had squashed him, was more desirable.

Brodie's many acquaintances sprung out of his business or collecting interests and no longer had occasion to remember him. His friends – which friends? Those of the past had drifted behind him as he sailed up onto the crest of the wave. His wealth embarrassed or upset them. They had left him, he hadn't left them, he assured himself. On the other hand, he admitted that he had not tried too hard to hold them back. There was no time for old friendship in the new world upon which he had burst with such brilliant determination. As for those other friends who had come with success, they were part of the rewards and glittering prizes. Like the lovely compliant women and the worldly men, they came with the Curzon Street house and the elegant furniture and dressings of the success-world, and they stayed with it. After a few weeks of diminishing references to the weirdness of his disappearance they would think no more of Brodie.

If they had known that he had bought a crumbling plantation-house on a cliff above a beach looking three thousand miles towards Africa, they might have thought that the place, when reconditioned, could be good for a winter out of England. Except that those

West Indian islands are so boring at night apart from Jamaica and simply everyone goes there. There was little chance then of Brodie being discovered. If he had been it is unlikely that any of his fashionable former associates would have recognized him up to his knees in sand and shell fragments, excavating, with a small trowel, an Arawak Indian midden.

Brodie bought the property named Indian Hall on the remote rocky eastern coast of Barbados because of the midden. To the rambling, fortress-like, grey weathered coral-block house with its bougainvillaea-overgrown castellated towers and termite-ridden fretwork wooden gallery, he did very little other than have a study and a bedroom put into shape and a kitchen and a bathroom made to work. The windswept barren acreage around the house he left untouched; but the beach, a wide, deep crescent of sea-hewn grottoes shaded by ancient bearded fig-trees, he at once set to work upon. So Brodie, the former wealthy connoisseur of fragments of the magnificent stone-age civilizations, became an amateur excavator of the broken shell-implements of the poorest of peoples.

Brodie was drawn as much by the obscurity of the Arawak civilization which had ceased to exist for no certainly known reason a century or so before the island was settled by the British, as by the lack of collectors' value of the simple shell axe-heads and hoes it had left behind. He had a need, it seemed, to bury himself among the poor, unconsidered shards of an unimportant and tragic people, whose life was as remote as his now seemed to him. The Arawaks had disappeared as completely as he had from the conflicted world. Success and failure meant as little to them as to him. Where he could formerly identify himself with the greatness of the Mayas and the ruthless magnificence of the Aztec peoples, it was now soothing to feel close to the unpretentious isolated simplicity of men who touchingly depended upon the fragmented queen conch for their livelihood.

Whenever he lifted from the white, clinging coral sand a smooth-ground ivory-like implement, it felt warm and familiar in his fingers. He too had in his time fought nature with inadequate weapons devised out of whatever was at hand. When he unearthed a small red pottery handle in the form of a shark's head or a pig's face it seemed a votive of his own to appease the inimical spirits of the wild creatures he had hunted and killed. Carefully he pieced together the shards of undistinguished pots, excited by the discovery of a little scratched decoration with a remote similarity to the Mayan. Eagerly he returned every sunrise to the debris of Arawak life, searching the mounds for something that would suggest what might be lasting in his own. So the rows of graded shell-implements in Brodie's study increased, and his collection of figured handles became the best in the island. The fine sand dust settled on the Rembrandt, his trenches on the beach grew wider and deeper. Somehow a year had passed, and then another, and still Brodie searched on and the sand yielded no conclusive answer.

The turning point came for Brodie one early overcast morning when, having dreamt of a woman's sweet profile beside him, he awakened to find the pillow empty and undented. The moon had been full and under it the sea boiled over the reef beyond his beach. That morning he told his labourer they would not be working. Then he wandered across the ruins of his long search, through the dim overhung grottoes down to the beach. Looking back at the wrecked graveyard of the past two years Brodie decided to present his collection to the local museum and move on. He felt suddenly empty and meaningless like a broken long-buried shell, the colour gone, the texture of dry bones. He was fit and brown, his hair white from the sun and the centuries he had lived through, yet though he had been alone for so long he felt for the first time the ache of loneliness about his heart. Whatsoever thy hand findest to do, do it with all thy might. He always had and the heart ached still. Finally Brodie abandoned himself to the pain, and in that moment made one of the most important discoveries in Amerindian archaeology.

From where he stood on a flat, worn coral rock looking out over the black churning sea, Brodie let his grief fly upwards from his vitals, gasping as it hit his throat, tangible as it flew like a small dark

bird above the waves. Following it into the foam and below, his attention was distracted by a number of reddish projections, obviously man-made, showing as the sea fell back and disappearing as it surged forward again. Climbing higher, Brodie watched for more than an hour with mounting excitement. There were eight projections. Through his binoculars he identified them as the tops of what must be very tall pots each some two feet in diameter. Later, when the tide had receded a little, Brodie saw that there were in each case several pots fitted on top of one another. But now two had already been partly destroyed by the pounding waves. Of those remaining, three had the upper portions missing and three were complete, each capped with a tightly fitting lid.

With his labourer Brodie tried to get at them by dinghy. But they were in a circular area protected by reefs and the sea was rough, he was only able to get near enough to establish that one of them contained bones.

Instead of risking the desperations of sleep that night, Brodie read till dawn through all the material he had on Arawak burial. Very few skeletons had been found on the island and little was known of their funerary rites. Tense with anxiety for his graveyard under the sea, Brodie went down to the beach at break of dawn to see if the tide had left him anything of his discovery, the tomb where the key to his life was buried, the answer in some cryptic seal or on a smooth fragment which he alone would understand.

Only one of the urns remained, but the sea was calm. Sweating with fear, Brodie pushed out the dinghy and rowed nearer than was sensible to the sharp-toothed reef. In the shallow transparent water he could see, scattered about the smooth sand, bones and complete pots, skulls and implements freshly broken by the sea from their shattered containers and as perfect now as on the day they had been immured. Beads and large seals and shell amulets were all there almost within his grasp, but Brodie ignored them. Instead he edged the boat through a narrow passage and let it slip, suddenly released from the pressure of the current, towards the complete urn.

Brodie was only able to dislodge the uppermost of the interlocked pots. As he heaved it away from the two supporting lower ones they split, spilling their bones softly to the sand floor. Brodie observed that one of them contained ribs and a skull while the other held leg and arm bones. The Arawak funerary rites apparently included truncation of the body and separation of the parts. The urn he was now straining to lift steadily into the dinghy without capsizing it was heavy, perhaps with equipment for the after-life. It also contained, carefully wrapped around a set of *zemis* or spirit-stones, and perfectly preserved, the talismanic object for which Brodie had been searching so long.

Felix Brodie it was, then, who rediscovered, analysed and recreated the miraculous synthesis of sea-island cotton with the pulp of a herb which is to be found only on the island of Barbados. This sample of the sacred material, used to enshroud the *zemis* of Indian heroes at burial, Brodie found to have properties which made it infinitely superior even to the fabrics which had lost him his fortune. But the right commodity finds finance as easily as the wrong one loses it. Now known all over the world as *Arawak* the new synthetic has made Brodie a power in the textile industry for the second time in his life.

As he sits in a Bond Street office scanning his superb collection of *zemis* mounted upon the sacred material which he brought back from the dead, Brodie's eyes sometimes meet those of the old man in his Rembrandt. The Rabbi looks down at him with sad regret, but Brodie shrugs and sighs as the telex begins to chatter the latest textile market figures. A man's hell is built into his life, he thinks. He must live out his time in it until the last. Only then, his organs separated from one another to make certain he cannot return, is he permitted to go away forever to the peaceful island of his ancestors.

Meanwhile Brodie ignores even the most dramatic fluctuation in textile prices on any morning when anything in the Amerindian line is being sold in the galleries of Sotheby's, which are so conveniently near to the offices and showrooms of Arawak International Textiles Limited.

I

Art

at

Issue

NEW ROLES FOR MUSEUMS *by Robert Harbison*

Architect's model of the new Guggenheim Museum, Bilbao by Frank Gehry, due for completion in 1997.

(BELOW)

The museum seems a particularly unstable category in our current historical moment. Much of contemporary art is conceived in opposition to the cataloguing and sanctifying functions of the museum, but there has been an unexpected twist in the process. A number of museums have radically redefined themselves to swallow and digest successive forms of anti-art. After more than a generation of such skirmishing it seems increasingly difficult to make anything that is too large, messy or unpleasant for a really determined museum to hold.

Among the built results of this struggle of art to burst the boundaries of the conventional museum building are a series of hangar-like spaces which lack almost all the qualities of nineteenth-century museums except monumental scale. These may be conversions of the most unlikely building types like warehouses (the Saatchi Gallery, London) or the provision of vast spaces in a new building in immediate proximity to traditional galleries filled with older paintings, which suggests a complete re-evaluation

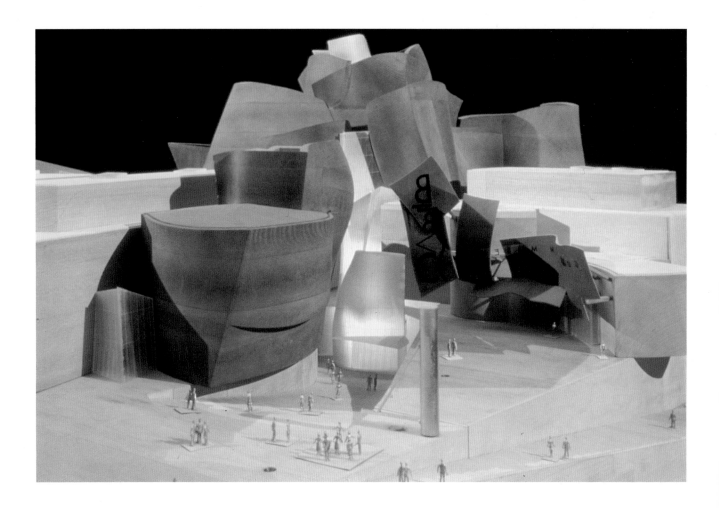

of relations between centuries (the new National Gallery, Ottawa). This last example is a meeting ground of two conceptions usually thought to form opposing poles – the museum as neutral envelope, and the museum as domineering monument, which overpowers its contents. Among archetypes of the latter are the Pompidou Centre, Paris (1972–77, Renzo Piano and Richard Rogers) and Frank Gehry's Guggenheim Museum for Bilbao in northern Spain, a city which hopes to put itself on the map with an extravagant, easily remembered building which will draw exhibitions and tourists who would not previously have made a stop. Whole histories of architecture have been written which make the desire to show off or outdo rivals the leading motive in the commissioning of the most interesting designs. Gehry's museum, now in the early stages of construction, probably owes something of its peeling, flopping forms, like five or six colossal unfurling bananas clad in shiny metal, to such impure motives.

Among demonstrative buildings this looks as if it will be a good one, but it is hard to imagine that the envelope will not always overshadow the contents. Visitors will be attracted by its advertised oddity, the more serious ones curious to see what kind of spaces can possibly arise from this sculptural congestion of forms.

The Pompidou apparently tends in another direction entirely, showing outwardly a lot of machinery which is usually kept hidden. It feels more like a children's toy than serious work, or like an oversized model in which ordinary ducts and linkages become mythic through enlargement. This building is one of the most popular tourist sights in Paris, a success which appears to be gained at the expense of its function as a museum rather than in fulfilment of it. A single aspect has come to dominate the rest, external escalators which take you to the top of the building. Because the structure has been turned inside out, conceptually, its circulation system can be detached and treated as a carnival ride.

Thus the Pompidou Centre becomes something like its rival the Eiffel Tower, valued for the view of Paris you get when you have climbed it. So the contents recede in a thoroughly post-modern manner – many visitors do not realize they are visiting a museum and come and go without actually entering the exhibition space. Interestingly enough, the progeny spawned by this building have so far been a series of office buildings and governmental complexes rather than further museums.

The foregoing sketch begins to suggest the instability or diversity in our current idea of what a museum can be, a self-effacing building type which puts itself at the service of a collection, or an assertive architectural statement bearing little relation to what is inside, or, a third category as yet unexplored here, the expressive container which means to reinforce the qualities of the collection. We are wrong if we think any of these options are entirely new. While it is true that every one of them has been pushed much further

Centre Georges Pompidou, Paris, Renzo Piano and Richard Rogers, 1972–77. (BELOW)

Sir John Soane's Museum in Lincoln's Inn Fields, London, improved over several decades until Soane's death in 1837. (RIGHT)

in the last few decades, the history of museums, like the history of architecture, is complicated. The idea that in 1850 or 1900 everyone could agree on what a museum should be or do is just another instance of the illusion that a particular moment in the past was uncomplicated.

The modern history of museums begins with princely collections of classical Antiquities in fifteenth-century Italy followed closely by those of humanist scholars whose assemblages were more modest. But a kind of bifurcation was built in from the start: on the one hand sarcophagi and large sculptural fragments, on the other coins and inscriptions which were in the nature of documents needing decoding. From these more purist beginnings devoted to the study of a single semi-buried civilization, classical Antiquities, we arrive at the Mannerist and later collection as a hodgepodge of wonders of all kinds including anything from rare minerals, biological freaks, historical relics and oddities, to live specimens. Francis Bacon advised having one's museum next door to one's zoo.

The urge to assemble marvels and rarities had never died of course; medieval relic-mongering in its more exuberant forms did sometimes approximate the later *Kunstkammer*, a cabinet of curiosities, enshrining tiny bits of farfetched bone or thorn in bejewelled, metal-mounted rock crystal. And the impulse hasn't disappeared since. Soane, Ruskin, Burrell and many museum directors have inherited the urge to concentrate all the diversity of the world in a single space, forming a whole that is deliberately incoherent, or coherent, according to principles so obscure it amounts to a private religion. Soane in his own house and Ruskin in his museum-school for workers in Sheffield mixed together copies and salvaged fragments, large and small, current and ancient, natural and artificial to create the most phantasmagorical and unclassical effect.

If we took these two assemblages as archetypes or standard versions of how museums functioned we would probably conclude that they exist to unsettle the mind, destroy certainties and subjectivize knowledge. Such environments encourage sensuous immersion and work against all intellectual system. One can even find the current

director of the National Gallery in London, an institution which ostensibly follows the sober line that great museums should show the history of art as systematically and with as few gaps as possible, voicing this view. Neil MacGregor has called the Gallery a wonderland of distinct worlds, which isn't far from admitting that its 2,210 paintings do not make a single giant narrative but propound 2,210 separate truths in incompatible languages which don't translate into each other.

This idea of the coherence or incoherence of the collection plays a determining role in what kind of house you devise to hold it. The history of museums after Soane moves, roughly speaking, from royal palaces to public institutions with palatial traces to large empty premises like the National Gallery in Washington or (a less ambivalently modernist building) the Boymans Museum in Rotterdam. Modernism in architecture arrives – of all places – in galleries of Old Masters, if a little belatedly. And it arrives representing as it does in dwelling spaces, a break with the past and a new start. By now it is so familiar that we have lost the sense of perversity of this freeing of historical relics from their historical context. What does it mean to want one's antiquities without their history? Picasso and Le Corbusier are not the first to attempt this metamorphic distortion, which is doomed to fail in the end but for the time being lets ordinary viewers feel that they themselves have invented Piero della Francesca, Vermeer or Friedrich. Much earlier, Johann Winckelmann and John Flaxman practised something very similar more successfully. For a long time now an effort to re-colour and re-primitivize the Greeks has made little headway against their powerful early Romantic idealization of Greece as pure, white, ethereal.

The current inheritors of a pure white idealized setting as the correct one for art are, unexpectedly, the vast sheds or barns which hold the latest struggles against the boundaries of art. As Le Corbusier turned to industrial prototypes when designing quarters for artists like Ozenfant, so current collectors are happiest with warehouses and power plants, not simply, as some think, because they yield the biggest spaces with least fuss or expense, but also because the industrial

association purifies art of certain inappropriate flavours of the past. When Bankside Power Station, London, is converted to the Tate's exhibition space for modern art it will carry a borrowed aura impossible nowadays to design from scratch. Art works will take the place of huge pulsing generators and banks of controls which awed their human tenders. New cults invariably reoccupy the sites of old ones – Christian churches where pagan burials and sacrifices occurred; art on the spot from which the powerful ghosts of science and technology have fled.

In the centre of Herzog and de Meuron's perspective of their winning Bankside scheme was collaged a photo of Rachel Whiteread's *House,* the ghost of a London terrace house formed by taking a cast from the last of a demolished row, then removing the house from the now-solid space inside it. This seemingly neutral and speechless work vibrated with tremendous historical energy but was razed completely before turning up again in Herzog and de Meuron's collage. Nonetheless there is something very apt in their borrowing. It puts a building in a building, the empty space of the smaller into the hollow shell of the larger. Both have been stripped or cleansed, leaving the messiness of reality for the neutrality of art. Each was generic not ornamental to start with and has become more so. The conjunction forms an allegory of the confrontation between container and content which museum designers and projectors must deal with, a mirroring in this case like endlessly bounced and rebounded radio signals, portentous but undecoded.

The context-free museum was a difficult discovery, always ambivalent, escaping from the accumulated weight of past culture yet more like reinterpretation than obliteration. The early purist phase is followed by movements which may seem like backsliding or rapprochement such as Carlo Scarpa's adaption of old fortresses and derelict palaces as display places for art in the 1950s and 60s. In an obvious sense this is locating venerable objects in the most logical settings, for building and contents are contemporaries. But the way Scarpa does it produces an effect not unlike Bankside. He clears the shell of later accretions, leaving it a lonely, untenanted

ruin. Then the art is distributed so sparsely and exquisitely that it increases the sense of loss. The final result feels both more scientific and more Romantic than the purpose-built, white-walled gallery. Paintings here stand out as survivors, and fragments are more fragmentary, their rough edges clearly silhouetted against a patch of colour or shadow. Modern insertions have no frame: they abut frankly on what remains. There are no disguises in Scarpa's remodellings in Palermo or Verona, yet these are some of the most insidious of all reinterpretations, where modern inserts are mellowed and ancient fabric made starker by their collocation. Today it seems unthinkable to build classical temples to hold classical sculpture as Klenze did so very solemnly in Munich.

Bankside Power Station, London by Sir Giles Gilbert Scott, 1957–60, in its present disused state. (FAR LEFT)

Projection of Bankside Power Station after its conversion by the Swiss architects Herzog and de Meuron for the Tate Gallery of Modern Art. (ABOVE)

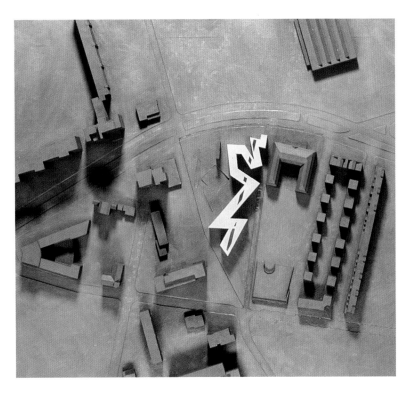

Architect's model for the extension to the Berlin Museum by Daniel Libeskind, completion in 1996. (ABOVE)

There are other compromise solutions to the problem of how a museum building can follow its own programme of expression and yet provide usable spaces for display. Gehry's Vitra museum in Weil am Rhein is regular on the ground and unruly overhead: a rectangular plan is swathed in a twisting system of roofs and skylights which, in their lower stages, are irrational sheaths or disguises for the rationality within.

Against the designer's intention Daniel Libeskind's extension to the Berlin Museum has been brought partway toward a similar result. The programme of this astonishing project is well known. By a series of triangulations on various key locations in German Jewish history such as Rosa Luxemburg's house, Kafka's fiancée's room, the meridian of Jerusalem and others, Libeskind discovered an elongated Star of David lurking in the map of Berlin. Using a somewhat unclear means of projection, he arrived at a zigzag fragment of this figure in the vicinity of the existing museum, which became the plan of his addition. Originally the outer walls of this roughly W-shaped figure sloped more steeply as they receded

from the current building, recoiling in horror or falling lopsidedly like its shadow. This feature has been edited out of the design as it presented difficulties of construction and use, but plenty of wilful irrationality remains. The building's fenestration resembles random scarification of its flesh, or strafing by war-planes, or graphic frenzies realized on an enlarged scale in three dimensions. This attack on the integrity of the walls runs counter to internal division into rooms and storeys, offering from outside violent slices through a series of zones, and from inside vertiginous glimpses of alien worlds and foreign dimensions. The most impressive stair arrives at a dead-end against a wall in a place where no one can stand up; another veers and its sides converge. Non-Jewish history is represented by the lightning flash of the floorplan. When it crosses the Jewish path, voids occur, tube-like spaces, eccentrically but dimly lit, beautiful in their way but unenterable.

The result is one of the largest collections of irrational spaces ever realized, which is presented by the designer as a historical vision. It is too early to say what these spaces will be like when inhabited by the museum's exhibits. Libeskind's building was intended to house the Jewish collection of the museum, among much else, but has come to be popularly known as the Jewish Museum, for it enshrines the Jewish vision of a Jewish architect who cannot forget the Holocaust.

The answer to the question of what the museum will do to the exhibits it houses is probably that it will exercise a strong deformative effect on them. In Libeskind's building you will not be able to look at anything without thinking of other things. Visitors will be constrained, haunted by the architect's vision of history, by meanings which it must be said are not otherwise much spoken of in Berlin. As it is a city presently in a phase of strong denial of its recent past, at least architecturally, this project's insistence is a welcome antidote.

Something in the idea of a museum inspires ambivalence. Like libraries, large ones invite comparison with tombs and it is perhaps in flight from this association that museum buildings like Libeskind's, which prevent or at least thwart display, arise. One of the starkest examples of this is the Johnson Museum of Art at Cornell University with a huge hole poked into it, through which rushes the wind from across the lake. This is I.M. Pei treating the building as an enormous Chinese character with Asian art isolated as if on a mountain top at the end of long vertical arms, a powerful expression of the displacement of these objects to upstate New York.

One of the most powerful versions of the museum-as-tomb occurs at the point where the Egyptian Temple of Dendur has been relocated in the Metropolitan Museum of Art, New York. More than any other, this museum specializes in reconstituting whole environments inside a crystalline bubble. When the modest local museum at Modica, Sicily lifts a dozen craftsmen's premises into its halls one gets a totally different feeling: a careful study of things nearby and unregarded. Reconstructions at the Metropolitan often have a slightly surreal flavour. The visitor is made vaguely uneasy by the huge rocks, big banana trees and deep pools in the Chinese garden because he has not really forgotten he is on the second floor. We can accept that China is above Egypt and next to the Impressionists but somehow a vast granite floor representing the banks of the Nile tests our sense of reality in a new way. This museum is offering us a substitute-reality made of real space. Like one of the landmarks blindfolded by the Bulgarian artist Christo we have been 'wrapped' or veiled, our primary reality dimmed. Like some experiments in virtual reality this museum makes us the appliances and itself the manipulator. All too often the struggle against the old boundaries of the museum has a similar effect: in liberating itself, art has found new ways of dwarfing us.

In the late 1980s the sculptor Donald Judd undertook one of the most thorough-going desertions of the museum. He began by looking for the point in the whole continental USA furthest from urban centres, major roads and commercial air routes. Of course there have long been provincial museums devoted to nearby archaeological sites or local traditions, but the comprehensive collection is almost

inevitably an urban conception, and one of the main ways a metropolis knows itself to be metropolitan, a centre.

Judd went straight from New York to Marfa, Texas, ostensibly because as his work grew larger he needed more space around it. The result is that searching for emptiness he ended up filling it, buying many of the buildings in the little town, which were stripped and then minimally inhabited by his monosyllabic work. He has turned a vast landscape into a museum for his own sculpture, which always brought order to far larger spaces than it actually filled. Surrounded by all this formerly neutral emptiness, Judd's installations must produce strong hallucinations in many of those passing through, who wonder just how far the sculptor's territory extends. Are the gaps in the sagebrush intervals in a vast, reticent composition? Is the scoured ground-plane an artistic datum? With minimal means Judd has achieved exactly what empire-building museum directors are after: a separate universe whose inscrutable rules it will take some study to understand.

The Herbert F. Johnson Museum of Art, Cornell University, Ithaca, New York by I.M. Pei, 1968–73. (ABOVE)

ART AND MODERN TECHNOLOGY *by Isabel Boucher*

Art and technology are hardly traditional partners. One has to go back to the early sixteenth century and Leonardo da Vinci to find a convincingly integrated approach to both. It is no coincidence therefore that the moving force behind the application of current technology to disseminating images of Western art, the chairman of Microsoft Corporation Bill Gates, bought Leonardo's *Codex Hammer* at auction last autumn. The sheets of drawings of natural forces such as waves and wind, and machines for harnessing their power served as studies for elements of Leonardo's paintings – now it is possible that they will be published on a CD-ROM disc by Gates's new electronic publishing company, Corbis.

Images, rather than text, have been the great challenges, and triumphs, of the computer age. However, putting digitized images, or scans of pictures that can be seen on a computer screen or sent down telephone wires, into databases or onto compact discs is only one aspect of what technology

Richard Land's work of virtual reality, *Mirror Images*, which reflects the face of the onlooker with increasing degrees of distortion. (BELOW)

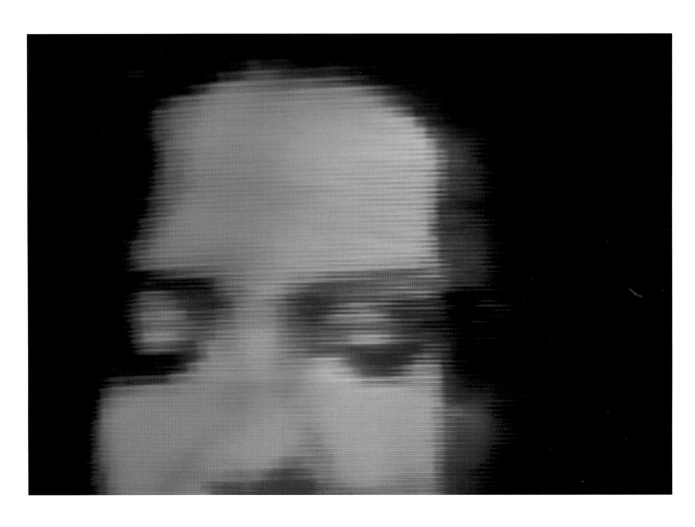

is doing for art today. It is revolutionizing the way museums make their contents available to visitors, both visually and aurally. A specially designed dialogue-driven image and text database is now in use by the Art and Antiques squad at Scotland Yard, assisting in the recovery of stolen art, and has recently been adopted by Interpol. New technology using moving images on a disc or 'on-line' through a telephone attached to a personal computer has the potential to preview auctions from the other side of the world. Three existing organizations – Thesaurus and ArtQuest in the UK and Centrox in New York – transfer auction catalogues onto their databases and charge for them to be searched at base or on-line.

There are problems, however, and the most difficult and as yet barely confronted, is copyright of images. Once a picture is released in a digitized format into, for example, the global telecommunications medium of the Internet, there is no longer any control over who may 'download' it into their computer, alter, or print it out. The Internet is essentially an information free-for-all: any image or text can be made available and there are no restrictions to what can be accessed and downloaded. Anyone with a personal computer, a modem and the appropriate software can join. Unpoliced and expanding at an ever-increasing pace, it is alarming governments concerned about controlling material such as pornography, and is challenging major companies who see the network as ripe for commercial exploitation.

Art directories on the 'Net' generally advise the user to keep the image file in its original state and not alter anything without permission. One warning in a directory for artists putting original

A screen image from the CD-ROM guide to the Louvre showing a detail of Géricault's *Death of Sardanapalous* enlarged for closer examination.
(BELOW)

La mort de Sardanapale, 1827, Eugène Delacroix
Toile 3,92 x 4,96 m

Détail

Salle 75

Loupe   Retour   Sommaire

electronic works into 'art galleries' on the Internet reads, 'To leave an image on "Art on the Net" is to give permission for it to be viewed, copied and distributed electronically. If you don't want your images distributed all over, don't upload them.' However, it is perfectly possible, for example, to call up on a computer screen, and print out, Impressionist pictures that have no stated provenance or copyright status. Monet's *Lady with a Parasol* from the Musée d'Orsay in Paris is one such example. With the harmonization of EU copyright legislation in July 1995, extending the force of copyright to seventy years after the artist's death, Monet's paintings are now back in copyright and his estate is entitled to charge a fee for their reproduction. It is as yet unclear what action will be taken retrospectively to limit the unauthorized distribution of images.

Museums wishing to increase their public profile and provide an information service are establishing themselves on the Internet via sites on the World Wide Web, an application that incorporates text, sound, photographic images and live-action video. On-line to date, and offering a virtual visit to the museum, are the Art Institute of Chicago, the Los Angeles County Museum of Art, the Andy Warhol Museum, the Tel Aviv Museum of Art, the Tokyo Fuji Art Museum and the Louvre, among others. Most present a brief guide to the permanent collection, with images that can be enlarged to fill the screen and explanatory captions, as well as edited highlights from the annual report and information on forthcoming exhibitions. In the first nine months of being on the World Wide Web the Smithsonian Institute in Washington DC had more visitors on-line than through the door.

Virtual reality of another kind could one day allow individuals to 'walk through' a gallery while sitting at a computer screen. The technology that enables 3-D artificial worlds to be created and facilitates a one-to-one (human to computer) experience with the aid of a headset and a keyboard has still not been fully explored. The promise of a 'virtual museum' was offered by a work exhibited at New York's Guggenheim Museum in October 1993. *The Networked Virtual Art Museum: the Temple of Horus* was developed by Carl Loeffler and Lynn Holden at the Studio for Creative Inquiry, Carnegie Mellon University. Based on the model of a computer network, the intention was that the new museum – a reconstruction of a 4,000-year-old Egyptian temple to the god Horus – would be simultaneously accessible to people at different points on the globe and would use virtual reality to allow the viewer to move around within this artificial space.

In 1995 Kevin Atherton, a lecturer in Combined Media at Chelsea College of Art and Design in London, produced a pilot project that explored the possibilities of virtual reality as a fine art medium. His computer-generated work *Virtual Retrospective* created a model of London's Tate Gallery in cyberspace within which he sited digital representations of four of his existing sculptures. Explaining his work, Atherton says, 'The viewer views the exhibition within the computer-generated gallery and by walking through the space, triggers various forms of interactions with the works, e.g. a sculpture consisting of a large stainless steel ball and three bronze figures is transformed from a summer image with summer sounds (bird song) to a winter image with snow and winter sounds (wind). Simply by stepping forward the viewer's movement is translated into a change of seasons, when they step back the work returns to summertime. Likewise, each of the remaining three works involve interaction that could only occur in virtual reality, thus in this work linking public space, gallery space and cyberspace.'

In fact, the excitement surrounding this and other earlier experiments seems to be evaporating as virtual reality is seen to have its limitations. The perception now is that machines are there to create new worlds, not to replicate, rather inadequately, that which already exists. Where virtual reality may have a real role to play is in conservation, as more and more archaeological and artistic sites are threatened by high numbers of visitors. The type of virtual-reality experience created by the Getty Conservation Institute of the tomb of Nefertari in Egypt, which allows visitors to experience the painted interior 'virtually' on computer while preserving the real art from wear and tear, may become a standard conservation measure.

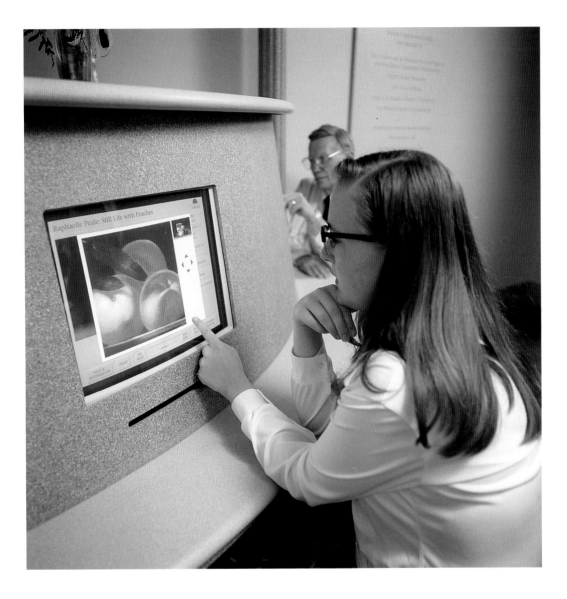

The San Diego Museum of Art was the first museum in the United States to develop a touch-screen computer guide for visitors called the IMAGE Gallery.
(LEFT)

With advances in imaging technology, more and more museums are making money to support their collections by publishing their art electronically. The National Gallery in London was one of the first to do this with their *Microsoft Art Gallery* CD-ROM, a definite success which, by March 1995, had sold over 150,000 copies since its launch in November 1993. This publication utilizes the text, images, animations and sound in the National Gallery's Micro Gallery (see below). As part of the publishing agreement with Microsoft, digitized images of the paintings were licensed for reproduction under a non-exclusive agreement.

These same images are held in the image databank conceived by Bill Gates and located near his Seattle headquarters.

Originally managed by Continuum Productions Inc., in 1989 Gates founded a totally new company called Corbis, independent of Microsoft, to manage the library of images and exploit their publishing potential through CD-ROM discs, on-line services and, in the future, interactive television. The archive of over 250,000 images covers science and technology, world cultures, history, fine art, natural history and geography. As with the National Gallery in

The virtual work *Winter* – a still from the virtual reality video *Virtual Retrospective* by Kevin Atherton, set in the Tate Gallery, London. (RIGHT)

London, the licensing agreements are non-exclusive, with Corbis acting both as agent for the digitized images and as electronic publisher.

The first fruit of the Corbis archive is a recently released CD-ROM, which successfully exploits this medium to the full. *A Passion for Art: Renoir, Cézanne, Matisse and Dr Barnes*, explores the Impressionist and Post-Impressionist paintings in the Barnes Foundation outside Philadelphia. It is ironic that the once little-known collection of Dr Albert Barnes, whose idiosyncratic visitor policy excluded art historians in favour of blue-collar workers, and who did not allow the reproduction of any works in colour because he considered it impossible to achieve faithful colour reproduction, should currently be on a prolonged world tour of galleries and among the first to be published electronically. A tour facility on the CD-ROM takes the viewer through the galleries to see where the paintings are hung, operating as a 'virtual museum'. Other features make the most of the ability of this new technology to combine

text, high-quality colour reproductions, recordings made by Dr Barnes and his contemporaries, a visual index which can be browsed through by artist or title and a zoom feature which allows details of paintings to be examined.

The most recent CD-ROM publication from London's National Gallery (this time in partnership with Cognitive Applications) is the *Complete Illustrated Catalogue*. All 2,210 works in the gallery are illustrated, and all but 300 are reproduced in colour. The advantages of the CD-ROM over the book, which was published simultaneously, are the facilities which allow images to be blown up on screen, and searches made of the text by any category. The cost of reproducing colour images electronically is far less than in book form and is of much higher quality.

While museums in the United States are generally behind their European counterparts in producing CD-ROM guides to their collections, and galleries in Britain are initiating publishing projects with independent software companies,

Winter is transformed into *Summer,* with birdsong, when the viewer steps back from the image in the virtual world of Kevin Atherton's *Virtual Retrospective* video. (LEFT)

the French State museums' publishing programme has been kept firmly in State hands. While government funding for museums and galleries in Britain leaves a considerable shortfall that has to be made up by the museums themselves, in France, government funding is total and generally adequate. In 1994 the Réunion des Musées Nationaux decided to sign an agreement with France Télécom rather than with Microsoft. 'National collections belong to the State', commented Joël Poix of France Télécom's multimedia division. 'It's up to the State to decide if or when to digitize them. We should not allow Europe to be pillaged.'

CD-ROMs from the Réunion des Musées Nationaux include publications on Poussin, Leonardo da Vinci and the Renaissance, Napoleon and a tour of the Louvre. To coincide with the major Cézanne retrospective at the Grand Palais in autumn 1995, and at the Tate Gallery, London in spring 1996, RMN is bringing out *Paul Cézanne,* a CD-ROM in French and English.

In the States only the Californian software company Digital Collections Inc. has published CD-ROMs of museum collections. Discs available to date are of the Frick Collection (*Great Paintings: Renaissance to Impressionism*), the Etsuko and Joe Price Collection (*Masterworks of Japanese Painting*) and the Brooklyn Museum (*Ancient Egyptian Art*). Most recently, in June 1995, Digital Collections Inc. released a *catalogue raisonné* of controversial photographer Robert Mapplethorpe's work on CD-ROM.

When the National Gallery in London opened its Sainsbury Wing in 1991 it incorporated a revolutionary computer guide to the collection called the Micro Gallery, a computer-screen guide to 2,200 of the gallery's works of art. A room off the main staircase houses banks of computers which visitors can use to access information on artists in the gallery, their place in history, techniques such as perspective, details of conservation, and images of the paintings themselves, which can be enlarged. The programme is

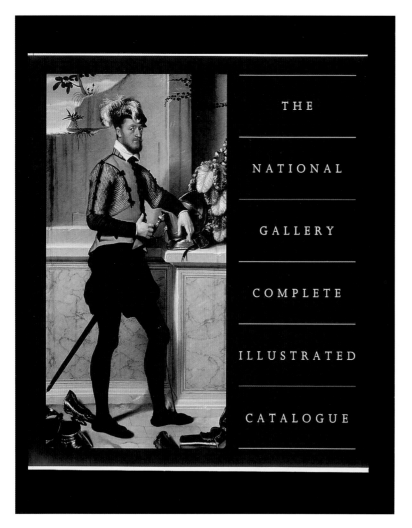

THE

NATIONAL

GALLERY

COMPLETE

ILLUSTRATED

CATALOGUE

The Complete Illustrated Catalogue on CD-ROM provides access to the entire collection of the National Gallery, London. (ABOVE)

covered by the collection. The aim is to guide visitors in the many ways of looking at a painting enabling them to ask questions for themselves. (As in London, the digitized images and data can eventually be marketed on CD-ROM.)

While CD-ROMs offer compact data storage with efficient search tools, scholars, museum curators and journalists are now logging into on-line databases, which offer immense possibilities for information access. The European Union-funded non-Internet project Remote Access to Museum Archives (RAMA) has been exploring how to link up image archives. Seven European museums are involved, each in a different country: The Antikensammlung (Antiquities Collection) of the Berlin State museums; the Beazley Archive of Greek vases at the Ashmolean Museum, Oxford; the Galleria degli Uffizi in Florence; the Museum of Cycladic Art, Goulandris Foundation, Athens; the Musée d'Orsay, Paris; the Museo Arqueológico Nacional, Madrid and the Museon in The Hague. Each museum has teamed up with a local telecommunications company which has independently devised a system allowing the museum to link up with its foreign partners and transmit text, still images, video clips and sound. It is even possible to search more than one database at a time and compare, for instance, an image of a Greek vase in the Beazley Archive with one in the Museum of Cycladic Art. RAMA's advantage is that many more objects are on each database than are on public display. The project has two purposes: to demonstrate that it is possible, without harmonized in-putting of data, for databases to be accessed, and to develop a broad-band telecommunication application in the cultural field which has the potential for a wider use within Europe.

Thanks to the project's standardized 'interface', or programme by which the various archives can be interrogated, very different categories of material, stored according to a variety of systems, can be downloaded in a choice of languages. Those running RAMA are keen to expand and add more museums to its network, but many are understandably anxious about the potential pirating of images once they are on-line. In the future, it should be possible to log

controlled by touching the screen to explore key words or use cross-referencing. The National Gallery in Washington used the same software company, Cognitive Applications, and the same sponsor, American Express, to install their own Micro Gallery, which opened in October 1995.

Washington's Micro Gallery is benefiting from advances in technology which produce higher resolution images with a wider range of colours and greater detail: each can be expanded to a metre in each direction, allowing the viewer to move across the surface via the screen to explore details which are hard to detect when looking at the original. An extra feature, not developed in London, is an in-depth examination of eight masterpieces, one from each major period of art electronically the use of photos so that museums can then charge the user. The latter would have to identify him or herself by a code in order to gain access to the system. There could also be controls over who may print out which level of image definition, choosing from a range of levels from fuzzy to sharp, high definition. 'Watermarking' of images and digital signatures are methods of identification and tracking that are still being tested. Their drawback is that anything incorporated into a screen image is visible (whether with magnification or not) and can be edited away with the sophisticated programmes now available. In general, it is the quality of the image that will determine its usefulness to a digital pirate and lawyers advise keeping the reproduction level deliberately low.

In the States these issues are being addressed in a practical way with the Museum Educational Site Licensing Project, recently launched jointly by the Getty Art History Information Program (AHIP) and MUSE Educational Media. With the specific task of resolving issues of intellectual property rights, network security and information standards, six American museums with image databases have been linked on-line to seven universities to examine the practical functioning of this type of service in the workplace. Faculties wishing to use the images, together with their libraries, the university computer departments, and the legal departments, will collaborate in proposing solutions to problems as and when they arise.

AHIP has also recently put its bibliographic and research databases on-line via the Internet. Apart from offering an information service, the move is experimental to test how large collections of information can be gathered, stored, processed and distributed across national and international boundaries. In addition, the site illustrates how separate databases of information can be linked together and searched as one 'virtual database'. With rapid advances in telecommunications technology over the past few years, and the prospect of faster link-ups in the future, the virtual global database is rapidly becoming a reality. AHIP is currently working on a thesaurus or universal index that would act as the first gateway to any existing art database, allowing it to be searched by a vast and standardized number of key words. Data interchange standards (also being developed) will mean that it doesn't matter how information is stored in a database as long as it is exchanged according to a standard protocol. This could mean that one day, from a home computer, one will be able simultaneously to search all the on-line art databases of the world for images, video clips, original documents and text on, for instance, Le Corbusier or Hans Memling.

While in Europe substantial EU funding is available for projects like RAMA which combine international co-operation in the arts and education with telecommunications development, comparable projects in the States have been largely privately funded and many feel that the humanities have been left behind in US central government grants made through the National Science Foundation. In September 1994 an alliance of major humanities and arts organizations issued a report urging the Federal government to recognize the value of the American people's cultural heritage in planning the National Information Infrastructure. In a plea for funding, the point made was that 'Even for fully automated cultural institutions, access to the Internet may be unavailable or costly. Indeed, such large museums as the Metropolitan Museum of Art and National Gallery of Art in Washington have no access to Internet services gallery-wide.'

When considering the extraordinary advances in imaging and communications technology, and how this has changed the way we experience art, whether it be through a museum micro gallery of a great collection that can be viewed on a home computer, or even browsing on the Internet, we should remain aware that this technology is still in its infancy. Its presence in our homes and consciousness is at a level comparable to that of the telephone or television five years after their introduction. Portable personal computers are now sold in the United States with CD-ROM drives as standard and for as little as $1,000. In ten years time they are likely to become accepted as an essential part of our lives. However, when it comes to art, the real will always beat the virtual hands down.

INSIDE THE ART WORLD

Glynn Williams talks to Eduardo Paolozzi

Eduardo Paolozzi in his studio assembling one of the maquettes for *Chinese Jugglers*,
a large commissioned sculpture for Kew Gardens, London. (ABOVE)

Sir Eduardo Paolozzi, Queen's Sculptor in Ordinary to Scotland, has been making sculpture for fifty years. A Scot of quite unambiguous Italian descent, he is one of Britain's most internationally regarded sculptors and nearly every honour has been bestowed upon him.

Now in his seventy-first year, the city of Edinburgh is paying him the tribute of a museum devoted to his works, which will include his studio reconstructed in all its fascinating and rich jumble. Indoor galleries will show a changing retrospective collection of his varied works and a three-acre garden designed by the artist will feature outdoor sculptures. Above all, the man himself will be periodically on site (at least once a month) working in the studio or conducting workshops. Great Britain unlike France, for example, is not generally good at acknowledging its artists in this way. The Eduardo Paolozzi Museum in the Dean Centre, Edinburgh is an unprecedented gesture of recognition and pride in the achievements of one of its own.

One might imagine that Paolozzi would have become an institutionalized manufacturing company with a production line of assistants turning out his public works – but one would be wrong.

Eduardo Paolozzi lives and works in a pair of quiet, modest-sized studios hidden away in Chelsea. Even to call them studios is to understate and generalize them. They are depositories of bits of everything that he has touched upon. Books ranging from philosophy to pin-ups, magazines on every popular subject, drawings, prints, toys, scale models and the ubiquitous white plaster casts of made and found objects. Shelves upon shelves, racks upon racks, floor to ceiling, wall to wall with no apparent order. The contents are literally bursting out onto the stairway. This is the ever-evolving collection-kit from which future works will undoubtedly be made.

It is hard to understand how anyone could work in such cramped surroundings, let alone Eduardo Paolozzi. He has an enormous physical presence – someone once compared him to the Minotaur – and there is a certain bull-like weight that makes him more like a sculpture than a sculptor. His hands are huge but agile and flexible and seem always to be itching to get back

to kneading some new world into life. Eduardo Paolozzi is a manipulator, he assembles and disassembles, mechanizes and dehumanizes, he commandeers and cannibalizes everything including his own previous works. He builds toys and models from kits, traces images and colours them in. He commandeers icons from any available source and playfully introduces them to each other irrespective of scale or subject. Assemblage is at the heart of all Paolozzi does and it is the process linking his fifty years of changing work.

He is someone who enjoys his life and has not become weary with the minutiae and the commonplace, although he is bored and irritated by the great and the good with their pomp and self regard and the invasion of sterile middle-class aesthetics in establishment art. He puts out a hard line on our visual world and doesn't withhold the ugly, prosaic or tasteless. Despite his age, his work has never been comfortable or predictable. He is an artist of enormous unevenness and to try and make a valedictory statement about him would be useless as he would disprove it immediately.

Paolozzi has participated in an enormous variety of related activities: lecturing and teaching sculpture, ceramics and printmaking; writing film scripts and making films; drawing; making prints and designing murals, tapestries and everything from door handles to gardens. All the work from the last thirty years has emanated from the clutter of his studio where I talked to him in June 1995.

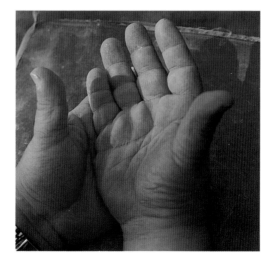

Paolozzi's hands, the tools through which the sculptor speaks, '... itching to get back to kneading some new world into life'. (LEFT)

Wealth of Nations

1993, length 9m (30ft)

This sculpture in bronze was commissioned by the Royal Bank of Scotland in Edinburgh. It is hoped that a future version might move around Europe on a flat-bed railway carriage.

(ABOVE)

G.W. Eduardo, can you describe your typical week?
E.P. Well I'm not a workaholic. I don't grind away all the time, it kind of stops and starts. A typical week might be sorting through a lot of images that I've cut out and then using them for a collage later on. I use a lot of ready-mades so there's always a lot of searching to do.

Whatever I'm doing there's a consistent making of things. A great deal of it has no direct reason behind it. Sometimes it might just be a small sphinx which is a copy of something out of a favourite museum which I make and cast just as presents for friends. I think Rodin was a great sharer. I'm much more inspired by Rodin as an idea and as an artist than, say, Henry Moore. It's interesting reading [a life of] Rodin in tandem with the last biography of Henry Moore. Rodin

really represents that whole era of intelligence and French sensibility whereas Henry Moore seems to retire after a certain period, and spend a lot of his time having his earlier maquettes enlarged by assistants. The enlargement, I think, sanitized the whole concept. His earlier roots, like a lot of English modern artists, came out of French Modernism, but they seemed to lose nerve. Certainly, in the case of someone like Barbara Hepworth, the whole idea of Modernism became – I don't like to use the phrase 'middle class' – but thoroughly sanitized.

G.W. There's a kindred spirit I suppose in the fact that Rodin was quite ruthless with the body, cutting it up into pieces with bits from one body added to another, things that were quite exceptional in terms of the tradition.

E.P. To me he's more modern than Henry Moore in the sense that he had boxes of bits which meant that they fed his mind continually. I went specially to Frankfurt to see an exhibition called *Fragmenta* which was roughly based on the work and ideas of Rodin. He just used to pile plaster casts one on top of the other. He was moving away from something that was monolithic and I think he must have planted seeds for some other sculptors, such as Picasso, because Picasso is a great assemblage artist and he recognized that the fragment could have its own importance. You need flexibility in making sculpture. What I really like is how things come together.

Henry Moore used to tell a story about Rodin, he told me the same story four times: Rodin was modelling a figure and was having big trouble with it and then by accident it fell on the floor. When he picked it up and put it back on the modelling stand it was exactly what he was looking for. That's almost a description of creativity isn't it, the invisible engine that makes you want to do it but you still don't know quite how to define it.

G.W. Henry Moore is purported to have said that the problem with sculpture was that it wasn't as powerful as the written word ...

E.P. ... or even the cinema perhaps ...

G.W. Maybe. Do you feel there are things you could have done more of? Do you believe the word is stronger than form?

E.P. No. I think that society is beginning to unleash my kind of potential, particularly outside just making sculpture ... I think Henry Moore and his notion of sculpture in landscape is over. I finally feel the sculpture park has had its day. I think you can restore dynamism back to sculpture by more people being involved with it. Fresh things are needed.

One of my ideas was a large bronze sculpture which was something like my *Wealth of Nations*. These hands and the feet and so on, on top of a big flat-bed railway carriage. I think it's much more dynamically interesting that a train sculpture could be in some siding in London and could then chug on through the tunnel to Paris. You could restore dynamism to sculpture in

all kinds of ways. I've demonstrated that artists working with museums could make their whole collection more dynamic, more accessible, more legible.

G.W. Can we now talk about your museum in Edinburgh? It's a unique event and currently work is starting on it. Were you involved in its inception?

E.P. Not at all. I think it was a series of accidents. We didn't know what to do with this fine building which belonged to Lothian Regional Council. It was fortuitous that all these local governments were being restructured and they were very keen to hand it over for a worthy cause. At the moment it's just a wonderful 1860s building designed by Thomas Hamilton, and new architects have been appointed to refurbish it. The main energy will be spent in lighting and making galleries and there is a rough idea where the studio will be. While I'm alive there'll be a sink, bags of plaster and regular workshops, and it will be used as a platform for all kinds of things that are necessary in Scotland now.

G.W. What are these things that are necessary for Scotland now?

E.P. Networking between the art schools. Breaking down isolation and bringing students together. We will have workshops with, say, four sculpture students from art colleges in Dundee, Glasgow and Edinburgh all working together, lectures for all interested parties, guest sculptors working there and guest curators organizing shows. I want it to be a catalyst for live sculpture in Scotland.

G.W. Sinks and plaster there whilst you are alive, but in what form will it continue when you are no longer here?

E.P. The place will never be static and fixed, it will always be flexible and changing with new displays and programmes. The responsibility for all of this will be with the people in Edinburgh and it will be up to them to decide how the studio can continue to best serve sculpture in the future. [They already] have all my thousands of photographs and slides and they are listing everything.

G.W. Can you tell me more about how the Museum will be organized?

The Dean Centre, Edinburgh, which will soon be opened as a museum devoted to the work of Eduardo Paolozzi. (RIGHT)

E.P. The museum, the Dean as it's called, has three acres of garden and they'll be designed with the blind, the disabled and children in mind and the sculptures will be like furniture that can be sat on. It might make children think of games that they can improvise. I did two big bronze sculptures sited at the top of Leith Walk in Edinburgh, a big hand and a big foot, and the children play games and even go up and down the foot on mountain bikes. That's dangerous but it's entirely their idea. Lots and lots of school children will be going to the museum and they will see for the first time in their lives that a door is open, they will see that all the things in a museum unexpectedly will be things they actually like. There will be animals and toys and things they recognize. I think a lot of the art teachers will say, 'Thank God, this place is going to make my job much easier'. I like that.

The programme will be flexible, in fact the sculptures may even be on wheels and move about the building. It will be more organic than any usual museum with different exhibitions curated by various people about aspects of my work. All parts of the museum exhibitions will be accessible to the public and they can view my studio, and the archive will be available for scholars to use. The whole thing will be an evolving centre for anyone of any age interested in art and I intend to give a children's lecture there every year.

G.W. *Does this sort of thing relate to other museums you like?*
E.P. No. It will be busy, noisy and active. The museums I like best are quiet, almost like sacred spaces. It's not good to say but I like museums that are more empty than full, where I can enjoy my time with the exhibits. No, the Dean will not be like that.

G.W. *In your work over fifty years, you appear to have always had your own space, you've not seemed connected to a current group or a style. Is this a deliberate thing?*
E.P. Well it's not so much deliberate, it goes way back to when I was at the Slade. I couldn't quite understand why I was disturbed by the other students and the fact they were so absolutely incomprehensible to me, but I suppose that future writers will describe that particular society, the teachers and most of the students, as homogeneous. They clearly understood each other's terms. I just couldn't understand, particularly the first inklings of what Modern art was all about. I couldn't relate them to what being an artist was, so I fled – although I was offered an extra year – I fled from the Slade without a diploma and I couldn't get to Paris quick enough. My grant ended in June '47 and I was in Paris in June '47 and fulfilling my reasons for being there by going to see real artists. I've been very much influenced by Paris and the way in which the French think, even the French

sensibility towards the movies. I'm like a curious kind of European hybrid on the English landscape; I still find Surrealism the big important seed that has been planted in me. I still find that it's a kind of petrol that makes me do things.

G.W. Your work ranges across a huge diversity of media. Do you see this as a whole or are each of the parts autonomous?

E.P. I'm interested in the total idea of being an artist. I like the possibility of perhaps working on several levels, and I like the idea of a challenge.

G.W. So the aspects all really come together as 'the work' rather than 'now I am doing printmaking, now I am doing sculpture'.

E.P. No – I like the idea of staying in one area at a time. When I did that print for Jesus College defining the notion of a portrait, I was doing a portrait without having met the sitter. On the face of Wittgenstein one can actually do the kind of things that would have been impossible, say a hundred years ago, certainly impossible without the Surrealists. Things such as putting geometric symbols and bits of writing on the face.

G.W. You've mentioned Wittgenstein. I know you've been interested in philosophy for a long time. You've read and quoted from philosophy but your work has never really been conceptual.

E.P. No. But on the other hand we tend to look at the arts in a kind of pre-ordered way. Sometimes what is not art is of interest ... Part of our society leads us to keep putting things in clear, specific categories. There are certain unclear areas that I'm interested in, such as an archive of popular art that I've given to the Victoria & Albert Museum which is robots and popular literature and magazines. As time goes on, when you get a sort of archeological distance, they're absolutely fascinating. I've an intense interest in all kinds of bric-a-brac and things which are also dismissed by established art. It was Surrealism that helped ... I was interested in popular art when I was young and there was a period going to art school that closed the door on that, but it's a nice way to recover your innocence by reassessing all that imagery.

What I don't understand is when people decide that they're no longer a child and they've become a grown-up. Why you leave your

An assembled area from the exhibition *Lost Magic Kingdoms* at the Museum of Mankind, London (1985–87). Paolozzi mixed the museum's artefacts with his own sculptures, objects and castings, giving a fresh approach to the usually static and sacrosanct atmosphere of the museum. (LEFT)

Revisiting rituals from a Catholic childhood: detail from *Props for a Musical about the Life of Hieronymous Bosch* from the exhibition *Noah's Ark*, 1989, in the Museum of Puppets at the Stadtmuseum, Munich. (BELOW)

innocence behind and why you can't still make simple toys like some frontier farmer in America. When I used to buy aeroplane kits I'd find it difficult to make them up sometimes because I just loved looking at all the details. They always seemed to lose a certain kind of potency when it was all put together. I still like making model aeroplanes. Part of my life seems to be going over

Portrait of Wittgenstein
1995

A print made for Jesus College, Cambridge mixing the visual languages of appearance and mathematical theory. (RIGHT)

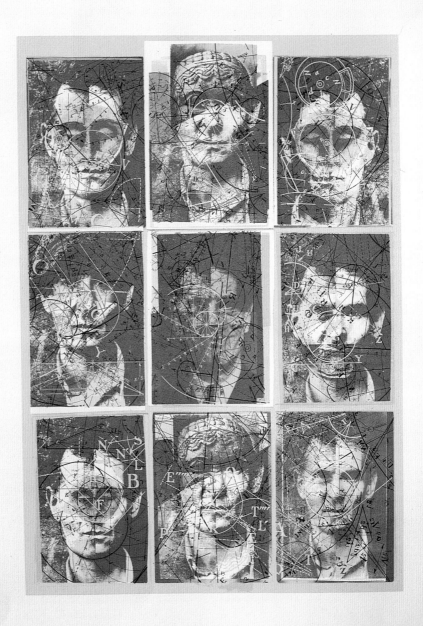

all the kinds of things I should have done when I was twelve and wasn't able to.

G.W. *Are there things in society that anger you and which you can attack in your work?*

E.P. Well, absolutely, but it can only be done as kind of historic metaphors. *Chinese Jugglers,* done for Kew, is perhaps more pure art in the sense that it's autonomous of any politics but it also has got to do with what Henry Moore might have called assembled 'impure form'.

G.W. *Tell me about that sculpture because it's the most recent piece to date.*

E.P. It really comes out of working over five or six years and being very moved by the most beautiful Greek museum that's ever been built, the Glyptothek in Munich. I'm moved by the details of these hands and feet in cabinets and how magical they are. I'm trying to reverse the process by having these elements and re-assembling them in a diagram of modernity. I enjoy museums and to work in a casual way with items that are usually sacrosanct is very exciting. Having done *Lost Magic Kingdoms* the people in the Stadtmuseum in Munich thought I could have a go with their museum, part of which was a puppet museum, and a lot of things were designed in the sense that I revisited the rituals of early years. You can see that I had a Catholic childhood.

G.W. *And is that still lingering ...*

E.P. Very much. It's a permanent scar.

G.W. *How does it manifest itself?*

E.P. I had to re-educate myself and am constantly doing that. For instance there was no Greek mythology allowed in the concept of a Catholic faith. Looking at it now, Greek mythology has just as much logic for me as the confessional has for the Catholic church.

G.W. *Have you always had assistants working in the studio along with you?*

E.P. No I haven't. When I first came to this room we're sitting in, I was very much into wax, shaping things in wax, and I used to do that from beginning to end on my own. I used Fiorini's foundry quite a lot. And what I did was to work over the weekend and take them in on Monday mornings. And I always used to take Monday off. But I was quite happy at that time, I mean I had

years of working on my own. It's just recently I've had one to two people here, but there's a lot, in sculpture, which is sheer hard donkey work.

G.W. *You talk about having Mondays off, and I know there are other things you don't like missing in the week like the radio. Are there habitual things you have to do in order to keep sane?*

E.P. It's quite important. I like listening to music, I find that the radio is a kind of muse to me. It's a kind of voice of the arts. There's such a rich mixture that I've been educated: everything I know about music I've learnt from the radio or even a great deal about plays and literature. I've learnt from the radio so I'm very dependent on it in a way. I find it gives me a kind of yeast to bake my bread.

G.W. *Do you have an optimistic notion of the future?*

E.P. Well ... I can't understand the society that we live in, it would never dream of building a Natural History Museum of that size or the British Museum – can you imagine building something like that now? I'm surprised that somebody hasn't come up with a blueprint for a new kind of building for teaching the arts in different ways, new kinds of ways.

On the other hand, I am quite optimistic about how two or three accidental events coming together can still lead to an inventive new opportunity. Some people have the imagination to see unheralded possibilities in disparate things, a bit like Surrealism. The Dean in Edinburgh is one such outcome, suggested by several coincidental factors, and will now provide a new sort of museum and a new sort of input into art education.

G.W. *Just to finish, Eduardo, can you tell me what you are reading at the moment?*

E.P. I'm reading Lindberg which is part of my childhood, which I find fascinating. And I'm reading Michelangelo's poetry. Because of that, I'm reading Ovid's *Metamorphoses.* And Ovid's *Metamorphoses* was a great source for Renaissance painting and was very influential on Rodin. He took the titles of some of his drawings from Ovid.

G.W. *So we'll end back with Rodin?*

E.P. Why not?

ART IN THE INTERIOR *by Fiona Biddulph*

Connoisseurs have always been plagued by the problem of display. This article focuses on how five of them have successfully incorporated very different collections into their homes. Using professional museum techniques only where appropriate to the feel of the room, and marrying them to know-how and imagination, they have devised their own solutions to issues such as framing, grouping and lighting. Two of the collectors have created historical settings, without being puritanical. Others chose to reject the methods of lighting and colour schemes favoured by galleries in order to preserve the warmth and intimacy of the domestic environment.

Alec Cobbe has dedicated much of his life to building a collection of keyboard instruments associated with different composers. He acquired his first antique piano when he was still an undergraduate in Oxford. Unable to afford the £300 needed for a modern baby grand, he bought an eighteenth-century piano by Longman & Broderip, a highly distinguished musical manufacturer patronized by Haydn, for a few pounds. Today, the grand piano played by Chopin at his London recitals and the square piano on which Elgar composed *The Dream of Gerontius,* stand within feet of each other in the pea-green library at Hatchlands Park.

This eighteenth-century country house in Surrey is rented by Alec Cobbe from the National Trust, in return for the loan of his collection of instruments, furniture and paintings (many inherited from his forbear Thomas Cobbe, and hung in mid-eighteenth century Irish frames). A picture restorer and designer by profession, Cobbe also masterminded the restoration of Hatchlands Park for the National Trust. But instead of returning the house to its original state when Robert Adam designed the interior in 1759, he incorporated later alterations, creating the eclectic, multi-layered look of a house that has evolved over the centuries.

Casts of great Antique statues bought from the British Museum's former plaster workshop look down on grand pianofortes owned by Mahler and Beethoven in the staircase hall. The marble statues compliment the late nineteenth-century white neo-Rococo plasterwork on the walls, while the rich tones of the mahogany doorcases and the pianos have been reconciled to the walls by painting the latter a soft yellow.

The drawing-room provides an elegant French-inspired setting for the French furniture and eighteenth-century instruments, including a graceful pianoforte reputedly made for Queen Marie-Antoinette by the Parisian manufacturer Sebastian Erard. A Rococo pier-glass hangs above a Louis XV ormolu-mounted marquetry commode bearing a contemporary green and

In the saloon at Hatchlands Park, crimson silk damask curtains, copied from pelmet draperies made for Blenheim Palace, frame a quadruple-stringed Graf with neo-classical ormolu detailing. (RIGHT)

gilt clock which bears the signature 'Cabot le Jeune, Paris'. Eighteenth-century family portraits and landscapes hang side by side on the delicate French-grey walls, made up of a white bodycolour covered with a thin glaze.

All Alec Cobbe's instruments are in full working order, making the collection 'a kind of working museum in which people can find out what Mozart, Beethoven or Chopin's compositions sound like on the different pianos the composers would have played'. Every summer, a series of recitals are performed on the instruments by concert pianists from all over the world. In order to support these concerts, as well as to maintain and restore the instruments, the Cobbe Foundation was set up in 1989.

The earliest instruments in the collection, two painted seventeenth-century harpsichords, are found in the sumptuous red saloon, a more 'Baroque' room than the simpler, eighteenth-century drawing-room. A magnificent display of predominantly Italian and Flemish Old Masters, lit by old, brass shell picture-lights, hang against panels of glowing, crimson silk damask. Silking creates a richer effect than would be possible using paint alone. The panels, with white and gilt mouldings echoing the ceiling and dado, are set into walls painted a matching red toned by a layer of burnt umber.

Crimson damask was chosen for the panels because it was a popular background for pictures in the nineteenth century. Gilded frames and plasterwork also look splendid against it. The deep, rich colours in Old Master paintings are well set off by middling shades of red, green or blue as long as they are not too bright or reflective, which would distract the eye. Colours which are too dark or too pale make it hard to adjust to the tones in a picture.

The harpsichords are framed by paintings hung three and four deep. An Italian instrument, dated 1622 and attributed to Girolamo Zenti, stands in front of Alessandro Allori's *Madonna & Child with SS Catherine of Alexandria and Francis of Assisi, circa* 1586. The scrolls of the carved and gilded picture frame are picked up in the harpsichord's swelling outlines.

In keeping with current thinking among

collectors and museum curators, Alec Cobbe chooses frames similar to the likely originals. The Allori hangs in a Venetian-style 'Sansovino' frame which cost more than the painting. Across the room the Allori is balanced by a Venetian late-seventeenth century *Pieta* hanging in a modern copy of an Italian frame dating from 1625–30.

Alec Cobbe emphasizes the importance of good hanging, 'rooms stand or fall by picture hanging'. As a general rule the best balance is achieved by hanging larger paintings above smaller ones. The inspiration for the rather dense display in the saloon came from the great picture galleries in Roman and Florentine palazzi. Contrary to the new fashion for brighter gilding, Cobbe believes that frames and furniture should be toned down in order to create visual harmony in a room full of old things. 'If you make it look brand new it jumps out like an electric shock.'

Alec Cobbe needed large grand rooms to dis-

A harpsichord by Andreas Ruckers of Antwerp (1636), also in the saloon, in front of a display of Old Masters. The landscape painting on the inside of the lid is contemporary with the instrument. (ABOVE)

In the School House, tall glass domes sheltering fruit and shells flank a portable font by Minton. A nineteenth-century innovation, these domes can be viewed as 'Victorian hi-tech'. (RIGHT)

play his pianos to best effect. Christopher Wood, on the other hand, looked for height and robust stone and woodwork when seeking a home for his collection of Victorian furniture and art. In the 1960s, when Wood began collecting, Victorian paintings and nineteenth-century furnishings were still widely derided. But Wood, a dealer and author, found himself drawn more to these supposedly inferior pieces than to rare eighteenth-century mahogany and satinwood furniture.

Wood felt that weighty pieces of oak furniture and Gothic Revival metalwork needed equally robust surroundings. Eventually, the ideal setting appeared: the School House, in the English West Country, built in 1857 at the height of the Gothic

Revival. Its central hall has a soaring vaulted ceiling with exposed beams. Everything seems to reach upwards, echoing the verticality of the space: the diamond-patterned wallpaper and window panes in the long, slender windows, the dark, ecclesiastical silhouette of the bookcase, the lancet-shaped frame surrounding a print of Chalon's coronation portrait of Queen Victoria, the organ in the corner of the room and the pointy-backed chairs flanking the window.

Christopher Wood is hugely inspired by the designs and strong, sombre colours of the visionary Gothic Revival polymath, Augustus Northmore Welby Pugin. The tiny entrance hall is paved with patterned Pugin tiles from a church.

purple slag glass. A Pugin stoneware plate produced by Minton, with the inscription 'Waste Not Want Not' is the focal point of a collection of decorative objects on a heavy oak sideboard carved with the inscription 'Tyme Tryeth Troth'. To its right and left are blue glass scent bottles by Day & Co, brass church candlesticks (ecclesiastical objects are used sparingly to prevent the house resembling a vestry) and tall glass display domes.

The study is dedicated to William Morris. The matching blue and cream wallpaper by Sanderson and the original curtains are both from designs by Morris at Kelmscott Manor. The carpet is also by Morris. Layer upon layer of pattern is added to the room with della Robbia plates, Maw lustreware and Burne-Jones photogravures from the *Briar Rose* series hung in their original frames. The grain of the oak shows through on the wide gilt mounts, reproducing the 'honest' effect recommended by Charles Locke Eastlake, in his influential book, *Hints on Household Taste* (1868): 'the sense of texture thus produced is infinitely more interesting than the smooth creamy monotony of gilt "compo" (gesso)'.

Collectors of photography, a much less established art form, have felt a greater freedom to invent new framing techniques. But innovative frames, or even unframed photographs, can look as effective in a traditional interior as in the minimal interiors beloved by New York collectors. Catherine Turner, who used to be a filmmaker, and now runs the Special Photographer's Company in London, has hung her collection in a warm, golden yellow drawing-room. Instead of spotlighting the photographs, which would have made this room look too clinical, light filters in beneath generously-draped olive-green antique silk curtains, and glows gently upwards from table-lamps with cream silk shades.

Some collectors use identical frames to create uniformity, but here every photograph is treated individually. William Wegman's *Silver Cloud*, an ethereal study of a 'wrapped' Weimeraner dog, appears to be floating within its limed frame, an effect created by placing a sheet of perspex underneath the photograph, leaving a seven-inch border around the image. Thus the photograph is sandwiched, as though suspended, in the middle

Gasoliers (now electrified) from Adare Manor in Ireland, hang from the high ceiling in the schoolroom. And a Pugin cast-iron grate does justice to the Gothic chimney-piece. However, Christopher Wood is not a purist. He resisted Pugin's flamboyant wallpaper designs in the schoolroom, in favour of a modest buff and red Laura Ashley copy of a mid-nineteenth-century wallpaper from Harewood House in Yorkshire. He felt that a Pugin wallpaper would be too overpowering.

Like Alec Cobbe, Christopher Wood demonstrates that good display is about being able to group things effectively. A mid-nineteenth-century cabinet with *trompe l'oeil* and brass strapwork is an appropriate way of showing a collection of

The polaroid negative transfer of a huge classical head by John Reuter in Catherine Turner's drawing-room has been coloured with pastels and dry mounted onto canvas. (ABOVE)

A clutter of treasures made of wood and other natural materials are displayed on a wooden chest in Rebecca Hossack's sitting-room.
(RIGHT)

of the frame area. A more radical alternative might be to hang the two perspex sheets, unframed, from the picture rail.

A huge polaroid negative transfer by John Reuter dominates the room. The edge of the mount is allowed to protrude at the sides, creating the impression of a slender frame. To one side, Horst's elegant platinum print, *Lisa with Harp* (1935), is treated quite differently. A cream mount, gilt slip and antique rosewood frame create space around the photograph, endowing this timeless black and white image with added grandeur. Catherine Turner's drawing-room testifies to her belief that 'you can frame photos any way you want', as long as you obey one cardinal rule: 'Never use coloured mounts, because they kill the subtlety of the image, or brilliant white, which makes black and white photographs look chilly and grey. Always choose shades of off-white through to cream.'

For a minimalist effect which also banishes reflections, frames and glass can be dispensed with altogether. Archival dry mounting, when the photograph is pressed onto acid-free foamboard with acid-free glue, allows the image to continue to the edge of the mount. Dry mounting onto aluminium sheeting can also be very effective. A recent exhibition of Richard Avedon's photographs, at the National Portrait Gallery in London, successfully used this technique. Non-archival dry mounting, though less expensive, is non-reversible, and not recommended for more valuable photographs. Images with information concerning provenance on the reverse should not even be archivally mounted, in case the back is damaged in the reversal process.

Rebecca Hossack's tiny eighteenth-century flat in Bloomsbury is an Aladdin's cave of ethnographic wonders and exotic colour. When she moved in the place was all dull 'beige carpets and magnolia walls', but images of Tibet, land of golds, reds and purples, inspired her to transform her walls with paint the colour of saris and spices. Gabbeh rugs made by wandering Iranian tribes and Tibetan tiger rugs now cover the dark wooden floors. Hossack's love of colour influences everything, including what she chooses to collect. The collection works in the setting because both were born of the same imagination.

The Australian Cultural Attaché in London and an art dealer, Rebecca Hossack inherited her taste for ethnographic art from her father, a doctor who worked in Papua New Guinea. As a child her bedroom was hung with Sepik masks which gave her a natural predilection for tribal art.

A large and disturbing painting entitled *The Big Shoot* by the Aborigine artist Mathias Kuage, dominates the yellow sitting-room wall above a deep sofa strewn with Rajasthani wedding dresses. It expresses the terror the artist felt on first encountering a white man, the doctor, who came to innoculate him and his schoolfriends. The absence of a frame demolishes the usual boundary which exists between a painting and the world of the viewer. The vibrant colours of the paintings are united with the similarly-coloured walls, creating a total environment in which we cannot distance ourselves from the pictures, and where we are forced to respond to them.

To the left three very fragile early Aboriginal paintings by Papunya Tula artists are, in contrast, enclosed by heavy wooden frames behind glass to protect them. The wide, rustic frames are in keeping with the rusticity of the wooden chests on which objects are displayed. Certain resonances are created by grouping things which share the same decorative patterns and symbols. This makes for an interesting 'cross-fertilization' of objects from different cultures. Bushmen tobacco-pouch holders, for example, have the same markings as an Ethiopian tribal gourd and the Papunya Tula paintings above. A Kuba chief's little conical hat echoes the shape of the gourd, while the bright-blue feathers in an Amazonian head-dress, given by Bruce Chatwin to the late Sally, Duchess of Westminster, sing out against a sunflower-yellow wall and amethyst woodwork.

The bedroom is peacock-green with yellow woodwork and deep rose-pink blinds edged with gold braid. Above the bed hangs a huge yellow feather mandorla by Simon Costin, which seems to reverberate against the bright green walls. The bedroom door is painted with symbols of the 'dreamings' of Aboriginal artist Clifford Possum, carried out after he once slept in the room. Thus his art becomes part of the fabric of the flat.

The corridor, hung with *coolomon*, the trugs used by Aborigines to carry berries, leads to the study, painted hot chilli-red. On the left wall hangs a circular picture *Rainbow Serpent Dreaming*, also by Clifford Possum. Two slithering serpents are depicted in slate greys, plums and ochres. The mesmerizing stippled paint strokes were created with the stump of a 'very expensive' brush given to Possum by Hossack, which he promptly snapped in two. The *motif* is picked up by two flanking snake candle sconces.

On the wall above the desk hangs a long green and turquoise landscape, *Burnt Wattle Creek*, by Robert Cambell, Jr., an Aborigine artist with no formal training. Illuminated by light streaming in from the curtainless window, the greens of the trees and grass are picked up by the emerald-coloured woodwork in the room. Hossack decided that the vivid colours of the picture, painted in the open air, looked best in daylight. After dark, twig lights, invisibly wired twigs with conical parchment shades, throw a soft, warm light upwards, without interfering or jarring with the woodiness of the objects. Like Catherine Turner, Rebecca Hossack chose not to spotlight her collection in order to preserve the pleasant warmth and cosiness of a sitting-room.

Two pairs of ceiling-to-floor glass cabinets with stained walnut frames face each other across Adrian Sassoon's drawing-room, dominated by Eva Jiricna's glass and steel spiral staircase. (ABOVE)

A collection of Vincennes and Sèvres porcelain is illuminated by tungsten-halogen lighting which throws an intense light, whiter than tungsten and warmer than natural daylight.
(ABOVE RIGHT)

The hot colours, clutter and earthy textures of Rebecca Hossack's tiny flat, decorated on a shoe-string budget, are a world apart from the order, clean lines, and cool, polished-plaster walls of Adrian Sassoon's airy Knightsbridge house, the interior of which was designed by the architect Eva Jiricna. A London art dealer and collector of ceramics, Sassoon dived into collecting with more courage than most. Whilst still at school he bought a ninety-piece eighteenth-century dinner service made of soft-paste Sèvres porcelain, which he saw in an auction catalogue. He hastens to add that he did consult an eminent dealer before bidding. Part of that original green *oeil-de-perdrix* service, painted with exotic birds from the Comte du Buffon's *Encyclopaedia of Birds*, is still in his possession. A gift from Louis XVI to the English diplomat William Eden, later Lord Auckland, it was purchased by the Prince Regent in 1814.

The experiments made by the early Vincennes and Sèvres potters are a particular passion. To show the porcelain to best effect, Sassoon asked Eva Jiricna to incorporate special display cabinets in her design. The backs of the cabinets are lined with mirrors, allowing the manufacturers' marks on the reverse of the plates to be seen, as well as opening out the rather narrow room by reflecting light from the windows and the adjacent terrace.

The shelves display a colourful variety of eighteenth-century Sèvres porcelain supported on perspex stands. Amongst the *bleu lapis* and *bleu céleste* there is a pair of *vases Danemark*, two rare Sèvres wine-bottle coolers with armorials and an unusual Sèvres 'peacock' *écuelle*. The cover of another enchanting *écuelle* (*bouillon* bowl) has a knop composed of a fish, shells and a mushroom: the ingredients in the soup. Dated *circa* 1750, the Vincennes bowl, cover and stand were once at

Mentmore in Buckinghamshire. A small oval Vincennes chamber-pot with rare chinoiserie hunting scenes is positioned to one side.

Although fibre-optics are rapidly becoming the museum curator's first choice of lighting, tungsten-halogen is still the preferred lighting for china and glass, and has been used in the display cabinets. Downlighters provide low-voltage, direct lighting, which sharpens colour, shows detail and makes the porcelain look bright and sparkling. The system can also be dimmed after dark, when it need not compete with the powerful natural light which floods the room in daytime. Additional light is provided by a discreet track with tiny bulbs fitted under alternate shelves and concealed by a narrow strip of sandblasted glass. These lights can be directed at specific objects or moved to prevent hotspots and avoid a flat, uniform effect.

As you descend the glass and steel spiral staircase to the ground floor, the colour of the walls changes from cream to pale green-grey. In the basement it deepens still further. Opposite the bottom of the staircase a slim glass-shelved display-cabinet is lit by spotlights at the top and base only, and no mirrors have been used. As the basement is darker than the drawing-room, the spots illuminate the shelves more evenly, making the intermediate bulbs unnecessary.

The cabinet displays a rare collection of 1970s delicate, white bone china by Jacqueline Poncelet and porcelain pieces by the late Eileen Nisbet, from the 1980s. This effect is created by the reflection of light from the door. At the bottom of the cabinet the light from the spots is diffused by a plate of sandblasted glass, adding an extra glow in the dark.

Works of art can be satisfactorily displayed in almost any interior, whether it be a grand country house or a tiny city flat. There are no hard and fast rules. Each of the above collectors has proved that there is no need to convert a house into a museum in order to make a successful display. Some have created settings intended for specific objects; others demonstrate how comprehensive collections can work in existing settings. Their achievement has been to enrich their collections, opening the objects to new interpretation, through the expression of their own taste.

In Adrian Sassoon's basement, bone china vessels by Jacqueline Poncelet and porcelain forms by Eileen Nisbet cast dramatic shadows against the marble-like grey walls behind. One of the Poncelet vases, the surface carved away in patterns, seems to fill with light which filters through its chinks when the glass door is closed.
(LEFT)

ART ON VIEW *by Richard Cork*

Nobody, looking back over exhibitions of the past year, could reasonably doubt the excellence of historical shows throughout the period. Despite the growing reluctance to lend by owners more and more conscious of their possessions' fragility, an impressive range of surveys added considerably to our knowledge of the past. My only reservation centres on the lack of major exhibitions devoted to Contemporary art. A distinct unwillingness to stage substantial shows of present-day work seems to have developed – fuelled, no doubt,

by anxieties about the availability of sponsors for anything other than blockbusters crammed with celebrated names.

The autumn of 1994 was especially rich in panoramic reassessments. At the Royal Academy, London, a mammoth survey brought together a resplendent array of painting, sculpture and drawing from eighteenth-century Venice. By that time, the city was in economic decline and fast losing its political power but its patronage continued, and the homegrown art embraced individuals as distinctive as Giambattista Tiepolo,

HENRY FUSELI

The Nightmare
1781, OIL ON CANVAS,
101 x 127cm (39¾ x 50in)
From the Collection of the
Detroit Institute of Arts

This work was included in the exhibition *The Romantic Spirit in German Art 1790–1990* held at the Hayward Gallery, London, from September 1994 to January 1995. (RIGHT)

Giovanni Battista Piazzetta, Canaletto and Francesco Guardi. No exhibition organizer can hope to convey the full, exhilarating impact of Tiepolo the fresco painter. But the artist's emotional range is surprisingly wide, and some of his finest canvases were borrowed, establishing that he was far more than a bravura decorator. Another revelation was provided by Piazzetta. Difficult to appreciate outside Italy, he is an outstandingly accomplished and eloquent interpreter of religious and secular themes alike.

Canaletto can easily look repetitive *en masse*, but the Academy chose well and emphasized the importance of his London sojourn. Painting the Thames and related subjects provided him with a fresh challenge, at a time when he was in danger of trapping himself within tired formulae. The show ended with a selection of carvings by Antonio Canova, none of which looked as impressive as the consummate *Three Graces*, finally secured for the nation after protracted international manoeuvring. The exhibition travelled to the National Gallery of Washington in 1995.

Few exhibitions span an era as vast or tumultuous as the Hayward Gallery's exploration of *The Romantic Spirit in German Art, 1790–1990*, which subsequently travelled to Munich. Not content with charting the rise of Romantic landscape painting in the early nineteenth century, the organizers drove the show forward to the late twentieth century. Controversy surrounded the outcome. If they had settled for a straightforward study of Caspar David Friedrich and his circle, the show would not have been faulted. After all, Britain is less familiar than it should be with Friedrich's achievements, and a strong representation of his work proved that Constable and Turner were not alone in revolutionizing the European vision of nature at that time. But by seeking to trace the continuation of the Romantic impulse right up to the present day, the exhibition risked blurring its definitions and came to resemble a comprehensive parade of major movements in twentieth-century German art, including Hitler's perverse twisting of Romantic precepts. By the close, where Joseph Beuys' apocalyptic floor-sculpture *The End of the Twentieth Century* dominated the final gallery, the

show seemed remote from the inspiration which had once nourished Friedrich's pioneering engagement with the natural world.

Several of the most outstanding individuals at the Hayward reappeared, in a very different guise, at *A Bitter Truth: Avant-Garde Art and the Great War*. As the selector of the show, which commenced earlier in the year at the Altes Museum in Berlin, I am in no position to assess its merits, but I wanted to reveal for the first time how major artists from Europe, Russia and the USA reacted to the traumatic events of this period. The exhibition's title came from Paul Nash, whose despairing and indignant images of Passchendaele are among the most powerful British paintings spawned by the killing fields. Appalled by the devastation, Nash wrote that 'it is unspeakable, godless, hopeless. I am no longer an artist interested and curious, I am a messenger who will bring back word from the men who are fighting to those who want the war to go on for ever. Feeble, inarticulate, will be my message, but it will have a bitter truth, and may it burn their lousy souls.'

At the beginning of the conflict, many reacted with enthusiasm and belligerence. But as the war proceeded, and increasing numbers of young lives were lost, artists in all the warring countries began to share Nash's stricken response. By the end, the pungent work of Max Beckmann, Otto Dix, George Grosz, Ernst Ludwig Kirchner and Käthe Kollwitz ensured that the German

PAUL NASH

The Menin Road,
1919
OIL ON CANVAS, 182.9 x 317cm
(72 x 124¾in)
From the Collection of the
Imperial War Museum, London

This work was included in the exhibition *A Bitter Truth: Avant-Garde Art and the Great War* held at the Barbican Art Gallery, London, from September to December 1994. (BELOW)

contribution was immensely forceful. A range of work from other nations also testified to a widespread determination to confront the full extent of the tragedy.

After all this relentless devastation, the James McNeill Whistler retrospective at the Tate Gallery, and afterwards at the National Gallery of Washington, came as a relief. The pugnacity of Whistler's public pronouncements on art contrasted with the quiet lyricism of his work. The most impressive room was devoted to his paintings of the Thames. Concentrating on the river at dusk, when most of the incidental detail had disappeared in the fading light, Whistler arrived at an extraordinarily simplified and refined vision. His desire to develop an extreme form of distillation still looks modern, even if we no longer believe that art should aspire to the condition of music. At a time when the Pre-Raphaelites and their successors insisted on freighting their images with an overload of pictorial information, Whistler's purgative approach was refreshing. So were some of his portraits – most notably an austere painting of Thomas Carlyle, where the writer is seen in profile as a haggard seer exhausted by his own unremitting labours.

Yet Whistler could not sustain the same level of achievement forever. Like Carlyle, he seems to have suffered from fatigue in his later years. The notorious libel trial with John Ruskin, who had denounced one of his paintings, was a pyrrhic victory. It affected Whistler profoundly, and the final room of portraits showed a decline in power.

Soon after the Whistler show opened, the Tate also played host to the latest Turner Prize shortlist. Four artists were included, and the range of work was wider than usual. Many years have passed since a landscape painter like Peter Doig has appeared in the Turner line-up, and Antony Gormley's body-casts contrasted dramatically with Shirazeh Houshiary's more abstract and mystical work. The Northern Irish artist Willie Doherty used a video installation to meditate on his country's violent history, but Gormley won the day with his sombre, stoical images of Everyman. The Turner Prize generates a great deal of publicity, providing an ideal opportunity to stage a really substantial show of new work. Yet it

always errs on the side of modesty. I hope that in future the Tate decides to expand the exhibition and give Contemporary art a proper airing.

Down at Dulwich, the superb Picture Gallery sounded an enterprising note around Christmas 1994. Lucian Freud was invited to show his recent paintings among the Old Masters and the outcome proved compelling. The room was dominated by Peter Paul Rubens' newly-cleaned *Venus, Mars and Cupid*, one of his uninhibited celebrations of woman at her most buxom and bountiful. Freud held his ground, with a monumental oil of *A Benefit Supervisor Resting*. This brazen image of an overweight, naked woman seated on a sagging sofa countered the conventional titillation of Peter Lely's *Nymphs by a Fountain*. On the other side of the Rubens, Freud displayed his equal mastery of the male body in *Leigh Under the Skylight*. His model, the performance artist Leigh Bowery who died soon afterwards, is shown standing askance on a table and vying with Rubens' Venus in the amplitude of his flesh.

The show proved that living artists can invade historical collections in an immensely stimulating way. Only a few years ago, such an intervention would have been unthinkable. But now even the British Museum is prepared to open its doors to contemporary work. For a few weeks, the august dignity of the Egyptian Gallery played host to a number of artists. The outcome was somewhat congested, and several of the contributions looked out of place among the pharaohs. Still, the sculptures by Stephen Cox and Marc Quinn seemed at home, enlivening the ancient carvings with their presence and forcing us to look at even the most familiar exhibits in a fresh way.

No such provocative ideas guided the organizers of the splendid Nicolas Poussin retrospective. Having started at the Grand Palais in Paris, this monumental show arrived at the Royal Academy, London early in 1995. It lacked the drawings included so prominently in the Paris version, but Poussin's paintings looked magnificent at Burlington House.

Never before had such an array of his finest work been assembled in Britain, despite the fact that so many of his major paintings are in British collections. The early rooms devoted to his Titianesque mythologies were enchanting and seductive, dispelling the notion that Poussin is always a cold, cerebral artist. But the change in his middle years is profound, marking the ascendance of Raphael as the cardinal influence. The prevailing mood now grows sombre. Poussin develops into a severe classicist, and the figures who had once seemed so sensual take on the rigidity of statues. He remains impressive, though, and the final room gave over the largest of the Academy's spaces to a grand group of his landscapes. The full extent of his contribution to European painting was thereby disclosed, helping to explain why Paul Cézanne admired Poussin so ardently.

Sometimes, however, the exhibitions which give most pleasure do not focus on the greatest and most predictable names. At the National Gallery, where an excellent small show had already been mounted on Michelangelo's long-disputed paintings in the collection, a quiet revelation arrived in the form of an exhibition devoted to *Spanish Still Life*. Great artists were included, of course – Diego Velázquez was there in force, most notably with his astounding *Old Woman Cooking Eggs* painted when he was only nineteen. But the opening room was dominated by Juan Sanchez Cotán, who executed a haunting image of a quince and cabbage suspended above an illusionistic window-ledge, each dangling from a length of string like the victims of a public hanging. A melon resting on the ledge has already been slashed open. With great severity, Cotán left most of the background dark and void, its blackness reminding the viewer that extinction awaits even the most robust of the larder's occupants.

The rest of the show maintained a high level of intensity, spanning the austerity of Francisco Zurbarán as well as the sumptuousness of Antonio de Pereda. It reached an unforgettable climax with the work of Goya, whose studies of a dead turkey, fish and sheep provide no comfort in their stark exploration of mortality. The sheep's severed, blood-clogged head seems to stare at us with his doleful eye, and we shudder to recognize our own expendability in this cheerless, uncannily modern image of still life as dead meat.

Man Ray attracted huge interest when his work was shown at the Serpentine Gallery. Although some of the paintings he produced throughout his long career were included, they did not possess the conviction of his work with a camera. Man Ray was, quite simply, a master photographer. Whether taking the portrait of a fellow artist, or juxtaposing a model with a Surrealist object, he was able to create memorable images with hallucinatory force. He may have felt frustrated about his inability to gain unqualified approval as a painter, but his restless inventiveness as a photographer, filmmaker and manipulator of found objects ensures that he remains a potent force today.

James McNeill Whistler

Nocturne: Blue and Gold – Old Battersea Bridge *c.*1872–75, OIL ON CANVAS, 67.9 x 50.8cm (26¾ x 20in) From the Collection of the Tate Gallery, London

This painting was shown in the exhibition of the artist's work held at the Tate Gallery, London, from October 1994 to January 1995. (ABOVE)

YVES KLEIN
Leap Into The Void
PERFORMANCE BY YVES KLEIN, PHOTOGRAPH BY HARRY SHUNK
OCTOBER 1960, 120 x 80cm (47¼ x 31½in)
From the Collection of Harry Shunk

This photograph was originally published in Klein's paper *Dimanche*, 27 November 1960, with the caption 'A Man in Space! The painter of space throws himself into the void!' and was featured in the exhibition *Yves Klein: Leap Into The Void* at the Hayward Gallery, London, from February to April 1995. (ABOVE)

So does Yves Klein, whose career was cut short with his death in 1962 at the age of thirty-four. His Hayward Gallery retrospective was entitled *Leap Into The Void* – a reference to his arresting image of the artist jumping from a fifteen-foot high wall. His appetite for experiment took a prodigious variety of forms. Whether he was performing judo throws, directing a gas jet at canvases to make fire paintings or smearing nude models with blue pigment to produce his scandalous body paintings, Klein opened up new possibilities for post-war European art. Wisely, the Hayward did not allow entertaining film footage of his body performances to completely over-shadow the products of these notorious events. The emphasis was placed on the art itself – above all, the luminous blue monochrome paintings, which looked extraordinarily radiant and pure on the gallery's white walls. The exhibition was later shown in Cologne, Dusseldorf and Madrid.

Over in Paris, spring was marked by the advent of Constantin Brancusi at the Pompidou Centre, an exhibition which later travelled to the Philadelphia Museum of Art. Because of their frailty, Brancusi's carvings are rarely brought together, but the loans secured for this survey were outstanding, enabling visitors to trace his formidable progress from provincial Romanian beginnings to pre-eminence as a sculptor venerated across the world.

Some of the most beguiling exhibits were found in the show's early stages. Brancusi underwent an astonishing transformation when he left his youthful academicism behind and started carving directly into the stone. The single-mindedness of his vision henceforth set new standards for other experimental sculptors, as he pared his work down to an ever more simplified sequence of forms. Sometimes, the sculpture at the Pompidou was clustered too tightly together, militating against the works' limpid stillness. But in other rooms a clearing was found for a trio of gleaming birds in space, or a solitary fish presiding over its gallery with effortless authority and grace.

The most ambitious contemporary exhibition was staged in Venice, where the Biennale celebrated its centenary with an elaborate survey of art and the human body. Staged principally at the Palazzo Grassi, it was curated by Jean Clair, the first foreign director to be appointed by the Biennale committee. Starting with works from 1895, Clair quickly emphasized the most vulnerable and disturbing aspects of his chosen theme. Self-portraits by Beckmann, Dix and Pierre Bonnard stood out, while British painters from Francis Bacon to David Hockney were strongly represented.

At the Giardini, the British Pavilion was devoted to recent paintings by Leon Kossoff. It stood out in a Biennale otherwise disappointing and lacking the vital element of surprise. Bill Viola contributed an excellent US Pavilion, transforming its darkened rooms into a virtuoso exploration of *Buried Secrets* which confirmed his stature as a leading video artist. Elsewhere, however, the Biennale suffered from Clair's inexplicable decision to abolish the Aperto section, where young artists often receive their first important international exposure. So the British Council deserved congratulations for organizing a lively survey of young British artists at the Scuola di San Pasquale instead.

Finally, in the summer, the Tate Gallery staged a survey of Contemporary art 'for the end of the century'. Although entitled *Rites of Passage*, it proved to be preoccupied with mortality. From the outset, where the septuagenarian John Coplans photographed his sagging flesh with disarming frankness, the Grim Reaper stalked the entire show. Mona Hatoum probed the glistening insides of her own body with a tiny medical camera, daring us to feel squeamish, and Susan Hiller offered a noisy, violent dramatization of the sadism inherent in a Punch and Judy show. The best works in this international survey were ambiguous in meaning, like Pepe Espaliú's empty birdcages, half forlorn and half lyrical. The fact that he died recently, of an AIDS-related illness, only added to the show's funereal mood.

The Tate's willingness to involve itself more fully with new work, whether in *Rites of Passage* or the recently-opened space devoted to Art Now, is a welcome development. Now that the Millennium Commission is likely to fund a number of new arts projects, Britain seems poised at last to give living artists the attention they deserve.

CONSTANTIN BRANCUSI
Princess X
1915–16, BRONZE, 61.7 x 40.5 x 22.2cm (24¼ x 16 x 8¾in)
From the Collection of the Musée National d'Art Moderne, Centre Georges Pompidou, Paris

This sculpture was included in the exhibition of the artist's work held at the Centre Georges Pompidou, Paris, from April to August 1995. (LEFT)

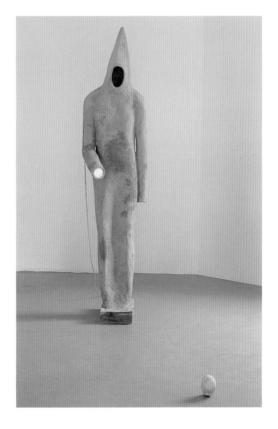

MIROSLAW BALKA
Shepherdess
1988–89, CONCRETE, GLASS, WOOD AND WIRE, 217 x 55 x 62cm (85½ x 21⅝ x 24⅜in)
From The Schyl Collection, Malmö Konsthall, Sweden

This work was included in the exhibition *Rites of Passage* held at the Tate Gallery, London, from June to September 1995. (LEFT)

II
Art
at
Auction

THE FINE ARTS *by Simon de Pury*

The rejuvenation of the world art markets in the 1990s has proved to be a hearteningly steady process, and we are arriving at a situation that is not only lively and successful, but also strongly rooted in a cautious – rather than a flamboyant – faith in the future. Such a base is a great deal healthier than the roller-coaster ride of the 1980s, but it hasn't prevented some splendid fireworks this last season. Because of a new confidence in conditions, exceptional objects are once again being released onto the market, some with exceptional results. In the field of the Fine Arts this market activity has been pronounced. In May 1995, Picasso's portrait of Angel Fernandez de Soto sold for $29,152,500, the highest price achieved for a painting since 1990. But there were other equally gratifying successes.

Old Master paintings, traditionally a conservative field with conservative collectors, generated highly energetic sales in both London and New York, and not a little drama. Two groups of delightful works from the British Rail Pension Fund were offered in London in December 1994 and July 1995. One of the paintings, Meindert Hobbema's A Wooded Landscape with Cottages, was bought by the Mauritshuis in the Hague for an impressive £3,741,500. Also in this group was a work Sotheby's had sold in 1976 and featured on the cover of the 1975–76 edition of Art at Auction, G.D. Tiepolo's The Tiepolo Family. In July this year it sold for £606,500.

Another group of Old Masters to generate considerable interest were the paintings from The New-York Historical Society, which brought some $12.2 million. These included the 'birthplate' of Lorenzo de' Medici, a painted salver representing 'The Triumph of Fame', which sold for $2.2 million.

In Europe, a fascinating discovery was made by the London Old Master paintings department of an early Georges de La Tour of St John the Baptist, the image presaging the ideas of Expressionism centuries later. This picture raised FF11,100,000. At the close of the season another remarkable picture, a powerful cabinet piece by Goya, was sold for £1,816,500 – far beyond its estimate.

GEORGE BELLOWS
Dock Builders
(detail)
SIGNED *GEO. BELLOWS, 1916*,
OIL ON CANVAS, 76.8 x 97.2cm
(30¼ x 38¼in)
New York $1,377,500
(£881,600). 1.XII.94
(LEFT)

ROSALBA CARRIERA
Portrait of Anton
Maria Zanetti
PASTEL, 22.5 x 17.3cm
(8⅞ x 6¾in)
New York $51,750 (£33,120).
10.I.95 (ABOVE)

RUFINO TAMAYO
El flautista
SIGNED AND DATED *0–44*, OIL
ON CANVAS, 114.6 x 94.6cm
(45⅛ x 37¼in)
New York $855,000
(£547,200). 17.V.95
From the IBM International
Foundation Collection
(ABOVE)

Of the earlier British pictures, one of the most charming was Gainsborough's Portrait of Master John Truman-Villebois and his Brother Henry. *This compelling work from around 1780 was sold in April for £661,500. More recent British paintings to make a mark included one of the main versions of Holman Hunt's ubiquitous image of the young Christ,* The Shadow of Death, *which sold for £1,871,500 in November 1994.*

As with the previous season, the dominant performer in the sales of nineteenth-century European paintings was Tissot: Le banc de jardin *achieved $5,282,500 in New York in October. Substantial figures were achieved by other artists, such as Gustave Moreau, whose ethereal* The Death of Sappho *was sold in June for £551,500.*

The second highest total ever for a Latin American art auction was achieved when our May sale in New York, which included property from the IBM International Foundation, brought $12.9 million. Over two days, eleven artists' records were set. Also encouraging was the marked increase in the numbers of international bidders at these sales. Frida Kahlo continues to be one of the most sought after of Latin American artists: her Autorretrato con chango y loro *sold in May for $3,192,500.*

The market for American paintings continues to be strong, and in May, works worth $29.8 million were sold in New York, the highest such total since November 1989. This sale included exceptional works from the IBM International Foundation, and broke a number of artists' records, among them Frank Benson, George Bellows and the ever popular Norman Rockwell.

The IBM collection also featured significantly in the season's New York sales of Contemporary art, which set records for such artists as John Chamberlain and Gerhard Richter. Sales of Contemporary art in London in June brought the highest total since 1990. Francis Bacon's Study for a Portrait of John Edwards *sold for £1,321,500, the first time the £1 million mark had been surpassed in London for a work of Contemporary art since December 1991. The renewed vigour of Bacon's status on the international art market was further shown by the sale of a powerful* Study for a Head *from 1960, which sold in November in London for £672,500.*

As in the last two seasons, the deep-rooted strength of the international markets was best revealed by sales of Impressionist and Modern art. The most impressive event was the sale in New York of the Donald and Jean Stralem

EDOUARD VUILLARD
Paysages et interieurs
1899, FROM A COLLECTION
OF TWELVE LITHOGRAPHS
PRINTED IN COLOURS,
39.5 x 31cm (15½ x 12¼in)
New York $162,000
(£102,060). 12.V.95
(ABOVE)

Collection in May. The quality and freshness of the works made this group highly desirable. The highlight was undoubtedly Picasso's Angel Fernandez de Soto, *but a delightful Matisse,* La pose Hindoue, *also did exceptionally well, selling for $14.9 million, and establishing a new auction record for the artist. The November New York sale was also notable, and featured a wonderful Modigliani portrait which sold for $5,942,500.*

November in London saw the sale of paintings, drawings and sculpture from the collection of the distinguished connoisseur, Alfred Richet. In June the star of the sale was Gauguin's Tahitiennes près d'un ruisseau, *a rare work from the artist's first visit to Tahiti. The importance of this painting was acknowledged by the market, and the price rose to £5.5 million. Other interesting works sold in London included the only recorded complete oil study for Kandinsky's work,* Improvisation 4, *which sold for £2.75 million.*

The season also saw a number of emerging collecting areas begin to establish significant status. Russian paintings gained notable success in their London June sale, with a new auction record being achieved by Ivan Konstantinovich Aivazovsky's Panorama of Constantinople, *which realized £326,000. Art in Israel also displayed signs of growth. 1994 was the tenth anniversary of Sotheby's, Israel, and the April sale featured rare works by Felix Nussbaum, as well as pieces by Chagall, Soutine and Rubin.*

Photography also had a special year – and London a remarkable sale – when an important collection of works by Man Ray was auctioned in March. Amongst the 500 works on offer was an exceptional group of photographs, including a portrait of Marcel Duchamp, which made £42,200.

New records abounded in the 1994–95 Fine Arts season, for individual artists and for specialist areas. No better indication could be given of the new confidence enjoyed by the markets, and this mood will hopefully help more works of quality to come to auction in the new season.

Christ among the Doctors, or 'Mid Pentecost'
1475–1500, FROM THE
FESTIVAL TIER OF THE
ICONOSTAS OF THE CHURCH
OF SAINT NICHOLAS IN THE
VILLAGE OF GOSTINOPOL ON
THE RIVER VOLKHOV,
53.5 x 42cm (21⅛ x 16½in)
London £232,500 ($372,000).
15.VI.95
From the Estate of Blanchette
H. Rockefeller

This work achieved a
world record at auction
for an icon. (BELOW)

OLD MASTER PAINTINGS

SALOMON VAN RUYSDAEL

A Wijdschip and Other Small Dutch Vessels on the River Waal, with the Town of Gorinchem to the Right

SIGNED WITH MONOGRAM *SVR* AND DATED *1659*, OIL ON OAK PANEL, 42 x 37.3cm (16½ x 14¾in)
London £1,541,500 ($2,450,985). 5.VII.95

The town of Gorinchem stands on the north bank of the river Waal and is seen here from the middle of the river looking downstream towards the west. The artist has exaggerated the prominence of the tower of the Groote Kerk for dramatic effect: in this and other important respects the view is far from accurate topographically. (ABOVE)

MEINDERT HOBBEMA
A Wooded Landscape with Cottages
SIGNED ..*HOBBEMA*, OIL ON CANVAS,
89.5 x 122cm (35¼ x 48in)
London £3,741,500 ($5,836,740). 7.XII.94
From the Collection of the British Rail Pension Fund

This picture and its companion piece, now in the National Gallery, Washington, are among Hobbema's finest works, painted between 1662 and 1668, when he was at the peak of his powers. Hobbema's most characteristic paintings show a type of wooded landscape associated with the less familiar eastern provinces of the Netherlands, such as Gelderland and Drenthe. His understanding of the texture of landscape elements, rendered with thickly applied unthinned paint, gives Hobbema's paintings a solidity and monumentality matched only by Jacob van Ruisdael at his best. (LEFT)

FRANS POST
The Church of St Cosmas and St Damian, and the Franciscan Monastery at Igaraçu, Brazil
SIGNED *F. POST*, OIL ON PANEL,
42.8 x 58.8cm (16¾ x 23¼in)
London, £1,211,500 ($1,889,940). 7.XII.94
From the Collection of the British Rail Pension Fund

Between 1636 and 1644, Frans Post was resident in the Brazilian town of Recife as a member of the retinue of Prince Johann Maurits of Nassau-Siegen. During this time, and after his return, he produced a large number of paintings depicting Brazilian landscapes. Demand for these scenes was enormous as Dutch collectors chose to associate themselves with their nation's military power and economic success by ownership of pictures which would have been seen as patriotic symbols of the country's aspirations. (RIGHT)

LORENZO DI ANDREA D'ODERIGO, CALLED LORENZO DI CREDI
Saint Quirinus of Neuss
OIL AND TEMPERA ON PANEL, 124.5 x 53.3cm (49 x 21in)
New York $1,212,500 (£776,000). 12.I.95

Lorenzo di Credi was the son of Andrea, a goldsmith. Although he
may have had some training as a sculptor, he enrolled in Andrea
Verrocchio's studio as a painter and remained there until
Verrocchio's death in 1488. Leonardo da Vinci was a fellow pupil
whose work had a significant influence on Lorenzo di Credi's art.
The subject of this painting has been in debate, but is now thought
to be Saint Quirinus, a military tribune of the second century who
was martyred by having his limbs sawed off, one by one. He is
generally represented as a young, early-Christian warrior holding
a shield and a banner with nine balls (or *palle*), as he does here.
It is thought that Lorenzo di Credi must have received the
commission from a patron with a very specific interest in
such an unusual saint. (LEFT)

GIOVANNI DI SER GIOVANNI DI SIMONE, CALLED LO SCHEGGIA, FORMERLY KNOWN AS THE
MASTER OF THE ADIMARI CASSONE AND THE MASTER OF FUCECCHIO

The Birth Salver of Lorenzo de' Medici. Recto: The Triumph of Fame, Verso: The Medici and Tornabuoni Coats of Arms

CIRCULAR, TEMPERA, SILVER AND GOLD ON WOOD IN ITS ORIGINAL FRAME DECORATED WITH TWELVE MEDICI FEATHERS,
diameter of painted surface 62.2cm (24½in)
New York $2,202,500 (£1,409,600). 12.I.95
From the Collection of The New-York Historical Society

Commissioned by Piero de' Medici in 1449 to celebrate the birth of his first son, Lorenzo 'il
Magnifico', this impressive painted salver is the first work of art associated with Lorenzo, one
of the most influential art collectors of the Italian Renaissance. The source of the depictions,
undoubtedly dictated to the painter by an intellectual adviser to Piero, is Boccaccio's *L'Amorosa
visione*, specifically Book VI. On the recto, shown here, winged Fame stands with arms
outstretched; in her right hand she holds a sword and in her left a statuette of Cupid with his
bow drawn. She surmounts a globe pierced by six portholes out of which six winged trumpets
sound, heralding the arrival of the newborn and his anticipated fame. The design exemplifies
the artistic rigour of single-point perspective and the format is consciously anchored by the
erect figure of Fame whose wings touch the edges of the compositional field and support the
curved frame; it is she who keeps the circular panel from visually spinning. (ABOVE)

GEORGES DE LA TOUR
Saint John the Baptist in the Desert
OIL ON CANVAS, 81 x 101cm (31⅞ x 39¾in)
Monaco FF11,100,000 (£1,323,004:$2,067,039). 2.XII.94

Previously unrecorded, this painting was recently discovered in France by a Sotheby's expert.
La Tour's work consists exclusively of religious and genre subjects and divides clearly into day
and night scenes. Hugh Brigstocke has commented of *Saint John the Baptist*: 'The
physiognomy of the head, the distinctive modelling of the saint's right shoulder and left knee
and the delicate chiaroscuro all point beyond any doubt to the hand of Georges de La Tour...
At the same time, the picture breaks totally new ground in our knowledge of the artist because
it is the only nocturnal picture by him in which there is no artificial source of light such as a
candle or torch, which strongly suggests that the artist was inspired directly by Caravaggio
himself as opposed to his northern followers.' (ABOVE)

DOMENIKOS THEOTOKOPOULOS, CALLED EL GRECO

Christ on the Cross, in a Landscape with Horsemen

SIGNED OR INSCRIBED IN GREEK AND INSCRIBED
ABOVE THE HEAD OF CHRIST IN HEBREW,
GREEK AND LATIN *JESUS NAZARE/
NVSREXIUDEOR*, OIL ON CANVAS,
96.5 x 61.1cm (38 x 24¹⁄₁₆in)
New York $2,312,500 (£1,480,000). 19.V.95
From the Gutzwiller Family

The subject of a living *Christ on the
Cross (Cristo vivo)* as a non-narrative,
devotional image, while not invented
by El Greco, became important to
him in the last quarter of the
sixteenth century and the beginning
of the next. Several of his works on
this theme were large altar-scale
paintings, datable to the first decade
of the seventeenth century, but he
also painted a number of smaller and
more personal depictions of the
subject for private devotion, of which
this is an example. These smaller
paintings appear to date from both
before and after the larger versions
of the subject. (LEFT)

FRANCISCO JOSÉ GOYA Y LUCIENTES
Sorting the Bulls
INSCRIBED ON THE REVERSE *5* AND *9*, OIL ON TIN PLATE, 42.6 x 32cm (16¾ x 12½in)
London £1,816,500 ($2,888,000). 5.VII.95

Goya's passionate interest in bull-fighting – his admiration for the skills of the *toreros*, his empathy with the crowd's
excitement and his feeling for the proud grandeur and stubborn courage of the bulls – was reflected in paintings
and etchings throughout his career. This work is one of a series of twelve painted in oil on sheets of tin plate, of
which six are devoted to bull-fighting and six to other themes from Spanish life including a shipwreck, a madhouse
and strolling players enacting an allegory. Goya wrote, 'I set myself to painting a series of cabinet pictures in which
I have been able to depict themes that cannot usually be addressed in commissioned works, in which *capricho*
(fantasy) and inventive creativity have little part to play.' (ABOVE)

Sir Peter Paul Rubens
Portrait of the Young Anthony van Dyck

Oil on panel, 36.2 x 26cm (14¼ x 10¼in)
New York $882,500 (£564,800). 12.I.95

This portrait has been almost universally accepted as representing the young Anthony van Dyck aged fifteen or sixteen years old, thus dating it to around 1615. It relates most directly to Rubens' copy after Willem Key's *Self-Portrait* in Berlin. Executed five or six years earlier, the *Self-Portrait* depicts the sitter turned to the left and just catching the viewer's glance. The subjects of both paintings wear hats and cloaks although in the earlier work Rubens reveals the artist's hand as well. The *Portrait of the Young Anthony van Dyck* has the intimacy of a self-portrait perhaps because it has been painted by a friend and mentor in an eloquent and spontaneous manner. (Right)

Giovanni Domenico Tiepolo
The Tiepolo Family

Inscribed *B.T.*, oil on canvas, red ground,
63.5 x 92.5cm (25 x 36½in)
London £606,500 ($964,000). 5.VII.95

Although traditionally attributed to Pietro Longhi and more recently to Lorenzo Tiepolo, this unfinished picture is now thought to be by Giovanni Domenico Tiepolo. The animated informal mood and the spontaneous execution suggest Giovanni Domenico's hand, rather than that of his younger brother, Lorenzo's, whose aesthetic aims were different. The picture probably shows Lorenzo making a pastel portrait of his mother, Cecilia Tiepolo. Behind her stands Giuseppe Maria Tiepolo, and to her left are the three younger daughters of the family, Orsola, Anjelica and Elena. The dog's collar is inscribed *B.T.* which is customarily interpreted as Battista Tiepolo. In view of the sitters' ages the picture probably dates from the second half of the 1750s. (Below)

OLD MASTER DRAWINGS

BERNARD VAN ORLEY

Johan IV van Nassau and his wife Maria van Loon-Heinsberg

PEN, BROWN INK AND WATERCOLOUR OVER TRACES OF BLACK CHALK, 34.8 x 49cm (13⅔ x 19¼in)
New York $387,500 (£248,000). 10.I.95

This and the accompanying drawing of Otto, Count of Nassau and his wife Adelheid van
Vianden are previously unrecorded preparatory studies by Bernard van Orley for two of eight
tapestries woven to his designs *circa* 1530. The series of tapestries known as the 'Nassau
Genealogy', now lost, was commissioned by Henry III of Nassau, one of Emperor Charles V's
most reliable councillors. They illustrate the line of the house of Oranje-Nassau, ancestors of
the Royal House of the Netherlands, from the early thirteenth to the early sixteenth century.
Apart from the present two drawings, five other preparatory designs are known, four in the
Staatliche Graphische Sammlung, Munich and one in the Musée de Rennes. (ABOVE)

GIOVANNI BATTISTA TIEPOLO
A View of the Entrance to a Farm
PEN, BROWN INK AND WASH, 18.9 x 28.3cm (7½ x 11⅛in)
New York $118,000 (£75,520). 10.I.95
From 'A Window on Venice: Eighteenth Century Venetian Drawings
from a European Private Collection'

Professor George Knox has pointed out that this
drawing is one of five views by Tiepolo of the same
group of rustic buildings seen from various angles.
The present work is most similar to a study in the
British Museum, also of the gateway but from a
closer view-point. Drawn from life, most of the
works in this series were executed between the
spring of 1757 and the summer of 1759. (LEFT)

JEAN-BAPTISTE OUDRY
'Rendez-vous au carrefour du puits du roi, Forêt de Compiègne' or 'Le botte du roi'
SIGNED *JB OUDRY*, PEN AND POINT OF THE BRUSH, BLACK INK AND GREY WASH OVER BLACK CHALK,
HEIGHTENED WITH WHITE ON FADED BLUE PAPER, 31.2 x 52.2cm (12¼ x 20½in)
London £100,500 ($160,800). 3.VII.95

The great *Chasses royales* tapestries, Oudry's most ambitious project, were commissioned by Louis XV
in 1733 to decorate the royal apartments of the Château de Compiègne, where they can still be seen.
Originally conceived as three panels, the series extended over the next thirteen years to nine. The
weaving, overseen by Oudry himself, began in 1736 at the Gobelins workshops utilizing cartoons
measuring twenty-eight feet in length. This drawing is a refined *première pensée* depicting
the moment before the royal hunt begins. (ABOVE)

BRITISH PICTURES 1500–1850

CIRCLE OF HANS HOLBEIN
Portrait of Henry VIII
OIL ON PANEL, 65 x 51cm (25½ x 20in)
London £298,500 ($480,585). 9.XI.94

This fine portrait of Henry VIII is an early derivation of Holbein's celebrated image
of the king in the mural painted for Whitehall Palace in 1537. While the mural itself
was destroyed in the palace fire of 1698, this portrait faithfully reflects the skill of
Holbein's original. The wide shoulders of the king and the intense effect of his gaze,
looking straight out from the panel, create an image of the all-powerful monarch,
emphasizing his new position as head of the Church. (ABOVE)

THOMAS GAINSBOROUGH
Portrait of Master John Truman-Villebois and his Brother Henry
OIL ON CANVAS, 155 x 129.5cm (61 x 51in)
London £661,500 ($1,051,785). 12.IV.95

This charming, beautifully constructed portrait is one of four major works by Gainsborough commissioned by the Truman family. Dating from *circa* 1780, it foreshadows the painter's celebrated 'fancy pictures', works depicting attractive subjects which combined portrait and landscape in a perfect fusion. The effect of the painting is wholly natural as if Gainsborough has observed the two boys at play without being noticed, and yet the composition is cleverly based on a triangle, loosely echoing the shape of the pile of cards. (ABOVE)

GEORGE CHINNERY

The Inner Harbour, Macau, Seen From the Casa Gardens

OIL ON CANVAS, 44 x 34cm (17¼ x 13½in)

London £98,300 ($156,297). 12.VII.95

On 29 September 1825 George Chinnery reached Macau at the end of his long journey from
India. Apart from brief periods in Canton and Hong Kong, Macau remained his home until
his death in 1852. The picturesque peninsula, first settled by the Portuguese in the 1550s,
provided Chinnery with an ideal source of material for his atmospheric paintings of local
scenery and this important work is among the most evocative of his Macau landscapes. (ABOVE)

JOHN CLEVELEY, SR.
Deptford Shipyard
SIGNED AND DATED *I CLEVELEY. PINXIT 1754*,
OIL ON CANVAS, 108.5 x 180cm (42¾ x 71in)
London £199,500 ($317,205). 12.VII.95

This is one of a small group of pictures by John Cleveley celebrating the launching of great men of war on the Thames in the early 1750s, a period in which such an event would have been an important public occasion. The artist's depiction of the river Thames teeming with life suggests the influence of Canaletto who worked in England from 1746–55. Like Canaletto, Cleveley transcended the purely topographical demands of the subject and produced a composition of considerable grandeur. (LEFT)

JAMES SEYMOUR
A Groom on Flying Childers, with Horsemen Beyond
OIL ON CANVAS, 98 x 123cm (38½ x 48½in)
London £287,500 ($462,875). 9.XI.94

Flying Childers, generally considered the first supreme thoroughbred racehorse, was known as 'the fastest horse that was ever bred in the world'. Owned by his breeder Colonel Leonard Childers and subsequently by William, 2nd Duke of Devonshire, the horse never lost a race and through his many victories at Newmarket in the 1720s he became the first popular hero of racing. This picture was commissioned by Sir William Jolliffe, Seymour's principal patron, who owned an important group of paintings by the artist. (RIGHT)

BRITISH WATERCOLOURS AND TOPOGRAPHICAL PAINTINGS

JOSEPH MALLORD WILLIAM TURNER
Christk Church College, Oxford
WATERCOLOUR HEIGHTENED WITH BODYCOLOUR AND
SCRATCHING OUT, 29.9 x 41.9cm (11¾ x 16½in)
London £177,500 ($282,225). 12.IV.95

In 1825, Turner was commissioned by
Charles Heath to produce 121 illustrations
for the artist's most important series of
engravings, *Picturesque Views in England
and Wales*. In the event, only 96 were
published between 1827 and 1837. This
watercolour shows the view looking north
along St Aldgate's towards Carfax, with the
college on the right. The building work on
the left was probably included by Turner to
symbolize Oxford's contribution towards the
building of knowledge. (LEFT)

THOMAS SHOTTER BOYS
**A View Down Pall Mall Looking
Towards Trafalgar Square**
SIGNED WITH MONOGRAM *TB*, WATERCOLOUR OVER PENCIL
HEIGHTENED WITH BODYCOLOUR AND GUM ARABIC,
31 x 44.5cm (12 x 17½in)
London £34,500 ($54,855). 13.VII.95

Recently discovered, this rare early London view
by Boys shows a prospect taken from the junction
of Lower Regent Street and Waterloo Place
looking east down Pall Mall. The National
Gallery and the spire of St Martin-in-the-Fields
are visible in the distance. (RIGHT)

ATTRIBUTED TO JEAN-BAPTISTE VANMOUR
A Panoramic View of Constantinople
OIL ON CANVAS, UNFRAMED, 204 x 443cm (80¼ x 174in)
London £78,500 ($124,815). 19.X.94
From the Estate of Henry M. Blackmer

In 1768, Horace Walpole visited Adderbury House in Oxfordshire and recorded in his journal having seen five
great views, including this panorama of Constantinople, alongside similarly styled paintings of Jerusalem,
Persepolis, Isfahan and Aleppo in the hall. Taken from the heights above Scutari looking west, the work
encompasses the Bosphorus and the Golden Horn. (ABOVE)

SAMUEL PALMER
A Cornfield, Shoreham, at Twilight
PEN, BRUSH AND BROWN AND INDIAN INK ON WHITE CARD,
14.5 x 16cm (5¾ x 6¼in)
London £161,000 ($255,990). 12.IV.95

Samuel Palmer's rare watercolours and paintings dating
from the period when he lived in Shoreham, Kent are
imbued with a spiritual intensity which is reinforced
by their small scale and sometimes sombre palette.
Technically highly accomplished and employing a
surprising range of methods, they demonstrate the
power of a masterful draughtsman with a passion
for the rich abundance of nature. (LEFT)

BRITISH PICTURES FROM 1850

WILLIAM HOLMAN HUNT

The Shadow of Death

SIGNED, DATED AND INSCRIBED *18Whh70.3/Jerusalem*, OIL ON PANEL, 104.5 x 82cm (41 x 32¼in)
London £1,871,500 ($3,069,260). 2.XI.94

This painting, executed in London in 1873–74, is the third version of Holman Hunt's *The Shadow of Death*, one of his
most famous and memorable compositions. In its portrayal of Jesus Christ stretching and giving thanks to God after his
day's labour, it portends the Crucifixion not simply by the shadow cast upon the cross of carpenter's tools but also in
additional details such as the red head-dress echoing the crown of thorns and the silhouette of the saw's handle prefiguring
the spear which pierces Christ's side during the Passion. In his diary entry for 19 August 1955, Evelyn Waugh described it
as 'a superb painting .... The light and shadow on the legs is the finest achievement of the period'. (ABOVE)

SIR EDWARD JOHN POYNTER
The Cave of the Storm Nymphs
SIGNED WITH MONOGRAM AND DATED *19EJP03*, OIL ON CANVAS,
148 x 112cm (58¼ x 44¼in)
London £551,500 ($904,460). 2.XI.94

The subject of this painting is ostensibly a classical
one – the three nymphs may be recognized as the
daughters of Zeus who as dryads and nereids inhabited
woods, streams and sea-caves. While usually
embodying the virtues of abundance and grace they
sometimes assumed a siren-like character to prey upon
travellers, as here they have lured a vessel to its doom
by the sweetness of their music. Poynter believed that
art should concern itself with subjects that were
entirely imaginary rather than dealing directly with
mundane human experience, with the aim of being
both edifying and uplifting. *The Cave of the Storm
Nymphs* represents the consummation of decades of
thought and experiment on Poynter's part and may
be seen as the masterpiece of his late career. (RIGHT)

JOHN WILLIAM GODWARD
Dolce Far Niente
SIGNED AND DATED *1904*, OIL ON CANVAS, 50.8 x 76.2cm (20 x 30in)
New York $563,500 (£360,640). 16.II.95

In *Dolce Far Niente*, literally 'how sweet it is to do
nothing', Godward portrays a languorous damsel
dreamily reclining in blissful idleness. As in so many of
the artist's works, the female figure engages the viewer
by gazing out of the picture. This device adds
emotional thrust to what might otherwise seem like a
grandiose set-piece painting. The Italian model used
here became a mainstay of Godward's facial type, in
much the same way that Jane Morris came to represent
the Pre-Raphaelite image of femininity. (LEFT)

MODERN BRITISH PAINTINGS

SIR JOHN LAVERY
La pêcheuse, Grez-sur-Loing
SIGNED AND DATED *1884*, OIL ON CANVAS, 73.5 x 96.5cm (29 x 38in)
London £221,500 ($354,400). 2.VI.95

La pêcheuse is among the earliest in a distinctive group of Lavery's works painted at the village of Grez-sur-Loing and represents his first departure from the studio into *plein-air* painting. Grez-sur-Loing had been an artistic community for some time before Lavery arrived. Visitors to the village included Jean-Baptiste Corot and Jacob Maris, along with the writer Robert Louis Stevenson who wrote in lyrical terms about the mood of the place and the work of its resident painters. (ABOVE)

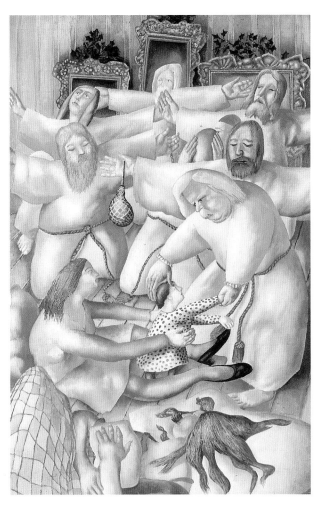

Sir Stanley Spencer
The Coming of the Wise Men
OIL ON CANVAS, 91.5 x 61cm (36 x 24in)
London £210,500 ($336,800). 21.VI.95

Painted in early 1940, *The Coming of the Wise Men* marks the beginning of Spencer's most important series of works in which he re-interprets the life of Christ according to his own beliefs and personal experience. The painting shows the magi arriving from the east to worship the infant Christ at His birth. Set in the Spencer family home in Cookham, the figures have been identified as various members of the artist's family. In the centre, Stanley's older sister Annie holds him as a child, while his oldest brother Will lays a hand on his head. In the foreground, Stanley's mother clasps a pillow to ease her bronchial chest, and the figures behind include Stanley's other brothers, his father and his sister Florence. (LEFT)

Sir Alfred Munnings
A Start: Moving up
SIGNED, OIL ON BOARD, 29.2 x 59.7cm (11½ x 23½in)
New York $431,500 (£271,845). 12.X.94
Sold to benefit the Cardiology Department in the Faculty of Medicine at the University of British Columbia, Vancouver

A Start was executed between 1952–53 at Newmarket, Munnings' favourite race course. The theme enabled Munnings to paint – as though using a zoom lens – a highly compact composition in which he could portray the excitement, tension and 'electricity' redolent in thoroughbred racing, the riotous colours of the jockeys' silks, the impressionistic light effects of the changing sky and the gleam of the horses' coats. (BELOW)

NINETEENTH-CENTURY EUROPEAN PAINTINGS

JAMES JACQUES JOSEPH TISSOT
Le banc de jardin
SIGNED, OIL ON CANVAS, 99.1 x 142.2cm (39 x 56in)
New York $5,282,500 (£3,327,975). 12.X.94

Between 1875 and 1882, Tissot was living in London with his mistress Kathleen Newton and her
children. Painted in the garden of Tissot's house in St John's Wood, *Le banc de jardin* was almost certainly
intended as an exhibition picture for the Royal Academy. Tragically, Mrs Newton died from consumption
before the work was finished and, distraught, Tissot returned to Paris where the painting was probably
completed. Although it was exhibited twice, Tissot retained the picture and it remained in obscurity until
its rediscovery at the Château de Buillon in 1964. Begun as a record of a high Victorian summer, it
became instead the memorial of a lost paradise. (ABOVE)

Joaquin Sorolla y Bastida
Llegada de las barcas
SIGNED AND DATED *1898*, OIL ON CANVAS,
48 x 101.5cm (19 x 40in)
London £496,500 ($789,435). 16.XI.94

Llegada de las barcas is an early
example of a whole series of
Valencian beach scenes painted by
Sorolla throughout his career.
Influenced by republican intellectuals
and politicians in Valencia and in
contrast to other Spanish artists of his
time, Sorolla set out to present Spain
as a joyful, healthy society, perfectly
integrated in contemporary Europe.
'One of my most cherished hopes', he
declared, 'is that in the longed-for
resurgence of my country Valencia
will take the lead in the industrial and
artistic movement as befits its
brilliant tradition and its inborn
artistic temperament.' (BELOW)

Giovanni Boldini
Portrait of Madame Georges Victor-Hugo
SIGNED, OIL ON CANVAS,
119 x 102cm (47 x 40in)
London £353,500 ($562,065). 14.VI.95

Madame Georges Victor-Hugo was
one of Boldini's favourite sitters and
featured in several of his paintings
and pastels. The preparatory sketches
indicate that Boldini pondered long
and hard over how to portray her.
Although society ladies were generally
portrayed in a pose of three-quarters
face, the slightly unorthodox pose in
this painting shows a full profile, and
was perhaps chosen to accentuate the
sharp features of the model. (LEFT)

ANGELO MORBELLI
In Risaia
(In the Rice Fields)
SIGNED AND DATED *1901*,
OIL ON CANVAS,
182.9 x 130.2cm (72 x 51¼in)
New York $2,202,500
(£1,409,600). 24.V.95

A member of the Italian
Divisionist movement,
Angelo Morbelli
employed the recently
discovered technique of
juxtaposing two colours,
as 'dots', 'points' or
parallel long, thin lines,
to optically fuse at a
given distance, making
all forms and effects of
light look as realistic as
possible. *In Risaia* is an
outstanding example of
this technique. Like
Jean-François Millet,
Morbelli was acutely
concerned with the
psychological and
physical condition of
alienated social groups
(the poor, the aged,
the insane) and this
canvas highlights his
empathy for the workers
and their seemingly
endless task. (RIGHT)

JEAN-FRANÇOIS MILLET
Le piège (The Bird Catcher)
SIGNED, CHARCOAL AND PASTEL ON PAPER, 61 x 50.2cm (24 x 19¾in)
New York $772,500 (£494,400). 24.V.95

Le piège is one of several pastels by Millet that pay tribute to
Pieter Brueghel the Elder, the great painter of peasant life, by
enlarging a small detail of that master's work into the theme of
an entire drawing. Here the homage is particularly touching in
that the pastel exploits a tiny incident in Brueghel's *Winter*
(variously known as *The Skaters* or *The Bird Trap*) which Millet
himself owned. But while the subject may have been inspired
by the sixteenth-century Flemish painting, the exceptional
composition, framing a tall, narrow slice of wintry, icy-bright
farmyard with a dark, dusty interior, is decidedly Millet's
own invention, a very nineteenth-century exploration of the
power of light and shadow to shape, define and ultimately
dissolve colour. (LEFT)

GIOVANNI SEGANTINI
Study zum Sein
SIGNED AND DATED *1898*, CHARCOAL
AND CONTÉ CRAYON ON PAPER,
80 x 136cm (31½ x 53½in)
Zurich SF317,800 (£172,717:$273,966).
12.VI.95

This drawing is the middle part of
a triptych entitled *Werden-Sein-Vergehen*, literally 'Becoming-
Being-Passing', which was first
shown in the Paris World
Exhibition of 1900. Although
largely self-taught, Segantini
evolved an extraordinary
technique for depicting light;
here, the enormous sky filled with
rays from the setting sun takes up
more than half the picture. (RIGHT)

GUSTAVE MOREAU
The Death of Sappho
SIGNED, OIL ON CANVAS, 81 x 62cm (32 x 24½in)
London £551,500 ($876,885). 14.VI.95

The myth of the Greek poetess Sappho and her tragic leap into the sea as a result of
her unrequited love for Phaon was a popular subject for writers and musicians, as well
as painters, during the nineteenth century. *The Death of Sappho* clearly shows an
artistic turning point for Moreau and his rich, flamboyant style displays the influence
of both the Romantic movement and Japanese art. The human figure is reduced to a
small scale giving extra emphasis to the fantastic landscape and rocks, and the use of
vibrant colours is remarkable. (ABOVE)

JULES BASTIEN-LEPAGE
The Sarah Bernhardt Portrait
SIGNED AND DATED *1879* AND DEDICATED *A SARAH BERNHARDT*, OIL ON CANVAS, 43.8 x 34.3cm (17¼ x 13½in)
New York $706,500 (£452,160). 24.V.95

The fame and magnetism of Sarah Bernhardt, the Divine Sarah, made her the most famous
female celebrity of her era. In 1879 she was visited by Bastien-Lepage who, while best known
today for his portrayal of rural life, was, at the time, equally famed as a Salon portrait painter.
He was captivated by Bernhardt – her vitality, fantastic tastes and independence – and caught all
her idiosyncrasies in this outstanding portrait. Seen in eccentric profile, she examines a figure of
Orpheus, an allusion to her love of sculpture and to the beauty of her voice. The steel frame
was almost certainly designed for the house Bernhardt had built on the rue Fortuny. (ABOVE)

RUSSIAN PAINTINGS

IVAN KONSTANTINOVICH AIVAZOVSKY

Panorama of Constantinople: The Golden Horn with the Nusretiye Mosque
SIGNED AND DATED *1856*, OIL ON CANVAS, 125 x 195cm (49¼ x 76¾in)
London £326,000 ($521,600). 15.VI.95

Aivazovsky enjoyed the patronage and personal friendship of four Russian emperors, as well as securing the patronage of a succession of sultans: Abdul Aziz, Murad V and Abdul Hamid II. Acclaimed for his views of Moscow and St Petersburg, Aivazovsky found in Constantinople the most perfect setting for his talent. Situated on a triangular peninsular at the junction of many waters, it is an unusual combination of city-, land- and seascapes. This painting shows the narrow channel of the Bosphorous which winds for seventeen miles between a double range of hills. It meets the river Marmara to form a natural harbour, the Golden Horn, where ships carry goods to and from Russia, Asia Minor and the East. This panorama set a new auction record for Aivazovsky's work. (ABOVE)

ART IN ISRAEL

Reuven Rubin
Market Scene
SIGNED, OIL ON CANVAS, 65 x 81cm (25⅝ x 31⅞in)
Tel Aviv $118,000 (£75,159). 22.IV.95

Painted *circa* 1923, this important early work dates from one of the artist's most fruitful periods in which he drew inspiration from the surroundings of his new home, Eretz Israel. Describing this time, Rubin wrote, 'A new life springs up around me. I feel the sap of creative energy rising in me too. I have thrown away all the ideas I had derived from the Bezalel Art School and the Paris Beaux-Arts. The world is clear and pure to me. Life is stark, bare, primitive.' (ABOVE)

Felix Nussbaum
Self-Portrait with a Mask
SIGNED AND DATED *1928*, OIL ON CANVAS,
62 x 50.5cm (24⅜ x 19⅞in)
Tel Aviv $101,500 (£64,650). 22.IV.95
From the Family of Felix Nussbaum

Felix Nussbaum (1904–44) was influenced by the psychological intensity of van Gogh's late self-portraits as is evident in this striking painting. Although the importance of Nussbaum's work was only discovered after his death, he is now widely considered to be the most significant visual artist to have perished during the Holocaust. This haunting, theatrical self-portrait seems prophetic of the artist's fate under the occupation of Europe, during which he was in hiding in Brussels before being denounced by the Nazis and gassed at Auschwitz in 1944. (LEFT)

IMPRESSIONIST AND MODERN ART

CLAUDE MONET
Vue de l'église de Vernon
SIGNED AND DATED *83*, OIL ON CANVAS, 64.8 x 80cm (25¼ x 31⅞in)
New York $3,742,500 (£2,357,775). 9.V.95
From the Estate of Mrs John Barry Ryan

Claude Monet moved to Giverny in 1883 but it took time for him to become accustomed to
his new environment. In some of his earliest paintings of the area, Monet concentrated on
distinct topographical features, such as churches and old buildings, before locating the more
unconventional *motifs* that he would later make his own. Three views of the small village of
Vernon, situated on the other side of the Seine from Giverny, date from 1883, including
Vue de l'église de Vernon. (ABOVE)

PAUL GAUGUIN
Tahitiennes près d'un ruisseau
SIGNED, OIL ON CANVAS, 73 x 92cm (28¾ x 36¼in)
London £5,501,500 ($8,692,370). 27.VI.95

Gauguin's trip to the island of Martinique in 1887 had awakened his interest in non-Western cultures and people, and in April 1891 he set off for Tahiti, eventually settling in the idyllic rural province of Mataieia where *Tahitiennes près d'un ruisseau* was probably painted. The artist presents the island as a scented paradise, a dream landscape in which virgin nature is in harmony with humanity, producing a sense of beauty and peace. The contrast between the uniform landscape background and the delicately brushed sections, and the power of Gauguin's colours, freed from reference to their representational function, confer a majestic and forceful quality upon this composition which transcends the recorded moment. (ABOVE)

EDOUARD VUILLARD

The Model in the Studio

SIGNED, OIL ON BOARD, MOUNTED ON CRADLED WOOD PANEL, 62.5 x 86cm (24⅝ x 33⅞in)
New York $1,927,500 (£1,195,050). 8.XI.94

This work is set in the painter's Paris studio on the rue Truffaut and was painted *circa*
1903–06, shortly after he and his mother had moved from the Batignolles quarter of Paris to
the rue de la Tour. On the mantelpiece is the plaster cast of Aristide Maillol's *Leda*, given
to Vuillard by the artist and which appears in a number of Vuillard's works. (ABOVE)

PABLO PICASSO

Au Moulin Rouge (La fille du roi d'Egypte)

SIGNED AND DATED *1901*,
WATERCOLOUR AND GOUACHE
OVER PENCIL AND CHARCOAL,
63 x 48cm (24¾ x 19in)
London £1,816,500 ($2,833,740).
29.XI.94

Picasso returned to Paris from Spain in May 1901 and threw himself into preparations for his first exhibition at Ambroise Vollard's gallery. Based at 130 boulevard de Clichy, the artist was conveniently close to the Moulin Rouge at no. 90 whose patrons and performers inspired many of the pictures executed for the exhibition. The present painting has been plausibly identified as number thirteen in the Vollard exhibition, entitled *La fille du roi d'Egypte*, slang for 'gypsy girl'. John Richardson has suggested that Gustave Coquiot, who wrote the exhibition's preface, devised most of the pictures' titles, their fancifulness being untypical of Picasso. (LEFT)

PABLO PICASSO
Angel Fernandez de Soto
SIGNED AND DATED *1903*, OIL
ON CANVAS, 69.5 x 55.2cm
(27⅛ x 21¾in)
New York $29,152,500
(£18,074,550). 8.V.95
From the Donald and Jean
Stralem Collection

Picasso met the brothers
Angel and Mateu
Fernandez de Soto in
1899 at the café Els
Quatre Gats in
Barcelona. Angel became
one of the painter's
closest friends over the
next four years during
which Picasso divided
his time between
Barcelona, Madrid and
Paris. Described by
Picasso as 'an amusing
wastrel', Angel worked
for a spice merchant
and occasionally
supplemented his
meagre income by
appearing as a theatre
extra in 'borrowed
finery', hence the playful
depiction of him as 'an
elegant boulevardier,
dashing officer or
habitué of Maxim's'
(John Richardson, *A Life
of Picasso (1881–1906)*,
1991). Executed at the
climax of Picasso's Blue
Period, this portrait,
with its exaggerated
forms and dynamic
rhythms, demonstrates
the painter's sympathy
for and understanding of
the Catalan dandy. (LEFT)

AMEDEO MODIGLIANI
Portrait de Jeanne Hebuterne
SIGNED, OIL ON CANVAS,
92.1 x 54cm (36¼ x 21¼in)
New York $5,942,500 (£3,684,350). 8.XI.94

Painted in late 1919, shortly before the
artist's death and Jeanne Hebuterne's
subsequent suicide when eight months
pregnant, this is one of approximately
twenty-six portraits of his companion
that Modigliani produced in the three
years they were together. The work
presents a particularly elegant solution
to the three-quarter-length portrait
format. The serpentine pose and the
rhythms established by the bands of
striped fabric result in a Mannerist *élan*
that co-habits with the Cézannesque
application of colour. (LEFT)

JUAN GRIS
Guitare sur une chaise
OIL, SAND AND COLLAGE ON CANVAS,
100 x 65cm (39⅜ x 25⅝in)
London £1,871,500 ($2,956,970).
27.VI.95

Although he was more
theoretically inclined than
either Braque or Picasso,
Juan Gris produced a body
of work that displayed a
remarkable range of styles.
By the spring of 1913 Gris
had developed a new
technique derived from
papier collé in which strongly
patterned and textured
planes are juxtaposed and
superimposed to create a
spatial structure within the
painting. The formal
intelligence that characterized
his best work is displayed
here where the fusion of
figure and ground, object
and setting is achieved with
consummate elegance. (LEFT)

PABLO PICASSO
Tête classique
SIGNED, BLACK CHALK AND
CHARCOAL ON ROSE PAPER,
63.5 x 47.8cm (25 x 18¾in)
London £1,981,500
($3,130,770). 27.VI.95

Executed in Fontainebleau in 1921, this is one of a group of large drawings of female heads which relate to Picasso's great neo-classical oil, *Femmes à la fontaine*. This period of classicism in Picasso's work was influenced by his first visit to Italy in 1917 when he accompanied Jean Cocteau to Rome. He stayed there for two months, visiting some of the major museums and churches and travelling to Florence, Naples and Pompeii. The impulse to look at classicism for inspiration at this time was not unique to Picasso but represented a more international trend at the end of the First World War when many artists responded to the general call for a 'return to order'. However, unlike his contemporaries, Picasso did not abandon his research into the language of synthetic Cubism and developed the two styles side by side. (LEFT)

ALEXEJ VON JAWLENSKY
**Prinzessin Mit
Weisser Blume**
SIGNED WITH INITIALS AND
DATED *13*, OIL ON BOARD,
68 x 49cm (26⅔ x 19¼in)
London £606,500 ($958,270).
27.VI.95

In 1899 Alexej von
Jawlensky abandoned a
military career to study
art at the St Petersburg
Academy under Ilya
Repin. Seven years later,
he left Russia to settle in
Munich where, in 1909,
he and Kandinsky were
among the founders
of the *Neue Künstler
Vereinigung*. Jawlensky
also visited France where
he worked briefly with
Matisse and saw
paintings by Gauguin
and van Gogh.
Significantly influenced
by this visit, Jawlensky
developed a non-
naturalistic style of
painting which
numbered among its
inspirations Fauvism,
Expressionism, Russian
icons and folk art. From
1910 he began a series
of heads in which the use
of colour became less
representational and
more symbolic. (LEFT)

EMIL NOLDE
Anna Wieds Garten
SIGNED AND DATED *07*, TITLED ON
THE STRETCHER, OIL ON CANVAS,
60 x 50cm (23⅝ x 19⅝in)
London £782,500 ($1,236,350). 27.VI.95

In 1906 Nolde began a series of
garden pictures which became his
first notably successful group of
paintings. Nolde loved flowers and
despite his poverty he planted a
luxurious garden next to his small
hut at Alsen. His garden and those of
his neighbours were the inspiration
for some of the artist's finest flower
paintings which demonstrate the
application of Expressionism to the
most beautiful of subjects. Nolde
later recalled, 'I loved the flowers and
their fate: thrusting up, blossoming,
radiating, glowing, gladdening,
bending, wilting, thrown away
and dying.' (LEFT)

WASSILY KANDINSKY
Skizze für Improvisation 4
OIL ON BOARD LAID DOWN ON PANEL, 1909,
70.5 x 98cm (27¾ x 38⅝in)
London £2,751,500 ($4,347,370). 27.VI.95

In 1909 Wassily Kandinsky began
Improvisations, a sequence of
paintings on a landscape theme.
He defined the series as those works
deriving from an inner impulse,
sudden and unconscious, the
emotion in the artist's soul. These
paintings were crucial in Kandinsky's
epoch-making breakthrough to
abstraction. *Skizze für Improvisation
4* is the only complete recorded oil
study for such a major painting,
and its freedom and spontaneity
contrast with the more contained
forms and careful organization of
the final composition, *Improvisation
4*, at Nizhny Novgorod Museum,
Russia. (RIGHT)

SALVADOR DALI

Cygnes reflétant des elephants

SIGNED AND DATED *1937*, OIL ON CANVAS, 50.8 x 76.8cm (20 x 30¼in)

New York $3,522,500 (£2,219,175). 9.V.95

During the period in which *Cygnes reflétant des elephants* was executed, Dali was championing
the *paranoiac-critical method*, his term for the controlled use of freely-associated imagery and
subjects derived from self-induced hallucinations. Dali's approach to the irrational was highly
planned and consciously manipulated to fulfill a pre-established conception. The sources from
which Dali drew his imagery were manifold: psychoanalysis, Surrealist literature, obsessive
private recollections and fetishes. In this painting the imagery is clearly derived from
conscious themes in his life and work. (ABOVE)

MARINO MARINI
Cavaliere
STAMPED WITH THE RAISED INITIALS *MM*, 1953, BRONZE, height 134.6cm (53in)
New York $1,102,500 (£694,575). 9.V.95
From the Estate of Lillian L. Poses

From the 1930s the theme of horse and rider dominated Marini's work. During the forties the sculptures presented firmly seated heroic figures, some with arms outstretched in exultation, others seemingly despondent, exhausted. By the fifties, however, the same subjects became charged with a wild almost uncontrolled energy. Marini explained the change, 'If you look back on all my equestrian figures of the past twelve years, you will notice that the rider is each time less in control of his mount, and that the latter is increasingly more wild in its terror, but frozen stiff, rather than rearing or running away. This is because I feel that we are on the eve of the end of a whole world.' (ABOVE)

CONTEMPORARY ART

FRANCIS BACON
Study for a Head
OIL ON CANVAS, 94.5 x 85cm (37¼ x 33½in)
London £672,500 ($1,049,100). 30.XI.94
From the University of Chicago

Painted in 1960, *Study for a Head* is Francis Bacon's only depiction of a pope in which the pontiff is shown from the shoulders upwards, without the papal throne. The linear structure encompassing the figure hides the lower part of his body and hands, in the same way that a confessional keeps priest and penitent apart. Divested of his attributes, the pope becomes a more archetypal figure of religious authority, and looms forebodingly from the darkness. (ABOVE)

DAVID SMITH
Three Circles and Planes
SIGNED, TITLED AND DATED *6.11.1959*, STAINLESS STEEL,
overall 285.8 x 105.4 x 44.1cm (112½ x 41½ x 17⅜in)
New York $1,982,500 (£1,229,150). 2.V.95

Three Circles and Planes is one of the earliest in a
group of monumental stainless steel sculptures begun
by David Smith in 1957 and continued
simultaneously with the *Cubi* series from 1961 until
the artist's death in 1965. Writing in 1959, A.E.
Navaretta described Smith as a 'constructor-sculptor'
and a major innovator of twentieth-century sculpture,
focusing on these towering configurations as a
summation of Smith's development as a mature and
assured artist. This sculpture is intended to be viewed
in the round, offering different compositions
depending on the perspective. (LEFT)

WILLEM DE KOONING
Untitled XVII
OIL ON CANVAS, 152.4 x 137.8cm (60 x 54¼in)
New York $717,500 (£444,850). 2.V.95
From the IBM International Foundation Collection

Untitled XVII was executed in 1977. Willem de Kooning's works during this period have been
described as 'landscapes of the body', and they exude a joyful freedom of expression. The
dancing rhythms of colour that undulate across this painting's surface form translucent ghostly
impressions. A melody of pinkish-white gestural strokes mingle with lipstick reds,
blues and greens, and possess a subtle but direct sensuality. (ABOVE)

GEORG BASELITZ

Verschiedene Zeichen

SIGNED, TITLED AND DATED *1965*, OIL ON CANVAS, 162 x 130cm (63¾ x 51⅜in)
London £507,500 ($801,850). 28.VI.95

In the early 1960s Georg Baselitz visited Florence on a scholarship and was greatly influenced by the
iconography and use of symbols in the paintings and frescoes. On his return to Germany he began to
paint the *Hero* series, of which *Verschiedene Zeichen (Various Symbols)* is one. This work is particularly
rich in symbols. The figure holds a palette, which identifies him as the artist. His left hand is trapped in
an iron and his freedom is further restricted by a low fence enclosing his legs. Baselitz uses the figure
both to examine aspects of the artist's identity and to personify post-war Germany. (ABOVE)

ALBERTO BURRI
Grande sacco
SIGNED AND DATED *54*, OIL AND BURLAP ON FABRIC,
150 x 250cm (59 x 98½in)
London £804,500 ($1,271,110). 28.VI.95
From The Newark Museum

As an Italian prisoner of war in Texas, Alberto
Burri created collages with whatever was available:
sacking, wood and fragments of rusty metal. He
later continued to use this raw material in a series
of experimental works, creating constructs of
elegance and beauty described by Sir Herbert
Read as 'a new world of form'. *Grande sacco* is a
seminal example of this work. Its large dimensions
give it a strong physical presence and the
composition, with its delicate balance of lines
and surfaces, has an architectural magnitude.
Small pieces of bunched up fabric are sewn
together, creating sensuous areas of texture.
This combination of monumentality and subtle
detail, lavished on such humble material, lends
pathos to *Grande sacco*. (RIGHT)

LUCIO FONTANA
Concetto spaziale attese
SIGNED, TITLED AND INSCRIBED
L'ULTIMO CRONO GELA IL TOUR,
PRIMO GIMONDI O POLIDOR ???,
WATERPAINT ON CANVAS,
115 x 146cm (45¼ x 57½in)
London £430,500 ($680,190).
28.VI.95

Executed in 1965, *Concetto
spaziale attese* is among the
largest and most beautiful
'Tagli' (cuts) made by
Fontana. The rhythmical
composition of the twelve
cuts combined with the
purity of the white canvas
infuses the work with
lyricism and poetic harmony.
The careful balance of
vertical and diagonal, wide
and narrow cuts incised into
the canvas calls to mind the
powerful yet delicate
arrangement of musical
notes. (LEFT)

GERHARD RICHTER
Familie Ruhnau
SIGNED, TITLED AND DATED 69, OIL ON CANVAS, 130 x 200cm (51¼ x 78¾in)
London £287,500 ($448,500). 30.XI.94

In 1962 Gerhard Richter began taking photographs as his subject matter. 'By painting from photos I was relieved of the obligations to choose and construct a subject. Admittedly, I had to choose the photographs but I was able to do this in a manner which avoided acknowledgement of the subject, namely through *motifs* which were less eyecatching and not "of their own time".' His portrait of the Ruhnau family resembles a snapshot which has been transformed into a fleeting image, moving in and out of focus. This effect is achieved by projecting the photographic negative onto the canvas and then brushing the finished painting across a horizontal plane. (ABOVE)

ROY LICHTENSTEIN
I ... I'm Sorry
SIGNED AND DATED 66, OIL
AND MAGNA ON CANVAS,
152.4 x 121.9cm (60 x 48in)
New York $2,477,500
(£1,536,050). 1.XI.94

I ... I'm Sorry is a
summation of
Lichtenstein's cartoon
paintings of women in
which he challenges the
conventions of art and
popular culture through
subject matter and
technique. By 1963–66,
the paintings of
prototypical blonde
women demonstrated
his mature command of
the content of his work
and of the stylized
pictorial elements
adapted from comics.
The women are
portrayed as openly
expressing their
emotions in contrast
to the comic book
war heroes who face
danger with stoicism.
Lichtenstein had 'noted
that people learned from
the culture around them
that it was okay for
women to cry but that
men were not expected
to show their feelings,
and he was struck by the
way comic-book
publishers played to this
gender distinction.'
(Diane Waldman, *Roy
Lichtenstein*, 1993) (LEFT)

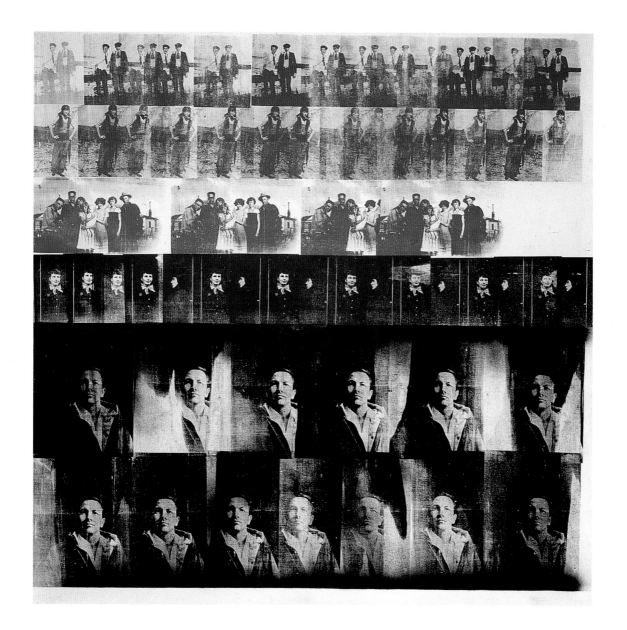

ANDY WARHOL
Let Us Now Praise Famous Men
SYNTHETIC POLYMER AND INK SILKSCREENED ON CANVAS, 208.3 x 208.3cm (82 x 82in)
New York $1,058,500 (£656,270). 1.XI.94
From the Collection of S.I. Newhouse, Jr.

Executed in 1963, this work is based on photographs of the American artist Robert Rauschenberg and members of his family including his parents, Ernest and Dora Rauschenberg. The title of the painting is taken from James Agee's prose commentary, *Let Us Now Praise Famous Men*. Agee (1909–55) was a writer for *Fortune* magazine, a film critic for *Time* and *The Nation*, and a screenwriter. (ABOVE)

AMERICAN PAINTINGS

FRANK W. BENSON
The Sisters
SIGNED *F. W. BENSON* AND DATED '99, OIL ON CANVAS, 101.6 x 101.6cm (40 x 40in)
New York $4,182,500 (£2,593,150). 25.V.95
From the IBM International Foundation Collection

The Sisters depicts the artist's youngest daughters, Elisabeth and Sylvia, playing in a grassy, seaside meadow, close to the New Hampshire village where the Benson family spent their summers during the 1890s. The painting's irresistible buoyancy and optimism captivated the imagination of public and critics alike, suiting the prevailing obsession with depictions of youth and beauty. Many of Benson's contemporaries responded enthusiastically to this idealized notion of childhood. The critic William Howe Downes stated, 'I would be at a loss to find a more sympathetic, intimate, charming representation of human babyhood'. (ABOVE)

FITZ HUGH LANE
Ships at Sunrise
OIL ON CANVAS, 51.4 x 87cm (20¼ x 34¼in)
New York $910,000 (£582,400). 1.XII.94
From the Estate of Dr Dallas Bache Pratt

Fitz Hugh Lane, one of America's pre-eminent marine painters, was the first of his contemporaries to evolve a personal style in the Luminist vein, devoting his time to a careful exploration of light and the atmospheric effects of nature on maritime and coastal subjects. The refined sense of colour, controlled nuances of tinted light, and distilled harmony and order between man and nature have all come to define Lane's particular pictorial vision. (RIGHT)

JASPER FRANCIS CROPSEY
Lake George, Sunrise
SIGNED *J.F. CROPSEY*, DATED *1868*,
OIL ON CANVAS, 61 x 111.8cm (24 x 44in)
New York $1,003,500 (£622,170). 25.V.95
From the IBM International
Foundation Collection

In the 1860s, Jasper Cropsey began combining his faithful renderings of nature with the atmospheric effects of light on water traditionally associated with the Luminist movement of the 1840s. With autumnal hues of golden yellow and brown, *Sunrise* depicts the warm reflection of the early morning sunlight as it glistens across the lake's surface. The rising sun casts a shimmering path which leads the viewer's eye to the travellers who are warming themselves by a fire, emphasizing the calmness and serenity of the scene. (LEFT)

ALFRED H. MAURER
The Beach
SIGNED *ALFRED H. MAURER*, OIL ON CANVAS, 74.9 x 91.4cm (29½ x 36in)
New York $800,000 (£512,000). 1.XII.94

The Beach is characterized by a monochromatic palette which is typical of Maurer's early works
and reveals his indebtedness to Whistler. The undeniable impact of Manet's bold brushwork
and reliance on broad areas of black is also very much in evidence. This painting was executed
circa 1901 at a high point in his career, the same year in which he had been awarded the
Carnegie Prize for his picture *An Arrangement*. Maurer subsequently broke with late
nineteenth-century naturalism, frustrated at what he viewed as his own artistic conservatism,
and worked with little success in the modernist vein until his suicide in 1932. (ABOVE)

WINSLOW HOMER
Diamond Shoal
SIGNED *HOMER*, DATED *1905*, WATERCOLOUR
ON PAPER, 35.2 x 55.2cm (13⅞ x 21¾in)
New York $1,817,500 (£1,126,850). 25.V.95
From the IBM International Foundation Collection

Winslow Homer's last dated watercolour represents his final achievement in his preferred medium. The theme of man's fundamental struggle against nature occupied the artist for much of his career. This painting captures the tension of two men struggling to regain control of their boat in the face of the unpredictable forces of nature. Danger exists in the changing weather and in the threat of Diamond Shoal, an underwater accumulation of sand and sediment hazardous to ships and known as 'the graveyard of the Atlantic'. (RIGHT)

MAURICE B. PRENDERGAST
On the Shore
SIGNED *PRENDERGAST*, OIL ON CANVAS,
56.5 x 86.4cm (22¼ x 34in)
New York $1,432,500 (£888,150). 25.V.95
From the IBM International Foundation Collection

Maurice Prendergast first became familiar with the works of the Post-Impressionists during a trip to Paris in 1907. This movement greatly influenced the development of his own decorative style which is also characterized by borrowed *motifs* from ancient, non-Western and children's art. *On the Shore* is an example of the idyllic subject matter that fascinated Prendergast throughout his career. Here the artist draws on the tradition of classical Greek sculpture in his depictions of maidens in togas and nude figures. (RIGHT)

GEORGE BELLOWS
Easter Snow
SIGNED *GEO. BELLOWS*, ALSO SIGNED AND TITLED *EASTER SUNDAY* ON REVERSE, 1915, OIL ON CANVAS,
86.4 x 114.3cm (34 x 45in)
New York $2,862,500 (£1,774,750). 25.V.95
From the IBM International Foundation Collection

George Bellows applied his own brand of realism not only to the gritty aspects of city
life, but also to many of its lyrical elements, forming a compendium of New York
scenes which document the multi-faceted nature of the urban landscape. Painted in
1915, *Easter Snow* depicts a fashionably dressed assemblage of holiday strollers,
walking along the promenade in the snow-covered landscape. Although clearly a hub
of genteel activity, the park appears uncrowded, quiet and semi-rural. Implicit in the
scene, however, is the vibrating energy derived from Bellows' slashing strokes from a
heavily loaded paintbrush, and colours of dazzling intensity. (ABOVE)

CHILDE HASSAM
Poppies
SIGNED *CHILDE HASSAM*, OIL ON CANVAS,
45.7 x 64.1cm (18 x 25¼in)
New York $2,642,500 (£1,691,200). 1.XII.94

Following an extended stay in Paris from
1886–89, Hassam spent many summers
on Appledore Island off the Maine-New
Hampshire coast. Celia Thaxter, an
established literary figure and artist in her
own right, ran a summer resort on the
island which regularly attracted a wide
circle of writers, musicians and artists.
Inspired by Mrs Thaxter's glorious
garden, Hassam painted several of his
most memorable oils and watercolours.
According to David Park Curry, 'the
delicate poppies and hollyhocks, larkspurs
and lilies of his early Appledore pictures
record not only the beauty of a poet's
garden in its glory, but also the flowering
of a young artist's dreams'. (RIGHT)

WILLIAM MERRITT CHASE
Seaside Flowers
SIGNED *WM. M. CHASE*, OIL ON
CANVAS, 74.9 x 99.1cm (29½ x 39in)
New York $2,422,500 (£1,550,400).
1.XII.94

Between 1891–1902 William
Merritt Chase founded and
taught at the Shinnecock
Summer Art School on the
eastern end of Long Island,
where he encouraged his
students to paint outdoors
and to capture the
momentary effects of light
and atmosphere. During this
time he produced some of his
most beautiful and technically
brilliant works. *Seaside
Flowers*, which features
Chase's wife and three
children, was painted around
1897 and conveys the artist's
obvious assimilation of
French Impressionist
techniques. (LEFT)

LATIN AMERICAN PAINTINGS

DIEGO RIVERA
Baile en Tehuantepec
SIGNED AND DATED *1928*, OIL ON CANVAS,
200.7 x 163.8cm (79 x 64½in)
New York $3,082,500 (£1,972,800). 17.V.95
From the IBM International
Foundation Collection

After Diego Rivera's return to Mexico from Europe in 1921, he travelled to the isthmus of Tehuantepec along the Pacific coast in search of a 'pure' Mexican art form. In his masterpiece from 1928, Rivera captures the folkloric dance *Zandunga*, depicting six dancers under a lush banana tree. This work, which is one of the largest canvases he ever painted, records the rich textures and vibrant colours which so fascinated him. *Baile en Tehuantepec* is Rivera's tribute not only to the people of Tehuantepec, but also to the customs and traditions of a people and nation whose history reaches back more than three millennia. (RIGHT)

FRIDA KAHLO

Autorretrato con chango y loro

SIGNED AND DATED *1942*, OIL ON MASONITE, 54.6 x 43.2cm (21½ x 17in)
New York $3,192,500 (£2,043,200). 17.V.95
From the IBM International Foundation Collection

Frida Kahlo's *Autorretrato con chango y loro* is a powerful self-portrait painted at the apex of her
career by an artist whose name is synonymous with self-portraiture. Kahlo depicts herself dressed
in the colourful and distinguished traditional folk costume and hair ribbons of the region of
Tehuantepec, a costume she had begun to wear at the request of her husband Diego Rivera.
Her firm, soulful gaze is a reminder that Kahlo's life was marked by physical and emotional
hardships following a tragic bus and trolley accident which left her with a lifelong disability.
The artist's pets became her surrogate children. In *Autorretrato con chango y loro*, she has chosen
a spider monkey and a parrot to surround her protectively in the composition. (ABOVE)

WIFREDO LAM
La mañana verde
OIL ON PAPER, MOUNTED ON CANVAS,
186.7 x 123.8cm (73½ x 48¾in)
New York $965,000 (£607,950).
15.XI.94

La mañana verde, a
monumental painting
executed in 1943, is one
of the artist's greatest
achievements, representing
his full psychic and artistic
maturity. Having returned
to Cuba after five years in
Europe, Lam synthesized his
Cuban heritage, its myths,
rituals, colours and music in
symphonic compositions
such as *La mañana verde*
and *La jungla* (at the
Museum of Modern Art
in New York). (LEFT)

CUNDO BERMÚDEZ
Mujer peinando a su amante
SIGNED AND DATED *45*, OIL ON CANVAS, 75.6 x 60.3cm (29¾ x 23¾in)
New York $343,500 (£219,840). 17.V.95

Cundo Bermúdez is one of Cuba's most important artists of the twentieth century, and *Mujer peinando a su amante* is a triumph in his *oeuvre*. Painted when the artist had developed his own visual language, the canvas is a testament to the ideals of Cuba's modernist movement. The vibrant colours are lavishly spread on the canvas to create a pictorial feast for the viewer. Bermúdez incorporates elements into his work which are endemic to Cuba and the tropics. He poignantly depicts the lovers separated from the outside world by two green hurricane shutters, as well as incorporating a colourful tile floor characteristic of Cuban architecture. In addition he repeatedly uses the flower *motif* which has always been associated with fertility and beauty. (RIGHT)

ARMANDO MORALES
Oracle sur Managua: Hommage à Ernesto Cardenal
SIGNED AND DATED *89*, OIL ON CANVAS,
162.6 x 201.3cm (64 x 79¼in)
New York $420,500 (£264,915). 15.XI.94

Armando Morales' *Oracle sur Managua: Hommage à Ernesto Cardenal* is a definitive painting from 1989 which fuses all the key elements characteristic of the artist's work. Nudes, carriages and horses, railways, boats and the ocean are all depicted in this quasi-surreal masterpiece. (LEFT)

CANADIAN ART

CORNELIUS DAVID KRIEGHOFF
Early Canadian Homestead
SIGNED AND DATED *QUEBEC, 1859*, OIL ON CANVAS, 61 x 91.4cm (24 x 36in)
Toronto CN$440,000 (£200,000:$317,460). 16.XI.94

This magnificent work is one of the finest paintings by Krieghoff ever offered at auction. Never exhibited, and unknown to the market, it has been in a private family collection since it was painted in 1859. Krieghoff was living in Quebec at the time, a period in which he achieved his greatest success as an artist. Owing to his vast output and the historical immediacy of his scenes of everyday life, the popular appeal of his paintings is unrivalled by any other Canadian artist of the century. (ABOVE)

AUSTRALIAN ART

FREDERICK MCCUBBIN
Bush Sawyers
SIGNED AND DATED *1910*, OIL ON CANVAS, 95 x 152.5cm (37½ x 60in)
Melbourne A$717,500 (£325,028:$523,946). 1.V.95

In 1901, Frederick McCubbin and his wife purchased a cottage at Mount Macedon
and named it 'Fontainebleau' after the French forest where Millet – one of his
greatest influences – had painted in the early nineteenth century. The surrounding
bush landscape was to provide a setting for many of McCubbin's most celebrated
compositions. *Bush Sawyers* is by far the most accomplished and satisfying of a series
of his paintings based on the theme of forest workers. The rhythm of their labour is
eloquently conveyed and the texture of the paint – brilliantly faceted with the palette
knife – creates a shimmering web of undergrowth in the gently fading light. (ABOVE)

PRINTS

ALBRECHT DÜRER

Samson Rending the Lion
WOODCUT ON PAPER,
38.5 x 27.8cm (15⅛ x 11in)
London £199,500 ($311,220). 2.XII.94

Usually dated to *circa* 1497–98,
this outstanding early work
by Dürer is notable for its
concentrated energy and variety
of line. A brilliant example, it
had been preserved in almost
flawless condition in an old
English collection. (LEFT)

REMBRANDT HARMENSZ. VAN RIJN

Christ Crucified Between the Two Thieves: *The Three Crosses*

1653, ETCHING, DRYPOINT AND BURIN, THE FOURTH STATE OF FIVE, ON EUROPEAN PAPER WITHOUT WATERMARK,
38 x 44.4cm (15 x 17½in)
New York $134,500 (£84,735). 12.V.95

The fourth state of *The Three Crosses* can perhaps be considered Rembrandt's second version of
the print. About five years after creating the drypoint, he entirely reworked the plate, making it
bolder and more dramatic. The change in composition follows the shift in subject to the
moment of Christ's utter despair, just before His death. Impressions of this print vary
enormously, depending largely on the type of paper on which it was printed and how
Rembrandt wiped the plate. (ABOVE)

HENRI DE TOULOUSE-LAUTREC
Miss Loïe Fuller
1893, LITHOGRAPH PRINTED IN COLOURS WITH POWDERED GOLD, FROM THE EDITION OF 50, 38.2 x 28.1cm (15 x 11in)
New York $60,250 (£37,958). 12.V.95

In one of Lautrec's most experimental prints, he depicted the American-born Loïe Fuller in the midst of her famous *danse de feu*. Lautrec's fascinating composition encapsulates the mood of the dance with its additional colour effects capturing the spectacular nature of Fuller's performances. Each of the fifty impressions was apparently printed with diverse colour variations, and the stone inked differently each time. This impression shows the gold dust particularly well, creating a brilliant play of light through the image. (ABOVE)

EDVARD MUNCH
Angstgefuhl
1896, WOODCUT, SIGNED IN PENCIL, ON FINE LAID JAPAN PAPER, 46 x 37.4cm (18⅛ x 14⅝in)
London £43,300 ($68,847). 27.VI.95

Angstgefuhl, 'Anxiety', is accepted as Munch's first woodcut and this immediate mastery of
the medium played a seminal role in the renaissance of the woodcut in the twentieth century.
Munch was able to exploit the broad surface of the woodblock to achieve an intense focus
on this powerful subject. (ABOVE)

JASPER JOHNS
Color Numerals: Figure 7
1968–69, LITHOGRAPH PRINTED IN COLOURS, SIGNED AND DATED IN PURPLE CRAYON, NUMBERED *22/40*, ON JAPANESE ARJOMARI PAPER,
70 x 56cm (27½ x 22in)
London £26,450 ($42,056). 28.VI.95

Jasper Johns' work is noted for its use of commonplace objects such as flags, numbers, maps, brooms,
footprints and targets, encouraging the viewer to question the relationship between art and reality. This print
features the Mona Lisa, as well as two of Johns' favourite devices: the handprint and a number, 7. (ABOVE)

FRANK STELLA
Talladega Three II
1982, RELIEF-PRINTED ETCHING IN COLOURS, SIGNED IN PENCIL, DATED AND NUMBERED *22/30*
(TOTAL EDITION INCLUDES 10 ARTIST'S PROOFS), 169 x 131.5cm (66½ x 51¾in)
New York $65,750 (£42,080). 13.V.95
The Property of Mr and Mrs Warner LeRoy

This print is from the suite, *Circuits*. The scrolling black lines to which the colour appears to cling are made from the laser cuts left in a piece of wood which was used as a backboard in the foundry where Stella's large cut-out constructions are made. When Stella saw the design left by the random marks, he decided to use the wood as the surface from which this large graphic work is printed. (ABOVE)

PHOTOGRAPHS

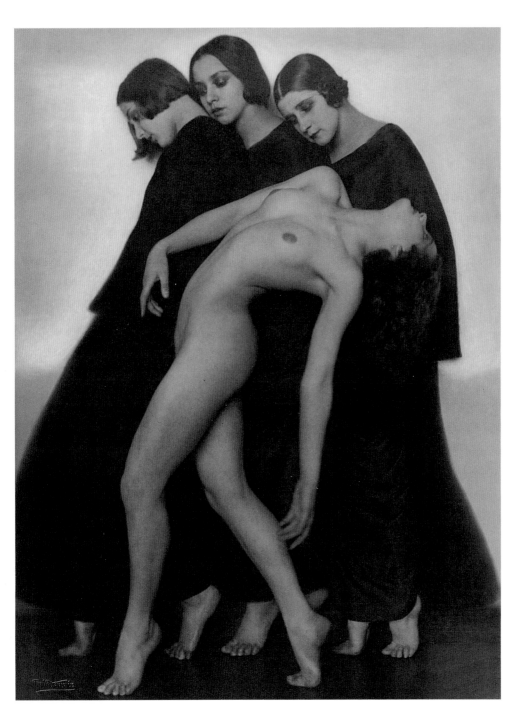

PROF. RUDOLF KOPPITZ

Bewegungsstudie (Study of Movement)

SIGNED *PROF. R. KOPPITZ, WEIN*, AND DATED *1926*, WARM-TONED CARBON PRINT, 37.5 x 27.9 cm (14¾ x 11in)
New York $112,500 (£69,750). 8.IV.95

Born in 1884, Rudolf Koppitz became a photographer in the Vienna of Gustav Klimt, Egon Schiele, Oskar Kokoschka, Josef Hoffman and Sigmund Freud. Although much of his work remains unknown, this picture has become arguably the most famous photographic image to emerge from Vienna at that time. The contemporary influences, particularly of Klimt, are clear in the curvilinear lines of the stylized poses; the repetitive, frieze-like figures in black; the solid, triangular massing of the composition and the luminous, sensuous flesh of the figure in the foreground. The influence of the new science of psychoanalysis can also be traced in the possible interpretations of Koppitz's tableau. (LEFT)

MAN RAY
Marcel Duchamp, solarised portrait
SIGNED AND DATED *MAN RAY 1930*, SILVER PRINT, 29.2 x 22.9cm (11½ x 9in)
London £42,200 ($67,098). 23.III.95
From the Estate of Juliet Man Ray, the Man Ray Trust
and the Family of Juliet Man Ray

Man Ray's relationship with Marcel Duchamp was one of the
most enduring and mutually inspiring friendships between
twentieth-century artists. Although they did not have a language
in common when they first met in 1915, they established an
immediate rapport. Both intensely individualistic, Duchamp and
Man Ray were always at the centre of Dada and Surrealist
activities but never committed 'members' of either movement. It
is appropriate that our image of the handsome and fastidious
Duchamp is to a considerable extent established by the
photographs of Man Ray who recorded him in many guises: as a
Dada prankster, as Rrose Sélavy (in his feminine manifestation)
and as a paragon of elegance in the solarised portraits. (LEFT)

CHARLES JONES
'Onions Ailsa Craig'
PENCILLED MONOGRAM *CJ*, *c.*1900, GELATIN SILVER PRINT,
19.5 x 25.5cm (7½ x 10in)
London £1,610 ($2,608). 4.V.95

Charles Jones's photographs have acquired an almost
cult following yet nothing is known of the man
himself. With great simplicity he systematically
recorded a wide variety of vegetables and flowers and
the impression his photographs give is of a man
obsessed with his subject matter. To late twentieth-
century eyes these images seem imbued with an
uncanny aesthetic strength. (RIGHT)

LITERARY PROPERTY *by Paul Needham*

T he firm of Sotheby's began a quarter-millennium ago with auctions of books and, despite the innumerable changes that have overtaken the auction world since the first sales, those of us involved in Sotheby's book sales today feel a distinct sense of continuity with our commercial ancestors. Besides the immediate satisfaction of achieving strong prices for our clients, there are subtler pleasures in watching important books and manuscripts move from one good home to another through our mediation, and in being able to note, in their provenance, that they were 'sold in our rooms' at some earlier date.

Sotheby's is the only auction house in the world to hold specialized sales of medieval manuscripts. High quality medieval miniatures have sold very well in the last year, including the collection of the distinguished art historian, the late Dr Rosy Schilling. One French miniature of circa 1410, which she had acquired at Sotheby's in 1948 for £24, was re-sold for £19,550. A highlight of the season was The Annunciation to the Shepherds by the Master of Mary of Burgundy which sold for £210,500, the highest price ever paid at auction for a fifteenth-century miniature. A pleasing trend is for manuscripts to be bought by public libraries in their places of origin. The last year has seen manuscripts return to the public libraries of Bamberg, Venice, Florence, Lyons and Avignon amongst others.

Hebrew books offered in the last year included a fine group which were collected by Baron Mayer Amschel de Rothschild (1818–74) and consigned for sale by the present Earl of Rosebery. The first printed edition of the Jewish history known as Yosipon (Mantua, circa 1474–77), brought an impressive £76,300. Major Hebrew manuscripts included, from the Schönborn Collection, a thirteenth-century Bible written in Germany (£183,000).

The 1994–95 season saw strong results in the field of Oriental manuscripts. The most spectacular was the £408,500 paid for a magnificent thirteenth-century manuscript of the Qur'an on vellum, setting a new world auction price record for a Qur'an. There was renewed interest in Persian manuscripts and miniatures, the competition for high quality pieces producing the strongest

JOHANN BLAEU
Atlas maior sive Cosmographia Blaviana
AMSTERDAM, 1662, ELEVEN VOLUMES, FIRST EDITION, folio
Milan L249,900,000
(£97,581:$152,471).
20.XII.94 (LEFT)

Portable antiphoner
SPAIN, EARLY SIXTEENTH CENTURY, IN LATIN, ILLUMINATED MANUSCRIPT ON VELLUM, 23 x 15.5cm (9 x 6⅛in)
London £3,680 ($5,925).
20.VI.95

In the lower left-hand corner of this manuscript is a miniature of a turkey. Native to North America, the bird shown here must have been one of the earliest specimens to reach Spain, and this may be the first illustration of American wildlife in an illuminated manuscript. (ABOVE)

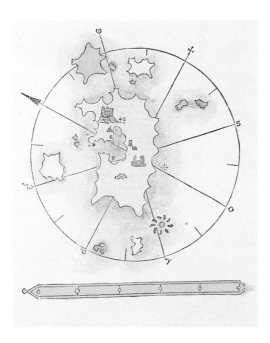

results for many years. A fine example was the £210,500 paid for a Sultanate and Mughal illustrated copy of Firdausi's epic, Shahnama.

Single-owner sales carry a unique cachet for auction houses. The major events for the London and New York departments were the first two sales of books from the library of Dr Otto Schäfer, the most important collector of illustrated books in the past fifty years. The first sale, in New York, consisted solely of Italian books and was a remarkable success, bringing just over $7,000,000 for 198 lots, with 23 lots realizing over $100,000, the highest single book-sale total seen in New York since 1989. The top price ($486,500) was attained by a Neapolitan humanist manuscript of the Ars moriendi *but the most surprising result was for the first illustrated edition of Frezzi's* Quatriregio *(Florence, 1508): conservatively estimated at $15,000–20,000, it was sold for $420,500. The London Schäfer sale of Parisian books in June numbered among its highlights a handsome copy of Redouté's* Les Liliacées, *which achieved a startling £155,500 and a paper copy of* Les Roses, *which sold for £106,000, while Tory's artistically revolutionary Book of Hours (1524) sailed beyond the pre-sale estimate of £40,000–60,000 to £122,500.*

Other single-owner sales of the season included two catalogues devoted to individual musical items. The autograph manuscript of Schumann's Second Symphony, perhaps the last autograph full score of a great nineteenth-century symphony that will ever come to auction, realized the astonishing sum of £1,486,500, twice the published estimate. Our old record of £1.1 million for a single musical work was decisively exceeded. The £661,500 paid for Haydn's String Quartets Op.50 nos. 3–6, likewise established a record for the composer.

The book-collecting taste of an earlier age was on display in the catalogue of the Continental Library of the 5th Earl of Rosebery. Rosebery was a noted bibliophile who maintained his collection at Mentmore, the home of his wife's family, the Rothschilds. The subject matter ranged from early Italian printed books to eighteenth- and nineteenth-century French literature and history, with some fine topographical works. The Merian Topographia, in a contemporary binding and with a seventeenth-century English provenance, realized £161,000.

Perhaps the most unusual sale of the season undertaken by the book department on either side of the Atlantic was the Collection of Dame Joan Sutherland, O.M. and Richard Bonynge, C.B.E. Bidders competed avidly for operatic memorabilia including costumes, jewellery, props, fans and opera-glasses. An autograph manuscript of part of Rossini's Zelmira achieved £26,450. Memorabilia of another type featured in the highly successful sale of the Northesk Collection, comprising 58 lots of papers, medals, swords and paintings, many relating to the Battle of Trafalgar, in which the 7th Earl of Northesk, commanding the Britannia, had been Nelson's third in command.

Sotheby's was privileged to receive for sale the library of the distinguished philosopher Sir Karl Popper. The collection included a number of his own publications, often extensively annotated and revised, together with two autograph letters from Albert Einstein about quantum mechanics. The catalogue proved so attractive that the Austrian government made an offer for the entire collection, enabling the library to be kept together in Klagenfurt. At the request of Sir Karl's executors, Sotheby's cancelled the auction, confident in the assurance that Sir Karl's library had found a permanent home in the land of his birth.

Manuscript Americana brought notably strong results during the season. It was a special pleasure to sell a selection of fine autographs from the collection of Roger Barrett which he had inherited from his father, Oliver R. Barrett, the greatest of all Lincoln collectors. The 1952 Parke-Bernet sale of Oliver Barrett's Lincoln Collection was a milestone in American auction history. The high point of the November Americana auction, at $288,500, was probably the most important Lincoln autograph to be reserved from the 1952 sale: a letter of 13 March 1864 to the recently elected free-state governor of Louisiana, suggesting, in anticipation of the Fifteenth Amendment, that he extend the franchise to 'some of the colored people' of the state. In the spring, this figure was nearly equalled by a very richly 'truffled' copy of Battles and Leaders of the Civil War, *containing some 900 autographs of Civil War military figures and political leaders ($255,500).*

Items from the
Northesk Collection
of Trafalgar
Memorabilia
London £122,748 ($191,487).
13.XII.94

Including the 'Order of Battle' sent by Nelson to Lord Northesk eleven days before Trafalgar, the Naval Large Gold Medal and the City of London sword of honour, both presented to Lord Northesk.

(ABOVE)

The predominant theme of New York's spring sales was the book beautiful. A collection of modern illustrated books and fine bindings, presented as The Book as Art, contained the most comprehensive assemblage of livres d'artiste *ever sold in New York. The collection included thirteen bindings by Paul Bonet. One of these, Verlaine's* Parallèlement *(1900) with lithographs by Pierre Bonnard, brought the best result of the sale ($123,500). The highest price of the entire New York book season at Sotheby's was brought by a magnificent album of plans and views of the Petit Trianon. One of a small group of such albums, presumably made by the architect Richard Mique at the request of Marie-Antoinette, it sold for $800,000.*

GUILLAUME APOLLINAIRE
AND RAOUL DUFY

Le Bestiaire, ou
Cortège d'Orphée
PARIS, 1911, SIGNED,
WOODCUTS, ONE OF 91
COPIES ON HOLLANDE,
OCHRE-TAN MOROCCO
WITH BLACK CALF ONLAYS
New York $68,500 (£43,155).
2.VI.95 (RIGHT)

PRINTED BOOKS AND AUTOGRAPH MANUSCRIPTS

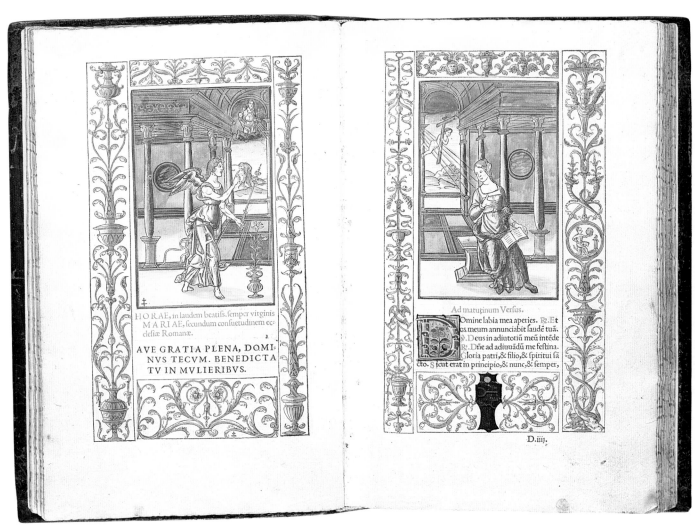

GEOFFROY TORY
Horae B.M.V.
PARIS, 1524, FIRST EDITION WITH WOODCUTS, 4to
London £122,500 ($193,550). 27.VI.95
From the Collection of Otto Schäfer

This issue of Geoffroy Tory's original, and artistically revolutionary, Book of Hours was described by William B. Ivins, Jr. as 'the first French book which from beginning to end was a highly conscious and deliberate work of art'. Tory's classical-Italianate woodcuts and borders were executed for him in an anonymous workshop which signed its work with the Cross of Lorraine. Care was not confined to illustration, the extended title refers specifically to the text's correctness in spelling and pointing. (ABOVE)

Ars moriendi, L'Arte de lo Ben Morire

Naples, c.1480, in Latin and Italian, translated by Junianus Maius,
illuminated manuscript on vellum
New York $486,500 (£311,360). 8.XII.94
From the Collection of Otto Schäfer

This is an apparently unique Italian version of the guide to dying a
Christian death. It describes five demonic appearances to a dying man,
tempting him to renounce his faith, abandon hope, lose patience, and
give in to worldly vanity and avarice. Each diabolic visitation is paired
with that of angels who counsel the resistance of such provocations,
enabling the man to come to a holy end. The manuscript, which has
53 text pages, took the scribe, Giovanni Marco Cinico, only 53 hours
to write out, justifying his nickname of *Velox* or Speedy. (ABOVE)

DANTE ALIGHIERI
La Commedia with commentary by Cristoforo Landino

Florence, 30 August 1481, first edition, Super Royal folio
New York $244,500 (£156,480). 8.XII.94
From the Collection of Otto Schäfer

Although incomplete, this is one of the most monumental illustrated
printed books of the fifteenth century. It is generally agreed that
the engravings for the first nineteen cantos of *Inferno* derive from
Sandro Botticelli and that they were executed by Baccio Baldini.
The original plan was to provide headpiece illustrations for each
of the 100 cantos but the reasons for its failure are not certain.
Of more than 125 surviving copies, only about twenty contain
the full complement of nineteen engravings. (ABOVE)

MERIAN (MATTHÄUS, THE
ELDER) AND MARTIN ZEILLER

Topographia

FRANKFURT, 1642–50, 13 PARTS
BOUND IN 12 VOLUMES, folio
London £161,000 ($259,210). 25.V.95
From the Continental Library of
Archibald, 5th Earl of Rosebery and
Midlothian, K.G., K.T.

The twelve original volumes of
the great Merian-Zeiller
Topographia series cover nearly
all of Germany, Austria and
Switzerland. They include 32
maps and 635 plates showing a
total of 965 town views, plans
and other subjects. Their
binding is of seventeenth-
century gilt-panelled vellum
with central arabesques enclosing
the Bridgeman arms. (BELOW)

Eusebius Pamphilius

PARIS, 1544, FIRST EDITION, folio
London £133,500 ($210,930). 27.VI.95
From the Collection of Otto Schäfer

The finest bindings
commissioned by Marcus
Fugger in the 1550s were on
Greek texts, under the influence
of the Fontainebleau programme
of Henri II. The royal binder
of this work was long identified
as Claude de Picques, but it is
now thought to be Gommar
Estienne. Issued when Estienne
had been appointed official
Printer in Greek to François I,
it was also the first substantial
book to be set in Claude
Garamond's *grecs du roi*, a
font commissioned by the
king specifically for printing
the texts of unpublished
Greek manuscripts in the
Royal Library. (LEFT)

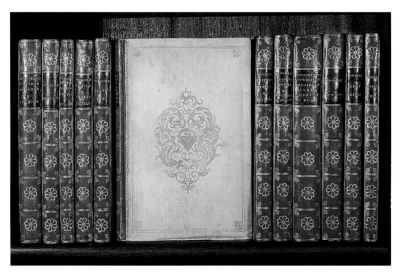

BRAUN (GEORG)
AND FRANS HOGENBERG
Beschreibung und Contrafactur der Vornembster Stät der Welt
COLOGNE 1576–1618, 6 VOLUMES BOUND IN 2,
GERMAN EDITION
London £60,900 ($95,004). 12.XII.94

The supreme value of the *Civitates* (as this series is widely known) lies in its survey of European towns and cities just at the time when draughtsmen were capable of conveying a wealth of information in a single portrayal, incorporating views and plans of almost every kind of urban settlement. The tranquility of the scenes depicted here is remarkable considering that, during the compilation and publication of this series, many of the towns of Austria, Hungary and the Spanish Netherlands were wracked by civil and military conflict. (RIGHT)

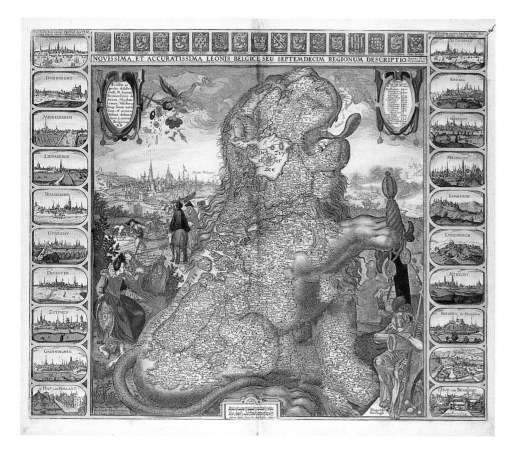

VISSCHER (NICOLAAS JANSZOON)
Leo Belgicus
AMSTERDAM, *c*.1621
London £17,250 ($27,773). 22.VI.95

In this portrayal of the Leo Belgicus, commemorating the Twelve Years' Truce (1609–21) between Spain and the Netherlands, the lion, although apparently resting, is watchful with his sword at his right paw, wary of danger. He is protecting the Seventeen Provinces, which are illustrated by peaceful scenes of farming, safe travel, and fruitful trade and commerce. From above, putti bestow riches, science, knowledge and blessings of God. (LEFT)

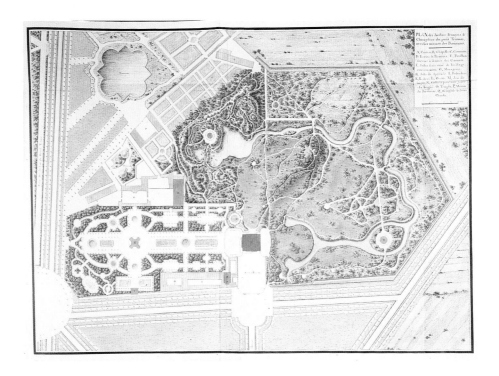

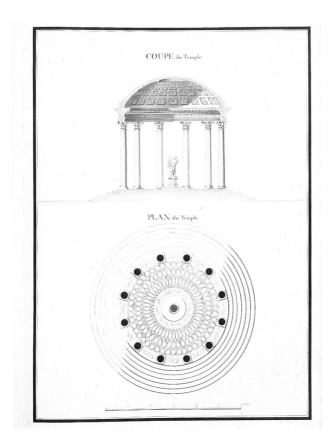

RICHARD MIQUE AND CLAUDE-LOUIS CHÂTELET
Recueil des plans du Petit Trianon
[PARIS?], 1781, BROADSHEETS, MOUNTED ON GUARDS AND BOUND IN ONE VOLUME
New York $800,000 (£504,000). 2.VI.95

Commissioned by Louis XV from Jacques-Ange Gabriel at the suggestion of Mme de Pompadour, the Petit Trianon was completed in 1768. After Louis' death in 1774 his grandson, Louis XVI, presented the château to his nineteen-year-old wife, Marie-Antoinette and it soon became her preferred residence, a private refuge from the formal constraints of the court at Versailles. This magnificent album celebrating the Petit Trianon's Rococo splendours is one of a small number commissioned by the queen of her favourite architect, Richard Mique, and landscape artist, Claude-Louis Châtelet. The album contains fifteen architectural plans, elevations, cross-sections and details by Mique of the château and its parklands and five lively watercolours by Châtelet. (LEFT AND ABOVE)

JANSCHA (LORENZ) AND JOHANN ZIEGLER
Collection de cinquante vües du Rhin
VIENNA, 1798, oblong folio
London £63,000 ($101,430). 22.VI.95

This beautiful book contains undoubtedly the most magnificent series of views of the Rhine.
With text and captions in French and German, it contains fifty finely hand-coloured plates
showing prospects engraved by Johann Ziegler after Lorenz Janscha. (BELOW)

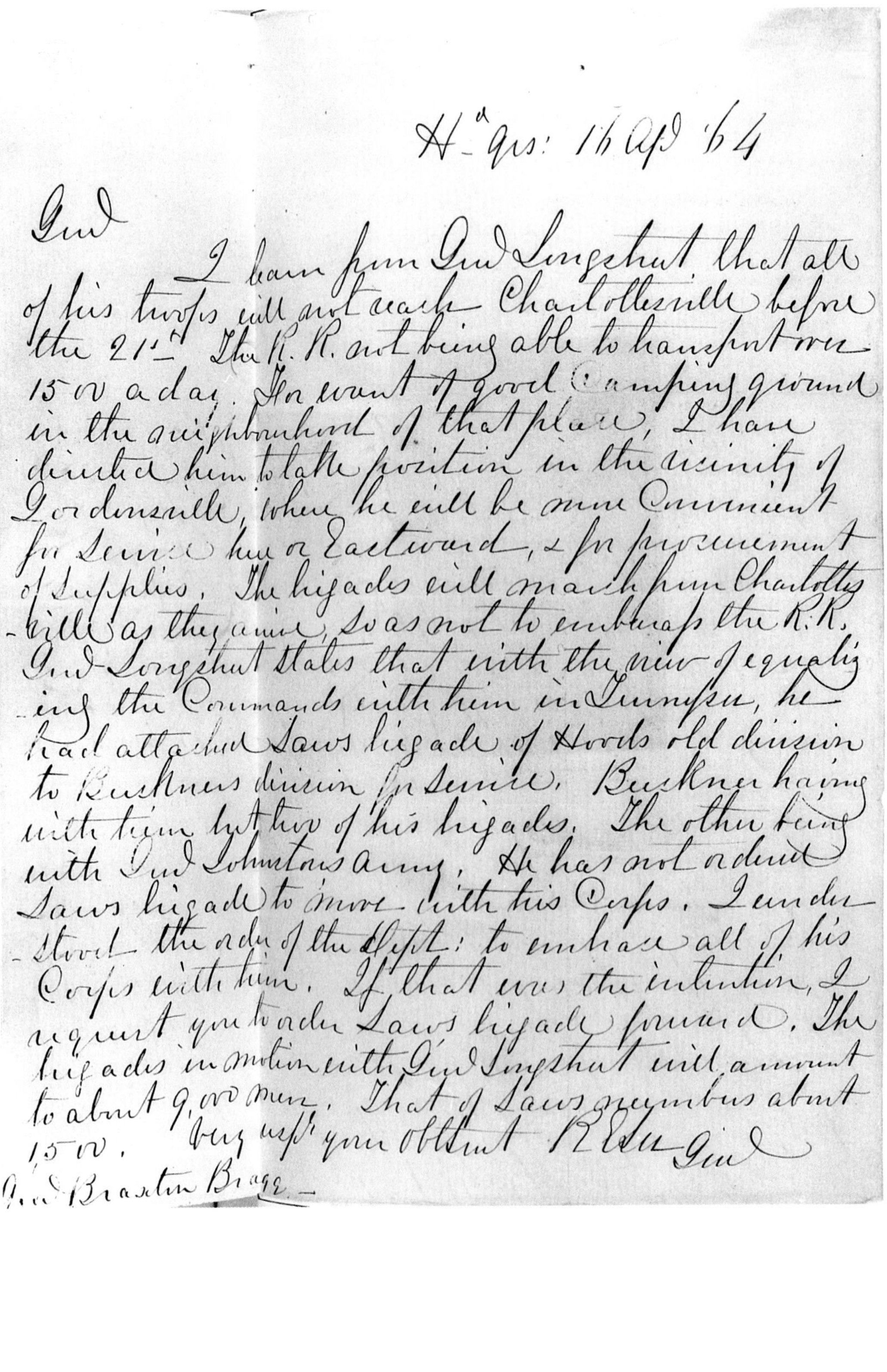

Hd Qrs: 16 Apl '64

Genl

I learn from Genl Longstreet that all of his troops will not reach Charlottesville before the 21st. The R.R. not being able to transport over 1500 a day. For want of good camping ground in the neighbourhood of that place, I have directed him to take position in the vicinity of Gordonsville, where he will be more convenient for service here or Eastward, & for procurement of supplies. The brigades will march from Charlottesville as they arrive, so as not to embarrass the R.R. Genl Longstreet states that with the view of equalizing the commands with him in Tennessee, he had attached Laws brigade of Hoods old division to Buckners division for service. Buckner having with him but two of his brigades. The other being with Genl Johnstons army. He has not ordered Laws brigade to move with his Corps. I understood the order of the Dept: to embrace all of his Corps with him. If that was the intention, I request you to order Laws brigade forward. The brigades in motion with Genl Longstreet will amount to about 9,000 men. That of Laws numbers about 1500.

Very respy your obt servt R E Lee Genl

Genl Braxton Bragg.

ROBERT UNDERWOOD JOHNSON AND CLARENCE CLOUGH BUEL, EDS.

Battles and Leaders of the Civil War

NEW YORK, 1887–88, 8vo

New York $255,500 (£160,965). 2.VI.95

From the Collection of Colonel H.H. Rogers

The insertion of more than 900 original letters, documents, signatures and signed manuscripts together with over 250 portraits and other illustrations has extended this collection from four to nine volumes. Virtually every notable flag officer for both the Union and the Confederacy, as well as cabinet members, legislators and war-time governors is included. In one letter dated 16 April 1864, shown here, Robert E. Lee writes to General Braxton Bragg, reporting on the movements of General Longstreet and his troops. (LEFT)

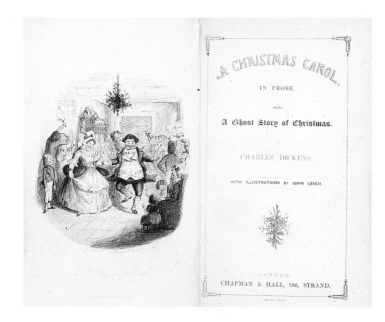

CHARLES DICKENS
A Christmas Carol
CHAPMAN & HALL, 1843, FIRST EDITION, FIRST ISSUE, FIRST STATE, 8vo
New York $63,000 (£40,320). 7.XII.94
From the Collection of Bronson Pinchot

This rare edition of *A Christmas Carol* is one of the eleven earliest presentation copies known to exist. The inscription bears the actual date of publication: 'Thomas Beard/From his old friend/Charles Dickens/Nineteenth December 184[3]'. Beard, a journalist, was a member of Dickens' most intimate circle of friends and had served as best man at Dickens' wedding to Catherine Hogarth in 1836. (LEFT)

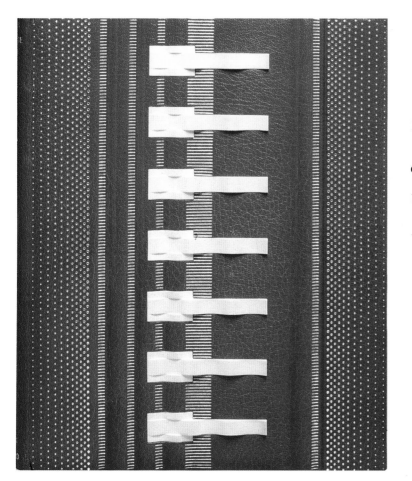

PAUL VERLAINE
Parallèlement
PARIS, 1900, NUMBERED 194 OF A TOTAL EDITION OF 200,
BINDING BY PAUL BONET, 1933
New York $123,500 (£77,805). 2.VI.95

Parallèlement is considered by many to be the first *livre d'artiste*. Pierre Bonnard's 108 sanguine-rose lithographs, among the finest works of his entire career, seem to wrap themselves around Verlaine's sensuous verse. In the early 1930s the Argentinian collector, Carlos R. Scherrer, commissioned Paul Bonet to design a suitable binding. A typed note on Bonet's letterhead, bound into the volume, reads, 'This is the first binding on which I have used ivory onlays. The colour of the illustrations determined that of the morocco, and I have tried to give a jewel-like quality to this architectural binding.' (LEFT)

MUSIC MANUSCRIPTS

ROBERT SCHUMANN
Autograph manuscript of the Second Symphony, Op.61
1846–47, 246 PAGES, 4to, 28.7 x 22.1cm (11¼ x 8¾in)
London £1,486,500 ($2,318,940). 1.XII.94

Schumann's Second Symphony has a central position in the modern concert repertory and is
one of the composer's most important works, linking the symphonies of the Classical school,
such as Beethoven and Schubert, with those of Brahms. This composing manuscript reveals
extensive layers of working and reworking, particularly in the first movement, providing a
valuable insight into the stages by which Schumann brought the work towards its final form.
Unrecorded for fifty years, the manuscript was assumed to have been lost or destroyed and
it is arguably one of the most significant music discoveries since World War II. (ABOVE)

JOSEPH HAYDN
Autograph manuscript of the String Quartets Op.50, nos. 3, 4, 5 and 6
1787, 123 PAGES, OBLONG 4to, *c*.16.5 x 26.5cm (6½ x 10½in)
London £661,500 ($1,038,555). 18.V.95

The string quartets Op.50 are central to Joseph Haydn's output and are regarded as among the greatest of the eighteenth century. Haydn is frequently referred to as 'the father of the string quartet' since he established the equal relationship between instruments to produce the conversational style celebrated by Goethe, in which accompaniments and leading parts exchange and 'discuss' a succession of musical motifs. This page contains the opening of the final movement of quartet no. 6 'The Frog' into which Haydn inserted a passage of four bars on a flap folded over the outer margin. (ABOVE)

WESTERN MANUSCRIPTS

THE MASTER OF MARY OF BURGUNDY
The Annunciation to the Shepherds
SINGLE MINIATURE FROM AN
ILLUMINATED MANUSCRIPT ON VELLUM,
SOUTHERN NETHERLANDS, POSSIBLY
BRUSSELS OR ROOCLOOSTER, *c.*1475–80,
12.5 x 9cm (5 x 3½in)
London £210,500 ($338,905). 20.VI.95

The Master is named after two
haunting Books of Hours which
belonged to Mary of Burgundy, wife
of Maximilian of Austria. This piece
is presumably from a Book of Hours
or other book of devotion. It stands
alone in its originality of composition
and representation of night. The
painter's comprehension of light is
unique. Although dark, the scene is
illuminated by the dawn sky beyond
Bethlehem, by the angel so bright the
shepherds need to shade their faces,
by the fluttering angels linking
Bethlehem to Heaven, and principally
by the dot of pure light from the
stable itself which must represent the
very moment of the Incarnation.
The latter is perhaps intentionally the
'light which shines in the darkness
and the dark comprehends it not'.
This artist was also one of the first
manuscript painters of northern
Europe to address the concept of
space and depth, devising several
methods of framing the foreground
through which one then looks into
the far distance. This miniature is
now in the J. Paul Getty Museum,
California. (LEFT)

THE BOUCICAUT MASTER
The Adoration of the Magi
SINGLE LEAF FROM AN ILLUMINATED MANUSCRIPT BOOK OF HOURS ON VELLUM, PARIS, *c.*1410,
18.8 x 14cm (7⅓ x 5½in)
London £19,550 ($30,498). 5.XII.94
From the Collection of Dr Rosy Schilling

The Boucicaut Master was one of the finest artists working in Paris at the beginning of the
fifteenth century. He takes his name from the great Book of Hours made for the marshal of
France, Jean de Boucicaut, and the figures of the magi here can be compared to those in the
Boucicaut Hours. There is a good case for identifying the Master with Jacques Coene, the
Bruges artist first recorded in Paris in 1398. The present miniature shows the pure colours and
tall rather disdainful aristocratic figures which are so characteristic of his work. (ABOVE)

Book of Hours in Latin with one prayer in French

ILLUMINATED MANUSCRIPT ON VELLUM, SOUTHERN NETHERLANDS, GHENT OR BRUGES, *c.*1510, 22.3 x 15.3cm (8½ x 6in)
London £139,000 ($223,790). 20.VI.95

The great glory of this manuscript is its calendar. It provides an extraordinary window into the
life of the southern Netherlands in the late Middle Ages, with details of buildings, costumes,
ships, carts, crockery, customs, pubs, tools, wine-making, flax-making and so forth, of a
richness and variety beyond description. Though the miniatures are technically only borders
around text, they are treated by the artist as landscapes with the panel of text as a superfluous
detail. In the manuscript workshops of Bruges, the art of secular landscape reaches its pinnacle.
For almost the first time in European art, there are townscapes and scenery standing on their
own. It is a development in the southern Netherlands which runs parallel to, or even precedes,
the evolution of landscape in oil painting. (BELOW)

MESHULLAM ZEIMEL BEN MOSHE

Seder Perek Shirah, V'sefer Tehillim, and other prayers, in Hebrew

MANUSCRIPT ON VELLUM, VIENNA, DATED *1721*, 19.5 x 13.6cm (7½ x 5¼in)
London £155,500 ($242,580). 5.XII.94

This book was written and illustrated by Meshullam Zeimel Ben Moshe of Palin, one of the most outstanding Bohemian scribes and book illustrators, who worked principally in Vienna. The miniatures here, in the style of engravings, show a detail and delicacy which is altogether exceptional. The *Perek Shirah* has 76 miniatures of all God's creatures, except man, joining to sing poetic praise to the Creator. These form a delightful eighteenth-century evocation of the world and include depictions of contemporary artefacts such as the classical pepper-pot (which shakes dew over the world) and a great sailing ship. This is followed by other prayers which open with elaborate decorative headpieces. (BELOW)

ORIENTAL MANUSCRIPTS

An Almohad Qur'an manuscript

ANDALUCIA OR NORTH-WEST AFRICA, c.1200, FINELY ILLUMINATED ARABIC MANUSCRIPT ON VELLUM,
31.5 x 29.5 cm (12⅜ x 11⅝in)
London £408,500 ($653,600). 26.IV.95

This is the largest known single volume Andalusian/Maghribi Qur'an in existence.
The manuscript is notable for the extraordinary quality of illumination, the size of
the panels, the intricacy of the work and the variety of designs. The marginal devices
are predominantly roundels or scallop-shapes, but there are also large trefoil and
quatrefoil devices and many large niche-shaped designs. The general character and
certain specific features of the script point to an Iberian, rather than a North African,
origin, but it is difficult to determine the geographical source of a manuscript purely
on the basis of the script, since scribes were often expatriate at this period. (ABOVE)

Sultan Ali Adil Shah II meeting with his general Afzal Khan

DECCAN, *c.*1660, ALBUM PAGE WITH COLOURED BORDERS DECORATED WITH GOLD
FLOWERING VINE, 20 x 16.7cm (7⅞ x 6⁹⁄₁₆in)
New York $28,750 (£18,400). 30.XI.94

The Sultan Ali Adil Shah, seated on a jewelled throne, delicately holds
a blossom in his left hand whilst grasping his sword in his right. Before
him kneels his general, Afzal Khan. The relative importance of the
figures is clearly delineated both by the gold halo encircling the
sultan's head and the variance in scale between the two men. The
artist's skill and attention to detail continue into the background of
the painting where a mango tree is laden with ripe golden fruit. (LEFT)

Shiva and Parvati Enthroned and Celebrated by Worshippers and Divinities

MANDI, SCHOOL OF THE ARTIST SAJNU, *c.*1810–20,
26 x 24.1 cm (10¼ x 9½in)
New York $21,275 (£13,403). 23.III.95

The artist Sajnu came to Mandi from Kangra in the first decade of
the nineteenth century and in 1810 completed a *Hamir Hath* series
for his new patron, Raja Isvari Sen. Sajnu brought with him stylistic
conventions of the Kangra valley which greatly influenced the new
brand of painting at Mandi. This work shows the divine couple,
Shiva and Parvati, enthroned on a lotus in a palace courtyard with
other Hindu deities including Brahma, Vishnu and Indra. (RIGHT)

THE DECORATIVE ARTS *by Philippe Garner*

A Japanese lacquer suzuribako (writing box)
NINETEENTH CENTURY,
24 x 22.5cm (9⁹⁄₁₆ x 8⅞in)
London £6,900
($11,040). 21.VI.95
From the Carlo Monzino
Collection (LEFT)

A marquetry filing cabinet (detail)
STAMPED *GENTY ET JME*,
c.1760–65,
height 137cm (54in)
Monaco FF388,500
(£46,305:$72,346). 3.XII.94
From the Collection of Baron
Guy de Rothschild at Château
Ferrières (BELOW)

The 1994–95 season has drawn to a close. It is tempting at this stage to try to identify the predominant patterns in the various market-places that come under the collective umbrella of the so-called Decorative Arts. Mercifully, the lean years of the recession seem to be over. A period of considerable difficulty has eased and the market has returned to a satisfactory level of stability, with a pleasing number of exciting individual prices and gratifying overall results.

The season has witnessed a steady demand for quality objects, but it must be acknowledged that the market of the mid-nineties has a different feel to it than that of the optimistic years of the eighties which preceded the short-lived speculative frenzy at the close of the decade. It is generally a more cautious, knowing and more professional market. Short-term turnaround profit is now recognized as a hazardous and often elusive goal.

The ubiquitous word in press reports is 'selective', a term which, in my view, defines a perfectly healthy state of affairs, that is to say a market-place in which potential bidders bring knowledge and discernment to the processes of viewing and bidding in sales. At the most difficult times in the market 'selective' might have been used to gloss over a regularly high rate of unsold items. Today it defines the acceptable reality that sales need to be carefully edited by the auction experts and the goods on offer must be correctly priced, for they will be subjected to a highly selective process of scrutiny. The trade in all categories has become wary of carrying extensive middle-range stock. In the current more realistic market buyers are resistant to even entering the bidding unless estimates are set at sensible levels, and then they will bid only if they are specifically attracted to a piece. As an auctioneer I have been conscious that if I invite bidding on a lot but attract no bids, nothing will be achieved by inviting bids at a lower level.

The Decorative Arts embrace areas appealing, on the one hand, to specialized collecting interests, such as Japanese Netsuke or pre-Columbian carvings, and on the other to the large market of potential buyers who are keen to buy antique furniture, furnishings and attractive works of art to

A sheet metal Angel
Gabriel weathervane
AMERICA, NINETEENTH
CENTURY, height 73.7cm (29in)
New York $44,850
(£28,256). 28.I.95
From the Collection of Mr and
Mrs G. William Holland
(ABOVE)

decorate their homes. The broad international market for useful antique furnishings and decorations provides a reassuring foundation for trading. The market is driven, however, by the informed passions of specialist collectors and their dealers. It is the desire of such collectors to possess the objects of their affections which make for the most heated bidding battles in the saleroom and the resulting records eventually carry the market with them.

It has been a feature of the modern market to expand the range of world cultures deemed worthy of serious artistic, as well as historical, interest. The arts of China and Japan have a relatively long collecting history; the collecting of tribal art is essentially a twentieth-century phenomenon, stimulated by the interest shown in the early years of the century by the Cubist painters and their avant-garde contemporaries. Tribal works of art have been reassessed for their complex aesthetic interest. Objects which were brought back from world travels more as curiosities or souvenirs came to be recognized as works of art of considerable beauty. Tribal art remains, nonetheless, a specialist subject, although Sotheby's New York has established itself as a strong selling centre in this field.

The American market has also shown an ever-increasing interest in the collecting of native American Indian art. This season witnessed successful sales in October 1994 and May 1995, with the highest price for the year of $387,500 achieved for a collection of important Sioux pictographic drawings. Pre-Columbian works of art are particularly popular with American buyers; a new world record was set during the year with the $123,500 paid for a Chinesco male figure (November 1994).

The changing patterns of global economies and politics will surely continue to have their impact on the art market. Sales of Korean art have proved themselves to be a growth area with successful results this season including the $948,500 paid for a seventeenth-century Choson Dynasty white-glazed jar (New York, March 1995). Sotheby's Australia consolidated its commitment to the subject of tribal and Aboriginal art and artefacts with its December 1994 auction in Sydney.

As we approach the close of the millenium another trend is becoming evident, namely a shift in attitude regarding the relative merits of the centuries. Twenty-five years ago, the principal areas of activity for Sotheby's, with the notable exception of certain Impressionist and Modern pictures, were in the most traditional fields of collecting, that is to say furniture and works of art from the eighteenth century or earlier. Today, there are several specialist departments successfully devoted to nineteenth- and twentieth-century works. In the past season, nineteenth-century sculpture sales have consolidated their place in the market with a good selection of works and high prices. These include notably the £107,100 realized for a fine bust of Henry Fuseli by Edward Hodges Baily, the £135,700 paid for Charles Henri Cordier's Jeune mulâtresse *(both London, November 1994)* and the $288,500 achieved in New York for Henri Weigele's group of two dancing female figures *(May 1995)*. Nineteenth-century furniture sales continue to make a solid contribution to the market with an increased awareness of the talents and individuality of major cabinetmakers. A gilt-bronze and parquetry medal cabinet by François Linke, circa 1890, sold for £56,500 *(March 1995)*.

It has been a strong season for twentieth-century works including two particularly interesting single-owner sales. An auction in London *(November 1994)* devoted to the Viennese avant-garde of the very early years of the century saw the setting of several record prices, notably the £331,500 paid for an inlaid cabinet by Koloman Moser. In New York, the sale of the John W. Mecom, Jr. Collection of Tiffany lamps set the highest individual price for any work of art within the Decorative Arts divisions with the $1,102,500 paid for a Virginia Creeper lamp.

Certain principles seem constant in the art market. Works of art which have an interesting provenance and which are fresh to the market-place seem consistently able to attract an extra degree of interest and this season has been no exception. Among the most interesting groups of property or collections to come to auction were two specialized sales of Japanese and Chinese works. The Carlo Monzino Collection of Netsuke, Inro and Lacquer sold in London in June 1995. The collection included rare examples which had been acquired in the fifties and sixties and the sale proved a great success with estimates comfortably exceeded. A record price was set for a wood Netsuke at £108,200. The sale of a hitherto unrecorded private collection of Chinese snuff bottles, formed in the forties, fifties and sixties, similarly attracted considerable interest when offered in London on the same day.

In a solid but unexceptional season of furniture sales, a strong provenance ensured a very good result with the sale in Monaco *(December 1994)* of furniture and works of art from the Château de Ferrières, the property of Baron Guy de Rothschild. The house now belongs to the University of Paris and four of the lots were pre-empted by the state to be returned for permanent display.

After a season whose other highlights included the $6,638,220 auction of the Cyril Humphris Collection of Works of Art *(New York, January 1995)* and the second and final sale of the Little Collection of American Folk Art, achieving a grand total of $12.3 million, *(New York, October 1994)* we look forward with curiosity to the inevitable surprises the 1995–96 season will deliver.

A Kakiemon porcelain bowl and cover
LATE SEVENTEENTH CENTURY, height overall 37cm (14½in) London £100,500 ($157,785). 17.XI.94 (ABOVE)

Tigers and Leopards in Mountainscape
ANONYMOUS, EIGHTEENTH/NINETEENTH CENTURY, INK AND COLOURS ON PAPER, MOUNTED ON BROCADE, 96.5 x 55.9cm (38 x 22in) New York $92,700 (£59,328). 3.XII.94 From the Collection of David and Rita Jordt (BELOW)

ISLAMIC AND INDIAN ART

A Gandhara bronze figure of Buddha
NORTH-WESTERN PAKISTAN, *c.*FIFTH/SEVENTH CENTURY, height 26.4cm (10⅜in)
London £78,500 ($126,385). 27.IV.95

The appearance of this figure on the market adds a further
example to a group of about a dozen such bronzes. The majority of
these appear to have been discovered in or near the Swat Valley in
Pakistan. Individual figures from approximately half the group can
be found in public collections including the British Museum, the
Victoria & Albert Museum, the Nelson Atkins Museum in Kansas
City and the S.P.S. Museum in Srinagar. (BELOW)

An Indian buff sandstone figure of a Chandella king
MADHYA PRADESH, KHAJURAHO REGION, LATE TENTH/EARLY ELEVENTH CENTURY,
height 68.6cm (27in)
New York $156,500 (£98,595). 23.III.95

This important and rare sculpture probably represents King Dhangadeva,
one of the most powerful monarchs of the Chandella Dynasty. King
Dhangadeva, or Dhanga, ruled over parts of northern India from
Khajuraho between 950 and 1102. Having conquered the Gwalior fort,
his territory extended to Vidisa in the east, and from Varanasi in the
north to the Narmada river in the south. Dhanga's long reign provided
him with the stability to promote the extensive building of temples, lakes
and gardens, and the arts also flourished under his patronage. (ABOVE)

A Gandhara grey schist figure of Maitreya
NORTH-WESTERN PAKISTAN, THIRD/FOURTH CENTURY, height 199cm (78⅜in)
London £177,500 ($285,775). 27.IV.95

This is among the largest Gandhara figures to have been offered at auction in recent years and
the price achieved is a world auction record for a work of art from the Indian sub-continent.
The moustachioed deity Maitreya is represented wearing an elaborate jewelled turban, several
necklaces and a voluminous *dhoti* tied with string at the waist. (ABOVE)

An Artuqid silver- and gold-inlaid bronze jug

JAZIRA, NORTHERN SYRIA, THIRD QUARTER OF THE FOURTEENTH CENTURY, height 15cm (5⅞in)
London £128,000 ($206,080). 27.IV.95

Of the same family as a group of related objects in Italian public collections, this work is inscribed
with a dedication to the Sultan Majd al-Din 'Isa al-Zahir, the Artuqid ruler of Mardin AD 1376–1404.
It also bears the following verse:
'Oh my possessor, may you ever remain in comfort,
And may you be free from all afflictions,
And may you always remain in abundance,
In favour, and happiness, and excellence'
The use of an elaborate intertwined *kufic* script for the main inscription is most unusual. Even more
striking is the extraordinarily finely executed group of six fish on the base, echoing a similar design used
on many examples of fourteenth-century Islamic metalwork. (ABOVE)

MAQBOOL FIDA HUSAIN
Plant III
SIGNED IN ENGLISH AND DATED '80, ACRYLIC
ON CANVAS, 99.1 x 124.5cm (39 x 49in)
New York $41,400 (£26,082). 12.VI.95
From the Chester and Davida Herwitz
Charitable Trust

Maqbool Fida Husain has been
compared to Picasso in the power of
his personality and the seemingly
inexhaustible flow of his work. Perhaps
no other artist has so successfully
captured the divergent images of India,
encompassing rural life, the British
Raj, the great Indian epics – the
Ramayana and the *Mahabharata*, the
cinema of Satyajit Ray, Buñuel and
Godard, the urban poor, the
discrimination against women and the
complex political situation. Husain's
methods are as varied as his subjects
and include massive murals, delicate
watercolours, tapestries, paintings on
wood and even film. (LEFT)

An Iznik pottery dish
TURKEY, *c.* AD 1575, diameter 29.5cm (11¾in)
London £32,200 ($51,842). 20.X.94

The central design of interlocking pointed and lobed
arabesques on this dish derives from earlier Iznik blue and
white prototypes, themselves influenced by Balkan silver
motifs of the period of Bayezid II. (RIGHT)

ORIENTAL CARPETS AND RUGS

An Agra carpet
NORTH INDIA, *c.*1870, 595 x 535cm (19ft 7in x 17ft 7in)
London £122,500 ($196,000). 7.VI.95
From the Toms Collection

Carpets made in India during the Mughal era were manufactured by small Imperial *ateliers* for
royal or aristocratic commissions and production had largely ceased by the early nineteenth
century. However, from the middle of that century, carpet weaving was revived as a
commercial activity, with much of the work stemming from the country's jails: Lahore, Agra,
Yeraoda and Montgomery in particular were renowned for the high quality of their product.
The earliest of the carpets made in this way were copies of classical Persian carpets in the
Maharajah of Jaipur's collection. This carpet set a world auction record for its type. (ABOVE)

A Heriz carpet

NORTH-WEST PERSIA, c.1900, 737 x 475cm (24ft 2in x 15ft 7in)
New York $112,500 (£72,000). 15.XII.94

The decoration of this carpet incorporates highly stylized flowers and geometrical medallions to
form an angular pattern. The wide main border continues the design. Delicate shades of blue,
green, red and brown are soft and clear upon a cream ground. (ABOVE)

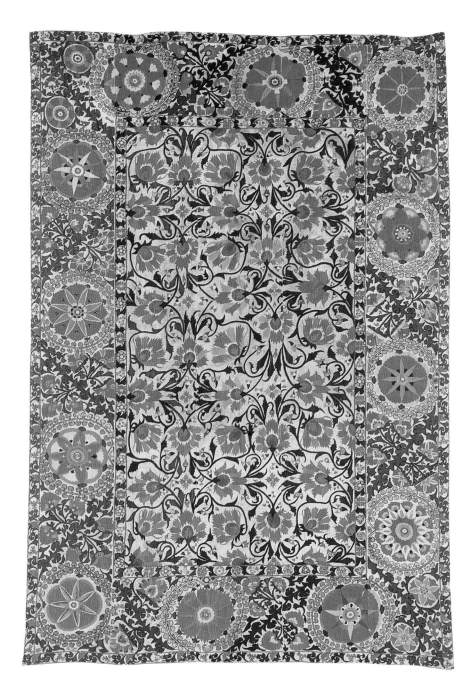

A Shakhrisyabz Susani

SOUTH UZBEKISTAN, LATE EIGHTEENTH CENTURY, 264 x 185cm (8ft 8in x 6ft 1in)
London £31,050 ($49,680). 26.IV.95

Intended as a wall hanging or cover, this Susani is embroidered with the rare design feature of
an 'in-and-out palmette' which is here used to beautiful effect, forming a swirling, colourful
composition. Only two dozen of this type are thought to exist including examples in the M.H.
de Young Museum, San Francisco and the Burrell Collection, Glasgow, and this piece set a
world record at auction. (ABOVE)

A Salor Engsi
CENTRAL TURKESTAN, MID-NINETEENTH CENTURY, 196 x 135cm (6ft 5in x 4ft 5in)
New York $90,500 (£57,015). 13.IV.95

Since the first Salor Engsi surfaced in 1973, a further seven have come to light. The appearance of an eighth in near perfect condition is an exciting event. In terms of both design and colouring it is very close to four other examples which probably date from around the middle third of the nineteenth century and thus represent the last phase of Salor weaving. A distinctive feature of this newly discovered example is its six-cord selvage decorated with a repeating pattern worked in red and dark green wool. Other examples have a two- or three-cord selvage wrapped with red wool. (ABOVE)

CHINESE ART

ZHANG DAQIAN
Dawning Light in Autumn Gorges
SIGNED *YUANWENG ZAO*, DATED *YI SI*, 1965, ELEVENTH MONTH, FIRST
DAY, WITH TWO ARTIST'S SEALS, SPLASHED INK AND COLOUR ON SILK,
269 x 90cm (105⅞ x 35½in)
Hong Kong HK$8,160,000 (£653,323:$1,056,995). 3.XI.94

Often regarded as the 'Picasso of the East', Zhang
Daqian is probably the most famous Chinese artist
of this century. His use of Western techniques and
abstraction in traditional Chinese ink paintings has
earned him wide acclaim around the world. The sale of
Dawning Light in Autumn Gorges set a new auction
record for a modern Chinese painting. (LEFT)

PAN YULIANG
Horses
SIGNED *YU LIANG* IN CHINESE WITH A SEAL AND DATED, 1956, INK AND COLOUR ON PAPER, 97.5 x 181.5cm (38⅜ x 71½in)
Taipei NT$4,670,000 (£104,944:$166,861). 16.IV.95

Pan Yuliang is famous for the eloquence and accuracy of her line and the manner in which she fused Chinese ink brush techniques with Western realism and perspectives. Strongly influenced by Impressionism and Fauvism, she spent many years in Paris where her insistence on having 'no foreign nationality, no love affairs and no contracts with art dealers' earned her the title of the 'Lady of the Three Nos'. Painted at the height of her career in the 1950s, *Horses* is one of Yuliang's biggest and most important ink and colour works. (ABOVE)

CHEN YIFEI
Eulogy of the Yellow River
1972, UNDATED, OIL ON CANVAS, RECENTLY RE-SIGNED IN PINYIN, *CHEN YIFEI*, 380 x 160cm (149⅝ x 63in)
Hong Kong HK$1,285,000 (£102,800:$166,021). 4.V.95

In 1978 and 1979 this painting was illustrated in numerous magazines and journals, including *Chinese Literature, People's Liberation Army Pictorial* and *Shanghai Pictorial*. (LEFT)

A blue and white jar (guan)
YUAN DYNASTY (1279–1368), height 27.6cm (10⅞in)
Hong Kong HK$7,940,000 (£635,709:$1,028,497). 2.XI.94

This jar is among the very finest surviving pieces of Yuan Dynasty blue and white, with a
painted figure scene of outstanding quality. The cobalt blue is perfectly controlled allowing
remarkable detail and subtly graduated washes. The subject is 'The Three Visits to the
Thatched Hut' from *The Romance of the Three Kingdoms*, in which Zhuge Liang, depicted
with his boy servants, is persuaded to return to politics from country retirement. (ABOVE)

An iron-red and underglaze-blue decorated dragon dish
MARK AND PERIOD OF YONGZHENG (1723–35), diameter 47.2cm (18⅝in)
London £287,500 ($457,125). 6.VI.95

This magnificent design of iron-red imperial dragons, combined with underglaze-blue
decoration, is one of the most striking found in the Yongzheng period when the production of
imperial porcelain was at its height. The design, with some variations, is also found in the
following reign of Qianlong. (ABOVE)

A marble Buddhist reliquary

SUI DYNASTY, INSCRIBED AND DATED TO THE EIGHTH YEAR OF
KAIHUANG CORRESPONDING TO AD 588, height 103cm (40½in)
New York $233,500 (£149,440). 22.III.95
From the Estate of Manly P. Hall

This reliquary is a synthesis of two burial practices: the
funerary urn and the stupa or pillar. The present
example is extremely rare in that it is dated, complete
and inscribed with the name of the monk for whom
it was made. (ABOVE)

An inlaid mother-of-pearl gold decorated black lacquer cabinet and hat chest

SIJIANGUI, KANGXI PERIOD, height 265cm (8ft 8½in)
New York $101,500 (£64,960). 29.XI.94

Inlaid mother-of-pearl lacquer cabinets are rare, partly because of the fragility of the
material: all lacquer furniture, if not properly conserved, will rapidly deteriorate. The
lacquer surface is resilient but once it has been compromised changes in humidity
will cause the wooden structure beneath to expand and contract, cracking and
buckling the lacquer surface. The turmoil in China over the past century has resulted
in damage to many such pieces and, as a consequence, there is more lacquer furniture
in the West and it is generally in better condition than that found in China. The
combination of the many varied techniques employed to create this cabinet is
extraordinary and possibly unique. (ABOVE)

A jadeite bead necklace

Beads graduating in size from
*c.*11.2–5.1mm (½–¼in)
Hong Kong HK$8,380,000
(£670,938:$1,085,492). 2.XI.94

Jadeite is a superior type of jade used
for jewellery and is especially prized
for its emerald-green tone. This
exquisite necklace is composed of
ninety-nine highly translucent
jadeite beads. (BELOW)

A pair of jadeite saddle rings

Hong Kong HK$3,210,000
(£257,006:$415,803). 2.XI.94

These rings are particularly well
matched, each possessing a rich
emerald-green colour and a fine
translucency throughout. (BELOW)

A jadeite cabochon ring

*c.*1935, approximate dimensions
2.53 x 1.93 x 1.1cm (1 x ¾ x ½in)
Hong Kong HK$5,740,000
(£459,568:$743,523). 2.XI.94

This oval-shaped cabochon of elegant
proportions is brilliantly clear and of a
rare, deep emerald-green tone. The
stone is set in a scrolled platinum
mounting. (LEFT)

KOREAN ART

White-glazed jar
CHOSON DYNASTY, SEVENTEENTH CENTURY, height 48.3cm (19in)
New York $948,500 (£597,555). 24.III.95

This superb white-wares jar is extremely rare due to its unusually large size and the
fact that it dates from the seventeenth century. The austere simplicity and elegance of
the shape is a classical example of work from the Choson Dynasty (1392–1910) and
embodies the prevailing aesthetics of the Neo-Confucian culture. (ABOVE)

JAPANESE ART

HASEGAWA TOHAKU
Atago Gongen
WITH ONE ARTIST'S SEAL *NOBUHARU (SHINSHUN)*, LATE
SIXTEENTH/EARLY SEVENTEENTH CENTURY, 81.3 x 36.3cm (32 x 14½in)
New York $343,500 (£216,405). 24.III.95

Hasegawa Tohaku (1539–1610) used the *Nobuharu*
seal, as seen on this scroll, in his early career while he
still lived and painted in Noto province, north-east of
Kyoto. His work in this period is known for a number
of figure paintings of Buddhist and Shinto subjects,
including this painting of Atago Gongen. The deity,
worshipped by warriors for victory in battle, is
considered an important early work by this artist. (LEFT)

TOSHUSAI SHARAKU

Portraits of the actors Ichikawa Yaozo III and Sakata Hangoro III
SIGNED, WITH PUBLISHER'S SEAL *TSUTAYA JUZABURO* AND CENSOR'S SEAL *KIWAME*, 37.4 x 25.4cm (14¾ x 10in)
London £95,000 ($152,950). 22.VI.95

This print illustrates a scene from the play *Keisei Sanbon karakasa* which was
performed at the Miyakoza Theatre in the seventh month of Kansei 6 (1794).
Ichikawa Yaozo III in his role as Fuwa-no Banzaemon, the villainous chief
conspirator of the play, is depicted squatting on one knee holding a sheathed sword
in his hand while Sakata Hangoro III, as the evil monk Kosodate-no Kannobo,
stands over him rolling up his sleeve. Other impressions of this print are held in
museums and institutions including the British Museum, the Museum of Fine Arts,
Boston and the Art Institute of Chicago. (ABOVE)

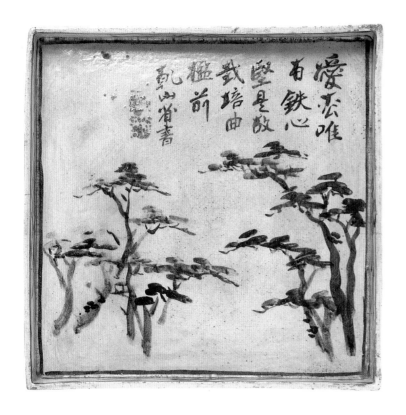

OGATA KENZAN
Two square plates (Kakuzara)
SEVENTEENTH/EIGHTEENTH CENTURY AND 1711, 21.6 x 21.6cm
(8½ x 8½in) and 22.2 x 22.2cm (8¾ x 8¾in)
New York $200,500 (£126,315). 24.III.95

Ogata Kenzan is Japan's most famous ceramic artist who had a tremendous influence on pottery traditions in both Japan and the West. In 1699 he established a kiln at Narutaki, north-west of Kyoto, and although other kiln sites followed, it was here that he began his long, illustrious career.

These flat, square plates are prized for their painted compositions and are typical of Kenzan's early work with underglaze decoration. The second plate in this lot (below) is remarkable for the beauty and size of the calligraphy which is undisputedly by Kenzan himself. It is also of note in that the inscription is dated to the year prior to the closing of the Narutaki kiln.

HOKKYO RYUKEI I

A wood Netsuke of a dancing islander

SIGNED *RYUKEI SAKU*, LATE EIGHTEENTH/
EARLY NINETEENTH CENTURY,
height 9.2cm (3⅝in)
London £108,200 ($173,120). 21.VI.95
From the Carlo Monzino Collection

The emaciated dancing islander
balances on one foot as he looks
up, and holds a drum and stick
before him. The slightly worn
wood bears a good colour and
the eyes are of ivory with dark
horn pupils. (RIGHT)

OGAWA HARITSU, KNOWN AS RITSUO

An inlaid black lacquer four-case inro

SIGNED *BUKANSHI RITSUO KIN SEI*, EARLY
EIGHTEENTH CENTURY, height 9.5cm (3⅞in)
London £58,700 ($93,920). 21.VI.95
From the Carlo Monzino Collection

The foreign ship decorating this
inro, or seal case, is a small
masterpiece of craftsmanship: the
mainsail is mother-of-pearl, the
masts' finials are coral, the three
visible crew are of inlaid pottery
and the boat itself is studded with
green and black stone. (LEFT)

Ko-Kutani tokkuri

LATE SEVENTEENTH CENTURY, height 22.2cm (8¾in)
New York $68,500 (£43,155). 24.III.95

Ko-Kutani ware is characterized by bold
designs and brilliant enamel decorations.
This bottle, freely painted in black with a
scrolling vine pattern underneath a clear
green enamel glaze, is distinctive in that it
is one of only three examples known to
have this decoration. (LEFT)

KOMAI

A pair of inlaid iron vases

SIGNED *NIHON (NO) KUNI KYOTO JU KOMAI SEI*,
MEIJI PERIOD (1868–1912), height 24cm (9⁷⁄₁₆in)
London £41,100 ($65,760). 29.III.95

The central decoration on each of these
vases is a cartouche containing two
figures. In one Michizane holds a plum
blossom and stands next to a seated
samurai in a Kyoto garden, in the other
an archer and his kneeling attendant have
their backs to Mount Fuji, just visible in
the distance. (RIGHT)

TRIBAL ART

A Lulua figure
Height 30.5cm (12in)
New York $189,500 (£117,490). 4.V.95
From the Detroit Institute of Arts

The Lulua believe that the spirits of their ancestors inhabit this type of intricately carved statue. Symbols of beauty and good fortune, such figures are also used to protect the health of children: after birth, both the child and the statue are covered with red earth, washed in warm water and wrapped in banana leaf, a ritual which is repeated regularly throughout the first months of the child's life. Such treatment accounts for the wonderful and varied patina encrusted on this exceptional figure. (RIGHT)

A Djenne figure

TWELFTH/SEVENTEENTH CENTURY, height 51cm (20in)
London £34,500 ($54,165). 28.XI.94

This statue belongs to a group of ten figures, all of which are notable for the elegance
of their posture and the serenely zoomorphic, almost alien, modelling of the heads.
Little is known about the origins of this style but it appears to bear some relation to
similar work produced in the Inland Niger Delta area of Mali, and may possibly
come from a site about 40 kilometres from the city of Djenne. (BELOW)

A Baule face mask
Height 23.8cm (9⅜in)
New York $57,500 (£35,650). 4.V.95

'Small Baule face masks are [worn] in entertainment dances of great antiquity.
Though new performances with new names, songs, music and dance steps seem to
have been introduced about every other generation, they all adhere to a common
pattern. Masks representing domestic and hunted animals, known individuals,
and such general types as "the slave", "the prostitute", "the dandy", "sun", and
"rainbow" appear one at a time in series of skits that mime village life. These skits
and the mask that represents the central figure in each skit are arranged in order of
increasing importance.' (S. Vogel, *Beauty in the Eyes of the Baule: Aesthetics and
Cultural Values*, 1981) (RIGHT)

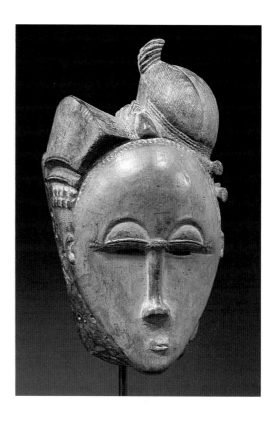

A Maori war canoe prow
Length 111cm (43¾in)
New York $51,750 (£31,568). 31.X.94

This rare and unusual canoe prow was discovered during the course of a two-year
round the world expedition by the ship *Korrigane* under the command of Count
Etienne de Ganany. After setting out from Marseilles on 26 May 1934, the ship
made stops at many of the South Pacific Islands, and the prow is likely to have
been retrieved from a marsh during a visit to New Zealand. Dating such objects
is notoriously difficult, but the present example was probably carved in the
early nineteenth century by the Arawa tribe from the Bay of Plenty region in
North Island. (BELOW)

PRE-COLUMBIAN ART

A Chinesco male figure, Type A
PROTOCLASSIC, *c.*100 BC–AD 250, height 60cm (23⅝in)
New York $123,500 (£77,805). 15.XI.94

Chinesco figures are attributed to a specific region of south-central Nayarit, near the Jalisco
border. Type A varieties, particularly male figures like this, are rare because they are believed to
originate from a single workshop or school of artisans. This subtly modelled example has a
heart-shaped face distinguished by bold facial tattoos and a small, jocular smile. The projecting
quids or lumps of tobacco visible in the chin are probably a type of hallucinogen. (ABOVE)

A Mayan limestone panel of a ballplayer
LATE CLASSIC, *c.*AD 550–950,
40 x 27cm (15¾ x 10⅝in)
New York $79,500 (£50,880).
16.V.95
From the Mr and Mrs Klaus
G. Perls Collections

The ballgame, known as *ollamaliztli* in Nahuatl, was one of the most widespread rituals in ancient Mesoamerica and held a unique place amongst the diverse practices of Mayan culture and religion. Over the centuries, at least two hundred ballgame courts were built in the Maya region, usually consisting of I-shaped masonry enclosures and located near the most sacred areas of the city. The game served many functions, ranging from exhibiting athletic prowess, to settling politically important royal disputes. The outcome was believed to be determined by divine authorities, with the defeated offered as sacrifice by decapitation. Symbolically, the game was viewed as a method of communication with Mayan ancestors whilst the ball itself represented the passage of the sun through the nocturnal Underworld. (LEFT)

AMERICAN INDIAN ART

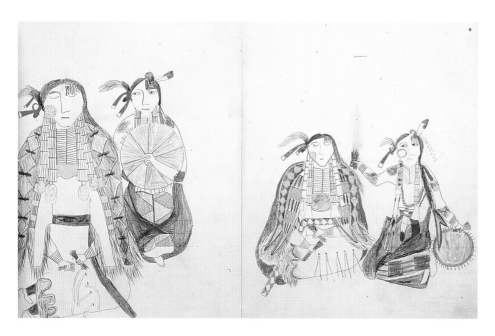

A collection of Sioux pictographic drawings

GOLD-STAMPED COVER: *INDIAN PICTURES DRAWN BY BLACK HAWK, CHIEF MEDICINE MAN OF THE SIOUX*, 41.3 x 26cm (16¼ x 10¼in)
New York $387,500 (£236,375). 21.X.94

These remarkable drawings were collected between 1880–81 by William Edward Caton, an Indian Trader at the Cheyenne Agency in Dakota. During a particularly severe winter, Caton heard that Black Hawk, the head of the San Arcs band of the Sioux, was experiencing great difficulties in supporting his many dependants. Knowing that Black Hawk had recently experienced an extraordinary dream, Caton provided paper and pencils and commissioned him to make pictures of his dream, offering him fifty cents for each one.

Caton started off by writing explanations to accompany each picture, but these were never completed. The final collection included fifty-six complete drawings with figures and nineteen complete drawings of animals and wildlife, using a combination of pencil, crayon, coloured pencils and coloured inks. (LEFT)

A Tlingit wood heraldic screen from the
Thunderbird House (*Xeitl Hit*)

JUNEAU *WOOSHKITAAN* CLAN

New York $233,500 (£149,440). 23.V.95

Property of Mrs Melba (Wallace) Sherer (*On-to*) of the Dipper House (*Yalth-Ta-Hit*) Raven clan and
Mr George Jim, Sr. (*Yawn-Ish-Took*) of the Sea Serpent House, Thunderbird clan, Juneau, Alaska

The design for this rare example of a heraldic screen was based on a blanket acquired
by *Kaajiwadaha*, clan leader of the *Wooshkitaan* group, from his grandfather
Dagasdinaa. The screen was commissioned, probably in the last quarter of the
nineteenth century, by the tribal spokesman at that time, Mike Moore. It was used in
numerous potlatches (the ritual giving away of property) and on other ceremonial
occasions including Moore's own funeral. (ABOVE)

ANTIQUITIES

A marble portrait bust of Emperor Septimius Severus

ROMAN IMPERIAL, AD 193–211, height 89.1cm (35⅟₁₆in)
New York $607,500 (£388,800). 14.XII.94

Septimius Severus was born in AD 145 in
North Africa and came to Rome as a youth.
Succeeding Pertinax as emperor in AD 193,
he waged many successful military campaigns
during his reign, including bouts in Asia
Minor, Mesopotamia, Egypt and Britain,
where he died in AD 211. This portrait
bust shows him wearing a tunic, corselet
and military cloak fastened with a domed
brooch in the form of a rosette. (RIGHT)

A fragment from an Assyrian gypsum wall relief
FROM ROOM B, THE THRONE-ROOM OF THE NORTH-WEST PALACE OF KING ASHURNASIRPAL II AT KALHU (NIMRUD),
c.883–859 BC, 61 x 42cm (24 x 16½in)
London £309,500 ($482,820). 8.XII.94

King Ashurnasirpal II of Assyria's vast palace on the banks of the Tigris, known as the North-West Palace, was discovered by Sir (Austen) Henry Layard in 1848. The walls were covered in reliefs honouring the king and depicting him surrounded by his court officials, his cup-bearer, the keeper of his bow and his eunuchs. This fragment shows the upper part of the figure of a courtier in profile bearing the royal bow and rosette-headed mace. On the complete relief the courtier originally stood behind the figure of the king as his arms bearer. (ABOVE)

Part of an Egyptian quartzite lintel from a temple

MIDDLE KINGDOM, TWELFTH DYNASTY, *c.*1836–1818 BC, height 52.6cm (20¹¹⁄₁₆in)
London £107,100 ($166,005). 8.XII.94

This relief was originally found in the garden of an English house that had been partially
destroyed by bombing in July 1940. It was identified by the British Museum in 1994.
Acquired by the Museum, it can now be seen near the three lifesize statues of Senusret III in
the Egyptian Gallery. The fragmentary cartouche at the lower left edge contains the throne-
name of King Senusret III, the most notable pharaoh of the Twelfth Dynasty. The figure of the
sun god Ra-Horakhty is just visible to the extreme left, and the text above him reads 'he grants
life, stability and dominion [like Ra]'. On the right, the upper part of the seated figure of the
god Atum faces right towards a falcon god wearing a double crown. (BELOW)

A monumental Egyptian diorite figure of the goddess Sekhmet

THEBES, EIGHTEENTH DYNASTY, REIGN OF AMENHOTEP III, 1390–1353 BC, height 109.2cm (43in)
New York $772,500 (£494,400). 14.XII.94
Formerly in the Collection of the First Marquess of Dufferin and Ava

Sekhmet was the divine consort of Ptah, chief god of Memphis, in Lower Egypt, and
was later identified with the goddess Mut, the consort of the chief god of Thebes, in
Upper Egypt, Amun. This figure of the lion-headed goddess of war and protector of
the king once stood among over six hundred images of Sekhmet which adorned the
courts and passageways of the great temple built by Amenhotep III in honour of the
goddess Mut at Thebes. (BELOW)

EUROPEAN WORKS OF ART

PIERRE REYMOND
A grisaille enamel and gilt copper casket
LIMOGES, 1547, 12.5 x 9 x 7.5cm (4⅞ x 3½ x 2¹⁵⁄₁₆in)
New York $178,500 (£114,240). 10.I.95
From the Collection of Cyril Humphris

Pierre Reymond specialized in working *en grisaille* across a wide range of tablewares which he produced in his Paris
workshop between 1534–84. On this casket, the design for the enamel plaque of four naked men fighting a lion
was taken from a 1532 print in the Cabinet d'Estampes, Paris. The lion hunt on the lid is after an engraving by
Agostino Veneziano and the side panel with the unicorn and other animals derives from an engraving by Virgil
Solis. The enamel of two dogs attacking the bull is a copy from a late fifteenth-century Italian plaquette. (ABOVE)

A pair of ivory writing tablet covers and three blank leaves with a *cuir boulli* case

TABLETS FROM FRANCE OR ENGLAND, SECOND HALF OF THE FOURTEENTH CENTURY, CASE FROM FRANCE, SECOND QUARTER OF THE FOURTEENTH CENTURY, tablets: 10 x 5.4cm (3¹⁵/₁₆ x 2⅛in); box: 10 x 7.2cm (3¹⁵/₁₆ x 2¾in)
New York $409,500 (£253,890). 31.V.95

Secular subject matter, including scenes of chivalry, were rare in the fourteenth century but small objects, ivory writing tablets and mirror backs for example, were the most suitable items for decoration with such illustrations. It has been noted by Richard H. Randall, Jr. that these tablets are also unusual in their architecture and in the character of the figures' faces which suggest that they may be of English origin. (LEFT)

A secular Gothic brass chandelier

NUREMBERG, *c*.1500, diameter 82.5cm (32½in)
London £166,500 ($266,400). 7.VII.95

Gothic chandeliers are exceptionally rare and even fewer are secular examples. They may be seen in Old Master paintings such as Jan van Eyck's famous Arnolfini marriage portrait and both Nuremberg and Flanders were centres of production for these beautifully balanced and fine examples of metalwork. (LEFT)

GRINLING GIBBONS
A boxwood high relief celebrating Psalm 148 with King David playing a harp
and Saint Cecilia playing an organ
ENGLAND, c.1670, MONOGRAMMED WITH TWO INTERLACED G'S, 37 x 24cm (14½ x 9½in)
New York $156,500 (£100,160). 10.I.95
From the Collection of Cyril Humphris

This virtuoso carved relief was probably executed for placing in an organ case. It takes its composition
from an engraving by Johannes Sadeler I which in turn was based on, and contemporary to, the painting
Audition d'un motet d'Orlando di Lasso by Peter de Witte, now in the Franz Hals Museum, Haarlem
(Orlando di Lasso had published his musical composition of Psalm 148 in 1565). This piece was
probably sculpted by Grinling Gibbons between 1667–71 when he was resident in York and was almost
certainly commissioned by the Barwick family whose coat of arms decorate King David's harp. (ABOVE)

FRANCESCO FANELLI

A silver and bronze bust of Charles II as the Prince of Wales

ENGLAND, PROBABLY OXFORD, *c.*1643, overall height 35.5cm (14in)

New York $442,500 (£283,200). 10.I.95

From the Collection of Cyril Humphris

By 1642 relations between Charles I, his people and Parliament had declined to such an extent that on 19 August the Royalist battle standard was raised at Nottingham, signalling the beginning of the Civil War. Fittingly, this bust depicts the future Charles II in armour, as do two of William Dobson's portraits of the young prince from around this time. Comparison of Charles' features with that of his profile on the 'Forlorn Hope' medal dates the bust to around 1643, when he was aged thirteen. In 1645 Charles took command of the Royalist forces in the west but by the end of that year his father wrote urging him to prepare his escape and on 2 March 1646 the prince boarded the *Phoenix* for the Scilly Isles, eventually joining his mother in Paris. (ABOVE)

NINETEENTH-CENTURY SCULPTURE

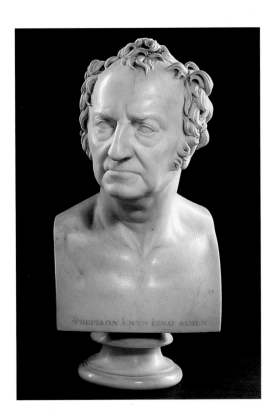

RAFFAELLO MONTI
Eve after the Fall
*c.*1850, WHITE MARBLE, height without plinth 126cm (49½in)
London £111,500 ($175,055). 12.V.95

Born and educated in Milan, Monti spent his early career working in Vienna and Budapest. His arrival in England coincided with the Great Exhibition of 1851, which provided an unprecedented opportunity for artists and designers to establish their reputations. Of the nine works exhibited by Monti, it was *Eve after the Fall* which was regarded by many as his masterpiece and was awarded a prize medal by the exhibition's jury. In their verdict they concluded that the figure is 'appropriately conceived; the motive is pleasing, and the execution is very careful'. (BELOW)

EDWARD HODGES BAILY
Henry Fuseli
SIGNED AND DATED *E.H. BAILY, R.A. SCULPT. LONDON 1824* WITH A GREEK INSCRIPTION, WHITE MARBLE, height 56cm (22in)
London £107,100 ($168,147). 22.XI.94

This highly important bust of Fuseli is the only documented sculpted portrait of the famous Swiss artist made when he was in England from 1764 until his death in 1825. It was commissioned by Sir Thomas Lawrence as one of four busts showing esteemed contemporaries to be placed in his art-filled sitting-room. Recently appointed Royal Academician, Baily carved all four: John Flaxman, Henry Fuseli, Thomas Stothard and Robert Smirke. The Greek inscription on the chest is taken from Plato's *Phaedrus* and translates as 'We speak of things now neglected', a testament to the great friendship and respect which existed between Fuseli and Lawrence. (ABOVE)

HENRI WEIGELE

Deux femmes dansant

INSCRIBED *H. WEIGELE* AND DATED *1914*, MARBLE, height 238.8cm (94in)
New York $288,500 (£184,640). 24.V.95

Henri Weigele executed life-size busts of young women often in a combination of marble and bronze. This sculpture, given its exceptional size, is extremely rare and considered to be a *chef d'oeuvre* of the artist. (LEFT)

EMILE CORIOLAN HIPPOLYTE GUILLEMIN

Femme orientale portant une cruche

INSCRIBED AND DATED *E LE GUILLEMIN 1872* AND WITH THE *F. BARBEDIENNE FOUNDEUR* FOUNDRY
MARK, BRONZE, POLYCHROME BROWN PATINAS WITH INSET LAPIS LAZULI, JADE AND OTHER
COLOURED HARDSTONES AND SILVERED EARRINGS, height 200.7cm (79in)
New York $250,000 (£160,000). 16.II.95

Emile Coriolan Hippolyte Guillemin was greatly inspired by the Middle East and its exoticism: representations of Indian falconers, Turkish maidens and Japanese courtesans firmly established his reputation as an orientalist sculptor from the mid-1870s. This figure dates from 1872 and is typical of the artist's late period. (ABOVE)

GARDEN STATUARY

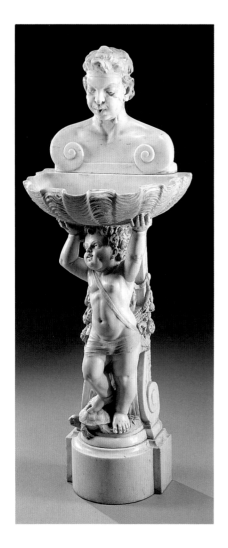

A marble figural wall fountain
NINETEENTH CENTURY, height 135cm (4ft 5in)
New York $18,400 (£11,408). 19.VI.95

This elegant marble wall fountain takes the
form of a large shell supported by a cherub
hung with garlands and surmounted by a
satyr mask. The mouth is drilled to allow
water to trickle into the font. (ABOVE)

A bronze sundial group
ENGLAND, EARLY TWENTIETH CENTURY, height 163cm (66in)
Billingshurst £63,250 ($99,303). 23.V.95

This unusual bronze group depicts two naked women
holding an armillary sphere pierced with the twelve
signs of the zodiac. Weathering has resulted in a rich
green patination of the bronze. (ABOVE)

IRISH ART

A carved wood mirror
ATTRIBUTED TO JOHN AND FRANCIS BOOKER, *c.*1750,
height 173cm (5ft 8in)
London £34,500 ($55,200). 2.VI.95

This mirror is of a type closely associated
with the furniture makers John and Francis
Booker, heirs to a family business originally
established in the 1720s. Working from
published designs, the Bookers developed a
distinctive style of mirror characterized by
the use of architectural elements of Baroque
and Palladian inspiration. From their
premises in Essex Bridge the Bookers quickly
assumed a leading position among the
furniture makers of Dublin and in the 1750s
and 1760s were involved in such major
projects as the decoration of Dublin Castle
and Mayoralty House, Dublin. (RIGHT)

JACK BUTLER YEATS
Singing 'The Dark Rosaleen', Croke Park
SIGNED, OIL ON CANVAS, 46 x 61cm
(18 x 24in)
London £496,500 ($794,400). 2.VI.95

Painted in 1921, the year of the Anglo-Irish
Treaty, this early masterpiece is a rare, and
characteristically oblique, depiction of a
political subject by the artist who so often
expressed his love for his country through its
myth and legend. Two singers accompanied
by a lone fiddler walk through Dublin's
Croke Park Gaelic Football ground. They
sing a ballad which, under the guise of a
simple love song, tells in fact of love for
Ireland. The crowd parts to let the men
through and a flower-girl, often used to
symbolize Ireland herself in Yeats' work,
turns to look at them. (ABOVE)

ENGLISH FURNITURE

A Regency library table

ATTRIBUTED TO MOREL & HUGHES, AFTER A DESIGN BY THOMAS HOPE, *c.*1810, height 75cm (2ft 5½in)
London £139,000 ($222,400). 7.VII.95

A table of strikingly similar design to this example is in the Whitbread collection
at Southill Park, Bedfordshire and was originally commissioned by Samuel
Whitbread II around 1810. Both tables were clearly produced by the same maker,
probably Nicholas Morel and his partner Robert Hughes who are known to have
been employed at Southill and whose documented work includes pieces of related
design. The form of the end supports and the Egyptian winged ornaments are
adapted from designs by Thomas Hope, published in 1807. (ABOVE)

One of a pair of George II gilt-decorated scarlet-japanned
side chairs (detail)
GILES GRENDEY, c.1735–40
New York $101,500 (£62,930). 22.IV.95

Giles Grendey's suite of furniture for the Duke of Infantado's castle at Lazcano in
northern Spain is the largest and possibly the most famous single set of eighteenth-
century furniture. In form the chairs are an archaic version of the Queen Anne style
which continued to be popular in Spain until the 1750s. With ample flat surfaces for
ornament, the style appealed to the Spanish taste for festive decoration. (LEFT)

A mahogany double-sided library desk
ATTRIBUTED TO THOMAS CHIPPENDALE, GEORGE III, c.1760, height 81.5cm (2ft 8in)
London £408,500 ($653,600). 7.VII.95

This desk corresponds closely to a design by Thomas Chippendale which was
engraved in 1759 and later illustrated in the third edition of *The Gentleman and
Cabinet-Maker's Director*. The quality of carving is consistent with Chippendale's
known work and the cut-brass handles are apparently identical to those on a related
table which Chippendale supplied to Lord Pembroke at Pembroke House, Whitehall,
around 1760–62. (BELOW)

A pair of George II mahogany library armchairs and a settee
ATTRIBUTED TO WILLIAM VILE, *c.*1755
New York $973,000 (£603,260). 22.IV.95

These three pieces, which include a settee not illustrated here, form part of an extensive
suite originally commissioned by Anthony Ashley-Cooper, 4th Earl of Shaftesbury, for
St Giles' House, Dorset. Their date would indicate that they were purchased by Lord
Shaftesbury following his second marriage in 1759, when the house at St Giles' was
redecorated in the fashionable Rococo style recently introduced from the continent.
Attributed at various times to Thomas Chippendale and William Hallett, Sr., the
most likely source is Hallett's pupil and protégé, William Vile, cabinetmaker to
George III. (ABOVE)

A pair of George III ormolu-mounted Derbyshire Spar three-light candelabra

MATTHEW BOULTON, c.1770, height 43.2cm (17in)
New York $162,000 (£102,060). 13.X.94
From the Estate of Polly Guggenheim Logan

Matthew Boulton and his partner, John Fothergill, founded their metalwork factory in Soho, near Birmingham, in the 1760s. The firm produced silver, Sheffield plate and ormolu ornaments of remarkable quality; George III and Catherine the Great were among their clients, and they even exported their wares to France. Vases accounted for the majority of the firm's ormolu production, which also included inkstands, ice pails, tripods, girandoles and obelisks. (RIGHT)

A mahogany globe-shaped secretaire

ATTRIBUTED TO MORGAN & SANDERS, c.1810, height 117cm (3ft 10in)
London £177,500 ($278,675). 24.V.95
From the Collection of the Late Sir Harold Wernher, Luton Hoo

This secretaire is a rare and exceptional example of a type known as *The Pitt's Cabinet Globe Writing Table*, in honour of the celebrated parliamentarian. Devised by the inventor George Remington, it was chiefly produced by the firm of Morgan & Sanders. While the provenance of this secretaire remains uncertain, so grand a piece of library furniture can only have been commissioned by a patron of wealth and discernment. The quality of workmanship testifies to the technical mastery of the secretaire's creators, while the ingenuity of its design displays a fascination with mechanical science which even today evokes the excitement of the Industrial Revolution. (BELOW)

CONTINENTAL FURNITURE

Two pairs of Italian marquetry commodes
GIOVANNI MAFFEZZOLI, CREMONA (LOMBARDY), LATE EIGHTEENTH/EARLY NINETEENTH CENTURY,
heights 93cm and 95cm (3ft ½in and 3ft 1½in)
London £344,000 ($536,640). 9.XII.94

Apprenticed to Giuseppe Maggiolini in 1791, Giovanni Maffezzoli became the most gifted of
the workshop pupils in Parabiago. The large neo-Romantic architectural scenes around the
sides of his commodes, incorporating Piranesian classical ruins and Gothic buildings, are
distinctive features of Maffezzoli's work, along with the use of candelabra decoration and
channelled ionic columns. The example shown here is from the larger pair in the suite. (ABOVE)

A Louis XVI ormolu-mounted Japanese lacquer and maple *secrétaire à abattant*

SIGNED *M. CARLIN*, LAST QUARTER OF THE EIGHTEENTH CENTURY,
height 104cm (41in)
New York $277,500 (£177,600). 9.XII.94
From the Collection of the Late Matthew Schutz

This piece bears out the maxim that appearances are deceptive: the top five drawers are, in fact, a fall-front which opens to form a green leather-lined writing surface and reveals four drawers beneath a shelf, thus performing the function of a *secrétaire*. The lower part is fitted with ten drawers flanking two box-form drawers. The lacquer decoration depicts pavilions, flowering branches and pastoral scenes. (RIGHT)

A commode decorated with imitation Chinese lacquer

LOUIS XV, 1745–49, STAMPED *D.F.* WITH THE CROWNED C MARK
Monaco FF2,050,000 (£265,201:$421,669). 1.VII.95

The initials *D.F.* stamped on this commode have recently been attributed to the cabinetmaker Jean Desforges, who produced elegantly constructed lacquered furniture from his workshop in rue du Faubourg Saint-Antoine, Paris. This example is one of the finest in a series of high quality imitation Chinese lacquer commodes constructed by Desforges between 1745–49, all of which display elaborate gilt-bronze mounts. (LEFT)

A K'ang-Hsi porcelain vase with Louis XVI ormolu mounts
EIGHTEENTH CENTURY, height 38cm (15in)
Monaco FF1,831,500 (£218,296:$341,061). 3.XII.94
From the Collection of Baron Guy de Rothschild at Château de Ferrières

Made for the export market and elaborately mounted in ormolu, this shell-shaped Chinese vase
is described in an inventory of 1791 for the property of the renowned Parisian collector, the
duc de Choiseul-Praslin. His collection was famous for its Dutch paintings, Boulle furniture,
lacquered Chinese and Japanese furniture and Beauvais and Gobelins tapestries. However, the
most unique items amongst these were the Far-Eastern ormolu-mounted porcelain vases,
including this turquoise pot-pourri vase, which the duke kept in his private rooms. (ABOVE)

A pair of Louis XV ormolu-mounted lacquer pot-pourri vases

MOUNTS BEAR THE CROWNED C MARK, MID-EIGHTEENTH CENTURY, height 35.6cm (14in)
New York $332,500 (£212,800). 10.XII.94
From the Dorothy and Wendell Cherry Collection

These pot-pourri vases are closely related to a pair in the Musée du Louvre. Mounted with matching ormolu finials and with similarly pierced rim and base, all are decorated with very nearly identical lacquer. The Louvre pair have been identified as forming part of the collection of Mesdames at Bellevue. Other design elements, such as the ormolu mount, assymetrical handle composed of coral and shells and the Japanese lacquer, appear on related articles in numerous private and museum collections. The crowned C, a tax mark used on any alloy incorporating copper, dates these pieces to between March 1745 and February 1749 when the tax was enforced. (ABOVE)

Two from a set of four Louis XV ormolu three-light *bras de lumière*
MID-EIGHTEENTH CENTURY, height 69.9cm (27½in)
New York $134,500 (£84,735). 20.V.95
From the Collection of Jaime Ortiz-Patiño

The backplate and intertwined branches of these wall lights are cast and chiselled with acanthus leaves, flowerheads and bulrushes. The baluster-shaped nozzles are fitted with pierced leaves which are drip pans. (ABOVE)

A pair of polychrome and parcel-gilt Italian blackamoors
VENETIAN, LATE SEVENTEENTH/EARLY EIGHTEENTH CENTURY, height 176cm and 171cm (5ft 9in and 5ft 7¼in)
London £106,000 ($170,660). 16.VI.95

For design and quality this pair of blackamoors can be considered one of the best examples of this genre of ornament. Throughout the eighteenth century, exotic decoration of this type became increasingly fashionable, particularly in Venice. (RIGHT)

NINETEENTH-CENTURY FURNITURE

A gilt-bronze and parquetry medal cabinet
SIGNED *F LINKE*, FRANCE, *c.*1890, height 142cm (4ft 8in)
London £56,500 ($90,965). 3.III.95

François Linke was possibly one of the most sought after cabinetmakers of the late nineteenth and early twentieth centuries. He made a wide range of furniture in mainly Louis XV and XVI styles, many of which were copied directly from eighteenth-century examples. This commode is based on the famous kingwood medal cabinet supplied by the Royal cabinetmaker Antoine-Robert Gaudreau in 1738 for the *Cabinet Intérieur* of Louis XV at Versailles. The decorative medals on the doors portray Roman emperors while the ovals contain the classical figures Ariadne, Hercules, Venus and Athena. (BELOW)

A pair of Louis XV style silvered bronze mounted glass urns

STAMPED *PICARD*, PROBABLY BY BACCARAT, PARIS, THIRD
QUARTER OF THE NINETEENTH CENTURY, height 74.9cm (2½ft)
New York $37,375 (£24,294). 13.IX.94

The glass bodies of these mounted urns,
decorated with birds and foliage against a
lattice framework, delicately taper down to a
circular silvered bronze base. The natural
theme of the ornamentation is continued
in the snakes which spiral up the scrolled
handles, and the lion masks flanking the
base's onyx-coloured panels. (ABOVE)

A pair of Cararra marble vases on stands

SIGNED *EUGENE CORNU INVENTEUR, G. VIOT & CIE EXP. 1867*, FRANCE, height with plinth 240cm (7ft 10½in)
London £199,500 ($317,205). 7.X.94
From the University of Evansville, removed from Harlaxton Manor, Lincolnshire

These white marble vases with their classical handles and deeply encrusted carved marble
shells and crustaceans almost seem to have been designed for the eccentricities of George de
Ligne Gregory's Baroque home, Harlaxton Manor, but the mysteries of who bought them
for the house and when they were placed in the hall remain unsolved. Exhibited at the
International Exhibition in Paris, 1867, each vase takes as its subject land or sea. Land,
shown here, is represented by the harvesting of corn in summer and grapes in autumn by
putti and bacchante; an abundance of sunflowers, pine cones, apples, ivy and moss suggest
bounty and fertility. The theme of the sea is energetically developed with masked mermaids,
cherubs riding dolphins, coral, seaweed, shellfish, bulrushes and cascading water. (ABOVE)

AMERICAN DECORATIVE ARTS

A Queen Anne carved and grain-painted maple chest-on-chest-on-frame

ATTRIBUTED TO THE DUNLAP FAMILY, BEDFORD, NEW HAMPSHIRE, 1777–92, height 196cm (6ft 5in)
New York $310,500 (£192,510). 22.X.94
From the Bertram K. Little and Nina Fletcher Little Collection

This chest was originally owned by the George family, early residents of the Bedford area of New Hampshire, and is attributed to Major John Dunlap. The chest-on-chest-on-frame is a 'regional preference' and displays many characteristics of the Dunlap family cabinet work: flowered ogee mouldings, sharp knees, S-scrolled brackets and 'spoonhandle' shell carvings. The colourful and dramatic painted graining – probably added in the early nineteenth century – attests to the New England desire to bring light, colour, pattern and movement into rooms otherwise dreary on long, sombre, grey-cloaked winter days. (LEFT)

A paint-decorated pine dower chest

ATTRIBUTED TO JOHANNES SPITLER, SHENANDOAH
COUNTY, VIRGINIA, c.1800, height 63.5cm (25in)
Charlottesville, Virginia $343,500 (£212,970). 27.V.95
From the Collection of Dr and Mrs Henry P. Deyerle

Johannes Spitler is best known for his
yellow pine blanket chests and tall-case
clocks. His work was influenced both by
his German background and the seclusion
of rural community life in Virginia, and
his designs were extremely diverse,
ranging from more geometrical patterns
to those which incorporated birds, flowers
and hearts. This chest is one of a pair
made for two sisters who lived in
neighbouring houses on the same
farm in Virginia. (RIGHT)

A classical gilt-metal-mounted mahogany and rosewood swivel-top card table

LABELLED CHARLES-HONORÉ LANNUIER,
NEW YORK, c.1810, height 74cm (29⅛in)
New York $288,500 (£175,985). 23.X.94
From the Estate of the Late George
Frederick Hastings

Charles-Honoré Lannuier was born at
Chantilly, north of Paris, on 27 June
1779; twenty-four years later he
emigrated to New York where much
of his early work continued to reflect
his training in the Louis XVI style.
The transition to the Empire style in
Lannuier's furniture is seen in a group
of superb card and pier tables, the
most distinguished of which are
supported on soaring gilded and
winged terms and acanthus-carved
animal legs, and decorated with
ormolu mounts and discreet bands
of brass inlay. The excellence of
construction and decoration reveal
that Lannuier was a superior
craftsman and artist. (LEFT)

A glazed redware figure of a goat

STAMPED *ANTHONY W. BAECHER, WINCHESTER, VIRGINIA, c.*1880, height 17.8cm (7in)
Charlottesville, Virginia $82,250 (£50,995). 27.V.95
From the Collection of Dr and Mrs Henry P. Deyerle

This stylized and amusing figure of a goat with its impressive horns is seated on a rectangular base which is stamped three times with the mark *Baecher Winchester*. The piece is covered in lead and manganese-glaze over a redware ground. (LEFT)

A. ELLIS

A pair of portraits

OIL ON PANEL, *c.*1830, each 73 x 53.3cm (28¾ x 21in)
New York $118,000 (£73,160). 22.VI.95
From the Estate of Mary Sugatt

Little is known about the life and career of A. Ellis, however the artist is believed to have been active in the Readfield-Waterville area of Maine during the 1830s. Best known for oil portraits executed on panels with pencil outlined details, Ellis incorporated solid areas of bright colour and portrayed figures with a linear quality. This use of colour and line suggests that he or she might have been more of a decorative artist than a portrait painter. These two pictures are mounted in what appear to be the original painted pine frames. (BELOW)

JAMES BARD

Schooner *Emma Hendrix*
OIL ON CANVAS, 82.6 x 132.1cm (32½ x 52in)
New York $200,500 (£126,315). 29.I.95
From the Collection of The New-York Historical Society

Born in New York City in 1815, James Bard was devoted to the depiction of steamboats and
he drew almost every steam vessel built at or owned around the port of New York. It has been
estimated that he completed one painting per week. His draftsmanship was meticulous and
each painting is so accurate that shipbuilders would claim they could lay down the plans of a
boat from one of Bard's pictures. This painting is unusual in Bard's *oeuvre* not simply because
its subject is a sailing vessel but also because it features the rare depiction of a woman. (ABOVE)

EUROPEAN TAPESTRIES AND CARPETS

WILLEM DE PANNEMAKER, AFTER JAN
CORNELISZ VERMEYEN

A metal-thread tapestry from the story of Romulus and Remus

BRUSSELS, MID-SIXTEENTH CENTURY,
212 x 275cm (7ft x 9ft)
London £56,500 ($88,705). 19.V.95

A Netherlandish painter of portraits and
religious subjects, Jan Cornelisz Vermeyen
was also a designer of tapestries. This piece
is based on his design depicting Romulus
and Remus brought before Amulius. Four
metal-thread pieces exist which are
evidently from the same set: two in Madrid,
and two in the former Seligmann
Collection. The Madrid tapestries are the
same height as the present example and
carry a similar border; they were presented
to Philip II of Spain in 1550. (LEFT)

An Aubusson chinoiserie tapestry depicting gardening and fishing

FROM CARTOONS BY JOSEPH DU MONS, AFTER
FRANÇOIS BOUCHER, FRANCE, c.1750,
323 x 688cm (10ft 7in x 22ft 7in)
New York $112,500 (£72,000). 13.I.95

King's Painter, François Boucher began
his association with the Beauvais tapestry
manufacture in 1734 and became
Director of the Gobelins factory in 1755.
His compositions *Le jardinier* and *La
pêche* were painted for the Beauvais
factory and Du Mons then incorporated
them in his work at Aubusson. Here the
two compositions were woven together,
probably as a special commission. (RIGHT)

An Axminster carpet
ENGLAND, c.1800, 871 x 579cm (28ft 7in x 19ft)
New York $96,000 (£61,440). 15.XII.94

England, like France, encouraged home manufacture of carpets in order to economize on the currency spent in importing oriental carpets which were in such demand. This example utilizes floral designs and shows the influence of architectural patterns. (ABOVE)

APPLIED ARTS

A Tiffany favrile glass, amethyst glass bead and bronze Virginia Creeper lamp
*c.*1900, height 46.4cm (18¼in)
New York $1,102,500 (£683,550). 22.IV.95
From the John W. Mecom, Jr. Collection

The Virginia Creeper lamp, formerly erroneously called the Maple Leaf lamp, is perhaps the most important and unusual of Tiffany's *oeuvre*. Its shade is the only one to incorporate glass tiles in the form of the leaf represented in the pattern. The tiles have been moulded in high and low relief and have been manoeuvred during manufacture so that the subtle shading around the veining can be seen when the lamp is lit. A technical *tour de force*, this piece was probably a special commission and not reproduced because of the difficulty encountered in the production of the leafage. It reached the highest price for any Tiffany lamp at auction. (ABOVE)

A Tiffany favrile glass floriform vase

*c.*1900–05, INSCRIBED *02417*, height 36.5cm (14⅜in)
New York $250,000 (£160,000). 19.XI.94

Louis Comfort Tiffany was born in
Brooklyn, Connecticut in 1848, the son of
Charles L. Tiffany, the founder of Tiffany &
Company. At a very early age Louis showed
an interest in the arts. Shortly after the Civil
War he studied painting with George Innes
in New York and later with Leon Bailly in
Paris, going on to specialize in landscapes.
Throughout Tiffany's long and illustrious
career as an innovator and arbiter of taste,
he continued to think of himself as an artist
and painter above all else. This vase is a fine
example of that early study of nature, the
milky-blue opalescent edges of the petals
merging into rose and periwinkle blue, with
lime green leafage at the base. (LEFT)

A Tiffany favrile glass and bronze cobweb lamp on a
mosaic wheat-sheaves base
1900–05, height 61.6cm (24¼in)
New York $783,500 (£485,770). 22.IV.95
From the John W. Mecom, Jr. Collection

This rare lamp is one of only three models in this size and it is a
marvellous example of Tiffany design and craftsmanship. Six cobwebs
in multi-hued shades of turquoise, sea-green, rose and emerald-green
textured glass are suspended from blossoming apple boughs heavy
with fruit. Patinated bronze wheat-sheaves, grasses and gnarled apple
tree branches reach up to the domical shade. The base is decorated
with mosaic tiles ranging in colour from blue-green iridescence to
deepest blue-black. (ABOVE)

A Gallé internally-decorated and applied cameo
glass vase: *Les Roses de France*
c.1903, SIGNED IN INTAGLIO *GALLÉ*, height 14.3cm (5⅝in)
New York $200,500 (£128,320). 19.XI.94

Emile Gallé ran a glass studio and factory producing works of art
at various levels of quality ranging from a production line
manufacture of decorative vases and lamps, to unique or very
limited series works which are among the most extraordinary
creations of their day. This latter category includes the series of
vases *Les Roses de France* on which the flowers are worked in full
relief. They are examples of virtuoso craftsmanship and a sensitive
symbolism, combining references to Gallé's love of nature and to
the patriotism heightened by the Franco-Prussian war. (ABOVE)

KOLOMAN MOSER, EXECUTED BY CASPAR HZADRIL

A cabinet with inlaid figures

*c.*1904, height 209cm (82½in)

London £331,500 ($537,030). 4.XI.94

This cabinet is part of a suite of bedroom furniture designed by Koloman Moser and executed as a commission for the apartment of Dr Hölzl in 1903–04. Of strict angular form, constructed in African chestnut with inlays of lemon wood, metal and mother-of-pearl, the cabinet incorporates two highly stylized female figures inlaid within the overall chequered marquetry design. These elegant women call to mind the exotic and richly decorated figures devised by Moser's friend and contemporary, Gustav Klimt. They also bear comparison with the stylized women incorporated by Charles Rennie Mackintosh into the doors of his celebrated white cabinet of 1902. This work thus demonstrates the varied elements which contributed to the burgeoning Modern Movement in Vienna. (ABOVE)

CHARLES RENNIE MACKINTOSH
An Argyle Street high-back chair
1896–97, height 137cm (54in)
London £210,500 ($338,905). 31.III.95

Mackintosh was commissioned by Miss Cranston to design this chair for the Luncheon Room of the Argyle Street Tea Room, Glasgow. Part of his first major commission for the decoration and furnishing of an interior, this is perhaps Mackintosh's most dramatic chair design and is the single piece of furniture most widely associated with him. Now almost a century old, the chair has acquired an iconic status as a symbol of the beginnings of the Modern Movement in architecture and design. (LEFT)

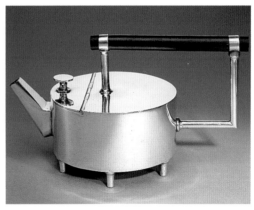

CHRISTOPHER DRESSER FOR JAMES DIXON & SONS
Electroplated teapot
1879, THE UNDERSIDE WITH DESIGNER'S FACSIMILE SIGNATURE *CH. DRESSER*, MAKER'S MARK AND NUMBERED *2275*, height 12cm (4¾in)
London £65,300 ($105,786). 4.XI.94

This is the only recorded example of this particular design, being a very slight variant of another teapot, also known in only one example. Dresser devised a series of teapots in dramatic geometric shapes which are documented in a costing book of 1879 for the manufacturers James Dixon & Sons. (ABOVE)

DEMETRE H. CHIPARUS
'Tango', depicting Rudolph Valentino and Natasha Rambova
1930s, MARKED *CHIPARUS*, height 62cm (24⅜in)
London £52,100 ($83,881). 31.III.95

Inspired by the Ziegfeld Follies, chorus lines and the Ballets Russes, Demetre
Chiparus' decorative, fanciful figures sparked a fashion for such pieces. This
particular work depicts the filmstars Rudolph Valentino and Natasha Rambova
performing the tango – a sensation of the early twenties. The delicacy of pose and
the representation of the relationship between the two makes this a fine and
charming example of the form. (BELOW)

CERAMICS AND GLASS

A Böttger black-lacquered red stoneware coffee pot and cover
*c.*1715, height 20.3cm (8in)
New York $222,500 (£137,950). 20.X.94
From the Collection of Margot Gottlieb

Böttger red stoneware was perfected probably towards the end of 1708 and was in full production during 1709, with the lustrous glaze of cobalt and manganese oxide in use by 1710. This superb coffee pot has a quadrangular pear-shaped body with a glazed black-lacquered background decorated with chinoiserie scenes in the manner of, and probably executed by, the court lacquer-master Martin Schnell. (LEFT)

**A Sèvres blue-ground vase
and cover** *(vase à glands)*
*c.*1768, SOFT-PASTE PORCELAIN, height 43.2cm (17in)
London £56,500 ($90,400). 15.XI.94

The unusual *bleu Fallot* background
colour of this superb Sèvres vase was
developed originally for a dinner service
delivered to the Austrian ambassador,
Prince Stahremberg, in 1766. The *fleurs
incrustées* decorating technique, which
involves scraping away the ground colour
to leave space for the fruit and flower
painting, is also rare. (LEFT)

A Chelsea 'Hans Sloane' silver-shape plate
c.1755, diameter 26.7cm (10½in)
New York $18,400 (£11,408). 19.X.94

Much of Chelsea's botanical decoration is adapted from illustrations of specimens in the Chelsea Physic Garden of Sir Hans Sloane (Queen Anne's physician and the founder of the British Museum), thus giving rise to the decorative term 'Hans Sloane' for such wares. The hexagonal rim of this plate is moulded with curved fluting issuing from three Rococo devices to form a crenellated edge, a shape first made in silver by the Chelsea factory's proprietor, the silversmith Nicholas Sprimont. (LEFT)

A Berlin cabinet plate
c.1820, diameter 24.7cm (9¾in)
New York $20,700 (£12,834). 20.X.94
From the Collection of Dr Edward G. Schiffman

This fine example of a cabinet plate is painted in an extraordinary 'micro-mosaic' pattern and depicts a pair of white swans swimming on green-shaded blue water against a dark blue sky. The border is decorated with panels of flaming urns and lyres painted on 'hardstone' grounds alternating with ovals of colourful 'micro-mosaic' butterflies. (RIGHT)

A London delft documentary 'Clapmash' dish

SOUTHWARK, PICKLEHERRING QUAY, DATED *1637*, diameter 38cm (15in)
London £56,500 ($89,270). 21.II.95

The form of this very rare dish is described in the factory inventories as a 'Clapmash' from the Dutch *Klapmuts*, a sailor's hat with a rounded crown and flat brim. The plate depicts St George on a spirited dappled horse, piercing the winged dragon with his lance, and bears the inscription *John Ayres, 1637*. Ayres was a London-based tailor whose business flourished between the years 1614–36. It seems possible that this dish was commissioned from the Pickleherring pottery as a retirement gift. (LEFT)

A Deruta maiolica yellow lustre dish

*c.*1520–40, diameter 43cm (17in)
London £32,200 ($51,520). 15.XI.94

This magnificent lustre dish depicts St George slaying the dragon on the flowery banks of a river, with a town visible on the opposite bank. The broad band of the rim is decorated with a bold pattern of scales. (LEFT)

A Baccarat faceted garlanded equestrian weight
NINETEENTH CENTURY, diameter 8.2cm (3¼in)
New York $40,250 (£25,760). 18.I.95
From the Collection of The New-York Historical Society

There are four documented examples of this weight, with its naturalistically modelled prancing horse. According to Dwight P. Lanmon (the former Director of The Corning Museum of Glass, New York), 'the tiny circular plaques [depicted in this type of weight] ... were made by engraving thin coloured overlays; after they were completed, they were encased in molten crystal to form the paperweight'. (ABOVE)

A German enamelled 'Ochsenkopfhumpen'
POSSIBLY FRANCONIA, DATED
1662, height 17.5cm (6⅞in)
London £14,950 ($23,621).
21.II.95

This glass or *humpen* bears a traditional depiction of the Ochsenkopf Mountain in the Fichtelbirge. A padlocked chain and various other symbols highlight the mountain's rich natural resources and these are also referred to in the inscription. It is one of several recorded examples from between the second half of the seventeenth century and the end of the eighteenth century. (LEFT)

A Webb two-colour cameo bottle vase
SIGNED *GEORGE WOODALL*, *c.*1880, height 40.5cm (15⅞in)
London £31,050 ($49,680). 15.XI.94

The squat globular form of this vase tapers into a tall neck with a matt clear tint overlaid in pink and white and carved with a lion mask and geometric scrolling acanthus decoration. Although stamped with the mark of Tiffany & Co, Paris Exhibition, 1889, this was probably applied at a later date. (ABOVE)

PRECIOUS OBJECTS *by John D. Block*

Throughout 1994–95 auction season for Precious Objects at Sotheby's produced excitement and newsworthy sales around the world. In New York, Geneva, Hong Kong and London collectors, retailers, dealers and museum curators filled the salerooms in search of beautiful, rare and historical pieces amongst the auctions of jewellery, silver, clocks, watches and objects of vertu held throughout the year.

In October, the first major jewellery sale of the season took place in New York and proved that the market was prepared to pay extremely high prices for the rarest gemstones. A magnificent 20.17-carat Fancy Blue diamond ring brought $9,902,500, a record price for any Fancy coloured diamond and, at the time, the fourth highest price for any lot of jewellery or precious stone at auction. In the same sale the 63.95-carat pear-shaped Anniversary Diamond fetched $965,000. Buyers who were looking for classically beautiful jewellery purchased items from the Estate of Rebecca Guggenheim Logan, including an important ruby and diamond necklace which sold for $332,500.

The trend of purchasing major gemstones continued in Geneva in November. A superb and rare unmounted Fancy Intense Yellow diamond weighing 10.37 carats fetched SF1,131,000 and a highly important diamond choker and matching pendant earclips by Reza, featuring nine, D-colour, Internally Flawless diamonds, fetched SF3,523,500. An exciting sale culminated with the purchase of a superb and rare unmounted heart-shaped, D-colour, Internally Flawless diamond weighing 62.42 carats which brought SF6,823,500.

Until the New York Extraordinary Jewels sale in April 1995, the auction market had never before seen such a variety of Fancy coloured diamonds. Among the rarest of these, a Fancy Yellowish Green brought $1,102,500, $515,000 per carat, and an extraordinary Fancy Pink diamond weighing 5.65 carats achieved $1,982,500. A record per-carat price for its type was fetched by a 4.92-carat Fancy Purplish Pink emerald-cut diamond, which sold for $2,092,500, approximately $425,000 per carat. Also included was

A gold and enamel hunter cased watch with Lange's patent jump seconds
LANGE & SÖHNE, NO. 61414, diameter 5.5cm (2⅛in) Geneva SF152,000 (£80,423:$126,667). 16.V.95 (LEFT)

A sapphire and diamond ring
*c.*1930
New York $266,500 (£167,895). 7.VI.95
From the Estate of Mrs Eleanor Robson Belmont (ABOVE)

a 3.53-carat Fancy Blue triangular-shaped diamond ring by Harry Winston which reached $992,500 and a superb Fancy Vivid Yellow diamond weighing 9.05 carats which realized $772,500.

In May, the most spectacular sale of the year concluded the season in Geneva. All areas of jewellery sold well including an exquisite diamond, coloured stone and onyx pendant by Cartier from 1921, which brought SF223,500. It was only fitting, however, that such an outstanding season should end with the sale of a 27.37-carat Burma ruby for SF4,843,500 and, best of all, a superb pear-shaped D-colour, Internally Flawless 100.10-carat diamond, which broke the world record for any lot of jewellery or precious stone ever, selling at SF19,858,500. This remarkable diamond was named The Star of the Season by its new owner, Sheik Ahmed H. Fitaihi, the Saudi Arabian department store magnate, who finally succeeded in claiming his prize after fierce competition from an anonymous telephone bidder.

A gold and enamel gem-set 'Egyptian-Revival' brooch
c.1900
St Moritz SF27,600
(£13,939:$22,080).
17.II.95 (Above)

As a whole, the market for English long-case and mantel clocks has remained fairly stable over the last year. Good prices were achieved for pieces from the top makers as well as for more uncommon items such as the George Graham table clock with silent escapement, which realized £80,700 in March. Clocks from the Black Forest area of South Germany attracted increased interest from the continent, with one example being an unusual and amusing automaton timepiece supporting a shaving monkey wearing a cocked hat and colourful coat and breeches, which fetched £5,980 in June.

Rare pocket watches in fine condition continued to attract runaway prices, with one of only six recorded 'Moses' automaton watches, bearing a depiction of Moses drawing water from a rock, realizing SF399,500 in Geneva. Additionally, a rare gold-mounted Meissen watch and chatelaine, made by Carl Heinrich Weisse and dated around 1755, sold for SF54,050. In London, a gold and enamel verge pocket watch with the coronet and cypher of the Jacobite Young Pretender, Bonnie Prince Charlie, was bought by a Scotsman for £8,050 after vigorous bidding. Fine precision watches from the turn of the century still retain their popularity due to the high quality and classic elegance of the design.

The wristwatch market continued to attract a new and varied following, resulting in an ever-increasing range of wristwatches being offered for auction. Patek Philippe maintained its position as the market leader and the season saw rare pieces continuing to achieve remarkable prices: in May, a gold chronograph with flexible lugs sold in Geneva for SF146,500 and in June, a gold cushion-form minute repeating wristwatch sold for $519,500 in New York. It not only set a record American price for a Patek Philippe wristwatch but was also the first cushion-form-style case to be offered for public auction.

Sotheby's continued to mount major sales of Russian works of art and objects of vertu. Strong prices for rare pieces were fetched in Geneva, New York and London. A silver samovar by Fabergé, boldly cast and chased in the form of an old man with windswept hair and beard, sold for SF251,000, nearly nine times its low estimate in the November Geneva sale. In New York, a rare Russian gold, enamel and diamond-set bonbonnière by David Rudolph, St Petersburg 1785, fetched $178,500 in December. Mounted with a portrait miniature of King John VI of Portugal as Prince Regent, it was presented to the Commander-in-Chief of the British Navy in the Mediterranean after his defeat of the Spanish fleet off Cape St Vincent on 14 February 1797. In the New York June sale a charming gold and enamel sealing-wax case by Fabergé brought $16,100, exemplifying the strong demand for small precious objects.

The high point of the silver season in New York was, in fact, made from gold – an eighteen-carat gold dinner service commissioned by the late Judge Elbert H. Gary, a founder of US Steel, from Tiffany & Co. New York circa 1910. Comprising 566 pieces and weighing a total of nearly 123kg (270lb) it sold for a record sum of $2,037,500.

In London in November, the eyes of the world's silver collectors were set upon a pair of recently rediscovered George II silver soup tureens by George Wickes, London, 1744 (the same year in which Sotheby's began). These extraordinary tureens, weighing 24.4kg (785oz), were designed by the architect William Kent for the 1st Baron Montfort and had last been seen publicly in 1921. They sold for a record-breaking price of £1,013,500.

In Geneva, May saw the sale of sixteenth- and seventeenth-century silver from the Collection of Joseph R. Ritman. Amongst the high quality items on offer was a coconut cup of an owl with Belgian parcel-gilt mounts from Antwerp 1548–49, which sold for SF454,500.

The thriving auction market for Precious Objects, whether crafted by man or created by nature, continues to draw eager buyers to the international salerooms. As new wealth is created in Asia, Russia and Eastern Europe, we can expect increasing competition in the race to acquire collections of dazzling precious objects.

A gold and enamel verge watch with coronet and cypher possibly of the Young Pretender, Prince Charles Edward Stuart
FRANCE, 1758, diameter 4.2cm (1¾in)
London £8,050 ($12,880).
2.VI.95 (ABOVE)

A silver-gilt and Limoges enamel chalice
PROBABLY PARIS, c.1540
Monaco FF399,600
(£47,448:$74,137).
3.XII.94 (BELOW)

JEWELLERY

The Star of the Season diamond
Geneva SF19,858,500 (£10,507,143:$16,548,750). 17.V.95

This magnificent stone established a new world auction record price for a jewel or
gemstone of any kind. At 100.10 carats, it is the largest D-colour, Internally Flawless
pear-shaped diamond of unmodified, classical proportions ever to be offered at
auction. It is exceptional not only for its size, colour and purity, but also because it
is beautifully proportioned and a superb example of the cutter's skill. As a pear shape
it is only exceeded in size at auction by the Mouawad Splendour, an eleven-sided
pear shape of 101.84 carats which Sotheby's Geneva sold in 1990, and is just eight
carats smaller than the world's most famous diamond, the Koh-i-Noor, which is
part of the British Crown Jewels. (ABOVE)

Fancy Blue diamond ring
New York $9,902,500 (£6,337,600). 18.X.94

Natural Fancy Blue diamonds are among the rarest of coloured diamonds and
this spectacular 20.17-carat example is the largest emerald-cut of its kind ever to
be offered at auction, setting a world auction record price for a coloured diamond.
The intense blue is evenly concentrated and is brought out to its utmost effect
resulting in a beautiful stone unique in quality and size. It ranks in importance
with some of the most famous historical blue diamonds such as the Hope, the
Wittelsbach and the Eugenie Blue, all of which belonged at one time to royal
or aristocratic families. (ABOVE)

A Fancy Vivid Yellow diamond ring
New York $772,500 (£478,950). 11.IV.95

The term 'Fancy Vivid' represents colours that are of a light to medium tone and of very high saturation. Although yellow is the most common of coloured diamonds, its rarity depends on the quality of its colour attributes, including hue, tone and saturation. Few stones warrant such an important grade and the highly saturated and 'even' colour of this 9.05-carat stone is superb. (BELOW)

A ruby ring
Geneva SF4,843,500 (£2,562,698:$4,036,250). 17.V.95

The fine colour and purity of Burmese rubies have made them the most sought-after of precious stones. Large specimens of over 20 carats which exhibit good pigeon-blood hue, like this example which weighs 27.37 carats, may be considered amongst the rarest of gemstones. (BELOW)

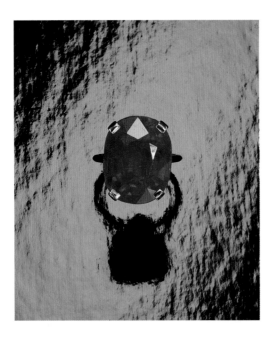

A Fancy Pink diamond ring
New York $1,982,500 (£1,229,150). 11.IV.95

This Internally Flawless diamond weighs 5.65 carats and has been cut into a marquise shape. (RIGHT)

A Fancy Yellowish Green diamond
New York $1,102,500 (£683,550). 11.IV.95

This extraordinary diamond weighs 2.15 carats. Due to their rarity and the complexity of determining natural colour origin, green diamonds are probably the least understood of the Fancy coloured diamonds. Most experts agree that, next to red, green is the rarest of all natural diamond hues. (LEFT)

A pair of emerald and diamond pendant earclips
Geneva SF850,500 (£450,000:$708,750). 17.V.95

Emeralds have been highly valued for thousands of years and, historically, Colombian emeralds such as these have always been the world's finest. This pair, weighing 12.22 and 12.38 carats, are extraordinarily well-matched in colour and combine a high degree of brilliance and purity. Surmounted by foliate sprigs of diamonds and supported by cluster tops of gemstones, the emeralds can be detached from their pendants. (LEFT)

Diamond bow brooch
LATE NINETEENTH CENTURY
New York $79,500 (£50,880). 7.XII.94

Delicately designed as an openwork lace bow-knot, this piece is set with several sizes of old European-cut diamonds mounted in platinum and gold and is decorated with a continuous pattern of foliate scrolls. (ABOVE)

Pair of diamond pendant earclips
TOPS AND CLUSTERS ORIGINALLY BY HARRY WINSTON
New York $1,102,500 (£705,600). 17.X.94

This pair of earclips is formed from two pear-shaped diamonds weighing 8.09 and 7.70 carats, which support clusters of ten marquise- and pear-shaped diamonds. The clusters are detachable so that the diamonds can be worn alone. (ABOVE)

A diamond and pearl corsage ornament
CARTIER, c.1905
Geneva SF234,500 (£113,835:$180,385). 16.XI.94

Jewelled stomachers, pinned to the front of the corset, have a long
history. They were introduced in the seventeenth century and were
worn intermittently up to the first decade of the twentieth century
when the new fashion for tunic-like dresses made the corset obsolete.
During the *belle époque*, Cartier stomachers, such as this example,
and *colliers de chien* set with diamonds and pearls were among
the prize possessions of society ladies. (BELOW)

A diamond and pearl tiara
CHAUMET, c.1915, length c.37cm (14½in)
St Moritz SF278,500 (£140,657:$222,800). 18.II.95

This piece is accompanied by an extract from a detailed statement
provided by Messrs. Chaumet, dated 1914 and 1915, from which it
appears that several other jewels were part of the same commission.
One illustration shows an earlier pearl and diamond tiara in the
garland style which was given to Messrs. Chaumet to be dismantled
in order to reuse the stones and pearls. Twelve of these stones in their
original settings are featured in the present tiara. (RIGHT)

Ruby and diamond necklace

Length approximately
38cm (15in)
New York $332,500
(£212,800). 17.X.94
From the Estate of Rebecca
Guggenheim Logan

This necklace is designed
with three rows of
cushion-shaped rubies
which continue to
double and single rows
at the sides and back,
making 95 rubies in
total. These are
supported by a line of
252 baguette diamonds,
some of which are
incorporated with 78
round diamonds to
form scroll *motifs* as
accents. (RIGHT)

A ruby, emerald and diamond flower brooch
PROBABLY FOR VAN CLEEF & ARPELS, *c.*1925
London £80,700 ($129,927). 22.VI.95

This flower jewel mirrors the series created by Van Cleef & Arpels in the 1920s. Diaghilev's collaboration with the Ballets Russes and the startling use of colour in his productions had a great influence on the world of haute couture, struggling to leave behind the privations of the First World War. This inspired the renewed use of coloured stones by leading jewellers which, in turn, initiated innovative demonstrations of the stone setter's art such as the 'invisible' setting developed by Van Cleef & Arpels, seen here. (LEFT)

A diamond cluster brooch/pendant
*c.*1910
London £45,500 ($72,800). 16.III.95

This circular brooch or pendant of interlaced garland and ribbon design is set with rose and cushion-shaped diamonds of which the largest four are detachable. The elegance and delicacy of the design is typical of early twentieth-century jewellery. (BELOW)

A gold, pearl, turquoise and diamond brooch
*c.*1840
London £4,025 ($6,279). 13.XII.94

On 10 February 1840 Queen Victoria married Prince Albert in the Chapel Royal, St James's Palace. The queen had twelve train-bearers, each of whom received an eagle brooch in turquoise, referred to as the 'Coburg eagle' and thought to have been designed by the prince. The back is inscribed with an interlaced monogram, *VR,* and the wedding date. (ABOVE)

An aquamarine and diamond necklace, bracelet, brooch, earclips and ring
*c.*1960
London £43,355 ($69,802). 22.VI.95
From the Collection of Dame Barbara Cartland, D.B.E., D.St.J.

Dame Barbara Cartland designed this suite herself at the invitation of her husband, Hugh, in the early 1960s and had it made up by Mr Digby Jones of Jones Bond Street Limited. It incorporates aquamarine stones in a variety of shapes, from step-cut to oval and pear-shape. The designs also feature eight- and brilliant-cut diamonds which make it a beautiful, striking set. (RIGHT)

A diamond choker and a pair of matching pendant earclips
REZA, choker's length 33cm (13in)
Geneva SF3,523,500 (£1,710,437:$2,710,385). 16.XI.94

The jewellery firm of Alexandre Reza was founded in Moscow in 1890 by the father of the
present owner who, having escaped from Russia in 1925, re-established the firm in Paris. His son,
also named Alexandre, took over the business in 1945 and transformed it into an internationally
renowned retail establishment. The nine principal marquise diamonds used here graduate from
6.10 to 8.84 carats and are all of the finest D-colour, Internally Flawless clarity. (ABOVE)

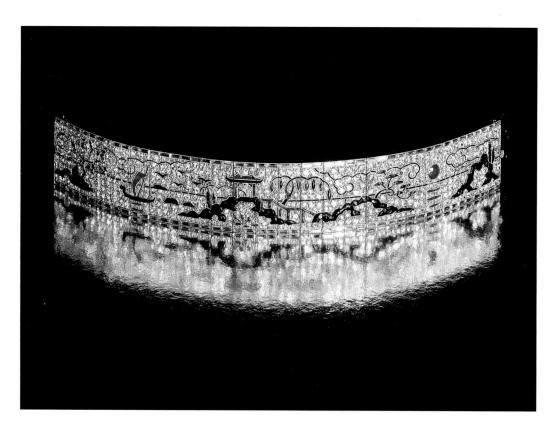

Art Deco diamond and coloured stone bracelet

LACLOCHE FRÈRES, PARIS, *c*.1920, length 18cm (7⅛in)
New York $178,500 (£114,240). 17.X.94

Inspired by Oriental and European *motifs* as well as the fables of La Fontaine, the house of Lacloche Frères mastered technical innovation in their decorative jewels. Their pieces were characterized by bright colours and strong geometric designs drawn with diamonds and precious stones and this bracelet exemplifies the fine workmanship and originality of design for which the firm is renowned. (LEFT)

A coloured stone 'tutti frutti' bracelet

CARTIER PARIS, *c*.1925, length 18.5cm (7¼in)
Geneva SF333,500 (£161,893:$256,538). 16.XI.94

Jewels encrusted with precious stones such as emeralds, rubies and sapphires carved as leaves, flowers or berries (hence the term 'tutti frutti') became very popular during the 1920s and 1930s. The best examples were produced by Cartier and were the result of Louis Cartier's ongoing fascination with exotic cultures as well as the increased exposure to traditional Indian jewels lavishly set with carved coloured gems. (RIGHT)

MINIATURES, VERTU AND FABERGÉ

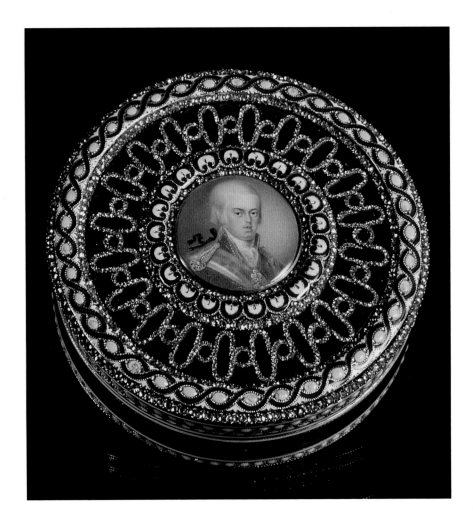

A Russian gold, enamel and diamond-set bonbonnière
DAVID RUDOLPH, ST PETERSBURG, 1785, diameter 8.6cm (3⅜in)
New York $178,500 (£114,240). 6.XII.94

This extremely rare bonbonnière is mounted with a portrait miniature of King John VI of Portugal as Prince Regent. It was presented to John Jervis, the Commander-in-Chief of the British Navy in the Mediterranean, after his defeat of the Spanish fleet off Cape St Vincent on 14 February 1797. The Commander was elevated to the peerage as Baron Jervis of Meaford, county Stafford and Earl of St Vincent. He lived with his wife at her family home, Rochetts in Essex, until his death in 1823. The interior of the cover is inscribed 'Given to the Earl of St Vincent by the Prince Regent of Portugal, and Left as an Heirloom to Rochetts'. (ABOVE)

A Fabergé silver samovar

MAKER'S MARK BELOW THE IMPERIAL WARRANT, MOSCOW, 1896–1908,
height 33.4cm (13⅛in)
Geneva SF251,000 (£122,439:$196,094). 17.XI.94

This remarkable samovar is boldly cast in the form of a hoary old
man with windswept hair and beard. The exuberance of composition
and vitality of execution of this work reveal the true creativity of the
house of Fabergé. (BELOW)

A lady

SAMUEL COOPER, c.1645, ON VELLUM, oval 8.2cm (3¼in)
London £89,500 ($142,305). 11.X.94

This remarkably spontaneous portrait is an
excellent example of Cooper's liberating approach
to miniature painting at the outset of his career.
His bravura technique effectively introduced the
spirit of the Baroque into the art of portrait
miniatures. The identity of the sitter remains
unknown. Previously thought to be either Mary,
Princess of Orange or Elizabeth Cecil, Countess of
Devonshire, both these identifications are now
considered unlikely because of irregularities in
dating and physiognomy. (ABOVE)

CLOCKS AND WATCHES

A month-going table regulator
PAUL GARNIER, SIGNED, *c*.1839,
height 50.2cm (19¾in)
London £21,850 ($34,960). 2.VI.95

The famous clockmaker Paul
Garnier (1801–69) exhibited a
similar table regulator in the Paris
Exhibition of 1839. The pendulum
used on this clock was based on a
design patented in 1819 by Franz
Josef Mahler, head of the Munich
firm Utzschneider & Frauenhofer
which supplied astronomical
regulators fitted with this type
of pendulum. (LEFT)

A mahogany long-case clock
THOMAS MUDGE, SIGNED, *c*.1775,
height 230.5cm (7ft 6¾in)
London £24,150 ($38,640). 2.VI.95

Thomas Mudge (1715–94) was
apprenticed to and worked for the
renowned clockmaker, George
Graham. Although principally
known for his work on watches
and chronometers, Mudge also
made a number of fine long-case
clocks. (RIGHT)

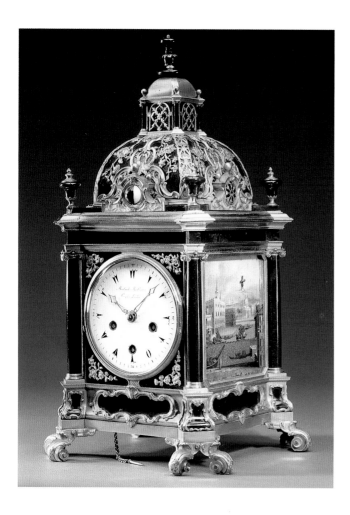

A miniature gold mounted bloodstone three train musical automaton table clock

MARKWICK, MARKHAM, PERIGAL, c.1800, height 29cm (11½in)
Geneva SF267,500 (£141,534:$222,917). 16.V.95

The rarity of an English musical clock in a gold mounted bloodstone case is such that it would be safe to assume that this piece was a unique commission for a royal client. The bell strikes every hour and plays one of six different tunes on six bells with twelve hammers. The glazed panels on each side enclose painted scenes of neo-classical buildings with automaton ships passing by and a windmill with revolving sails on a hillside. (LEFT)

An ebony veneered quarter repeating table clock with silent escapement

GEORGE GRAHAM, SIGNED, c.1725, height 39cm (15¼in)
London £80,700 ($129,927). 3.III.95

After the invention of the rack and quarter repeating work in the late seventeenth century, clocks were designed especially for use in the bedroom at night, when the striking train could be silenced unless it was activated by pulling the repeating cord. The natural development from this was to invent a means of quietening the loud tick-tock of the clock and it is possible that Graham adapted Thomas Tompion's method of silencing when he worked on this example. (RIGHT)

A gold repoussé triple cased half-quarter repeating alarm watch

ELLICOTT, c.1758–59, diameter 6cm (2⅜in)
New York $70,700 (£43,127). 24.X.94

This watch is extremely rare as it is possibly the only one known by Ellicott in gold combining the features of repeat and alarm. The repoussé case, depicting the Roman general Coriolanus before his kneeling wife Volumnia, their two small sons and his mother Veturia, is of the highest quality and exemplifies the work of H. Manly. (RIGHT)

An oval silver verge watch with astronomical dial and engraved miniature of King James I

DAVID RAMSAY, SIGNED, c.1620,
height including bow 6.2cm (2⅜in)
London £28,750 ($46,288). 3.III.95

David Ramsay was one of the finest of the early makers. He was appointed Chief Clockmaker to King James I in 1618 and became the first Master of the Worshipful Company of Clockmakers at its formation in 1632. A similar watch is in the Victoria & Albert Museum, and it appears that these are the only known watches by Ramsay containing engraved miniatures of the king. (ABOVE)

A gold early English lever watch

JOSIAH EMERY, SIGNED, 1790, diameter 5.4cm (2⅛in)
London £56,500 ($90,965). 3.III.95

This rare watch is fitted with Emery's lever escapement and has a mechanism at the edge for stopping and starting the action. According to the owner, the watch belonged to her grandfather who acquired it in lieu of a debt. (LEFT)

A gold and enamel quarter repeating 'Moses' automaton watch

CHARLES DUCOMMUN, c.1810, diameter 6.4cm (2½in)
Geneva SF399,500 (£211,376:$332,917). 16.V.95

Hitherto unrecorded, this watch depicts Moses drawing water from a rock (Exodus 17: 1–7 and Numbers 2: 1–13). Only five other watches of this type are recorded. According to family tradition, the piece was a gift from the Empress Eugenie of France, wife of Napoleon III, to their close personal friend Field Marshal Sir Lintorn Simmons G.C.B. G.C.M.G., the great-great-uncle of the owner. (RIGHT)

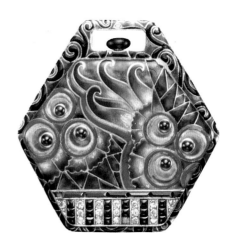

A gold openfaced minute repeating perpetual calendar split second chronograph watch

VACHERON & CONSTANTIN, SIGNED, c.1915, diameter 5cm (2in)
New York $112,500 (£68,625). 24.X.94

It is unusual to find a fully signed Vacheron & Constantin watch which combines the multitude of features found here. These include four subsidiary dials indicating day, date, months calibrated for a four-year cycle combined with a register for sixty minutes and constant seconds, as well as the age and phases of the moon. (ABOVE)

A gold, cloisonné enamel- and jewel-set hexagonal and openfaced watch

LONGINES, SIGNED, diameter 4.7cm (1⅞in), New York $26,450 (£16,135). 24.X.94

This watch was made for the 1925 Paris Exhibition of Modern Decorative and Industrial Art. The case is completely enamelled, the reverse in opaque polychrome blue, red and green with a pattern of peacock feathers picked out with six cabochon sapphires, and the base with a band of striped single-cut diamonds, onyx and sapphires. The front is similarly decorated. (ABOVE)

A gold cushion-form minute repeating wristwatch

PATEK PHILIPPE & CO., c.1930, width 2.8cm (1in)
New York $519,500 (£327,285). 13.VI.95

The manufacturer's archives record that this watch, begun in 1927, was finished and sold in 1932. Minute repeating mechanisms are found in Patek Philippe wristwatches as early as 1906, with originally cased pieces beginning sometime after 1925. The minute repeater was available in gold and platinum with a variety of case styles: the current watch is the first cushion-form style case to be offered for public auction. (RIGHT)

A gold and platinum rectangular eight-day wristwatch

PATEK PHILIPPE & CO., c.1930, length 4cm (1½in)
New York $288,500 (£181,755). 13.VI.95

This watch is the second known example of a Patek Philippe eight-day wristwatch. These watches could be seen as the company's answer to the self-winding watches made by competitors which were growing in popularity. The scarcity of this movement can probably be attributed to the fact that the production of eight-day movements proved too costly to manufacture in a series. Patek Philippe introduced their own version of the self-winding watch in 1953. (LEFT)

SILVER AND GOLD

A pair of silver soup tureens
GEORGE WICKES, LONDON, 1744, DESIGNED BY WILLIAM KENT, length 57.5cm (22½in)
London £1,013,500 ($1,621,600). 10.XI.94

Made for the 1st Baron Montfort of Horseheath, this pair of tureens was designed by the celebrated Palladian architect, William Kent and made under the direction of George Wickes, goldsmith to Frederick, Prince of Wales. On his death in 1755, Lord Montfort was described in a letter by Mrs Elizabeth Montagu as a 'true Epicurean character [who] loved a degree of voluptuousness that his fortune could not afford, and a splendour of life it could not supply'. Considered 'lost' since 1921, the fact that these tureens have survived is extraordinary because their remarkable weight, 24.4kg (785oz), would always have represented substantial value. (ABOVE)

The Judge Elbert H. Gary eighteen-carat gold dinner service (detail)
TIFFANY & CO, NEW YORK, c.1910
New York $2,037,500 (£1,283,625). 19.X.94

Elbert H. Gary, who grew up on a farm in Wheaton, Illinois, successively established himself as a
distinguished judge, then mayor of his home town, before becoming one of the most successful
business barons of his day, co-founding the United States Steel Corporation in 1901 and sitting for
twenty-six years as its first Chairman of the Board. Judge Gary's dazzling, 566-piece Tiffany table
service weighs in at 122.5kg (270lb) and includes an item for every possible dish of the grand and
sumptuous feasts that millionaires tried to outdo each other in hosting. According to family history,
the service was used on only one occasion, at a dinner honouring the Sultan of Turkey. (ABOVE)

A Dutch silver-gilt model of a horse
UNMARKED, ATTRIBUTED TO MELCHIOR VAN NEURENBORCH, GORCUM, c.1600,
height 34cm (13⅜in)
Geneva SF344,500 (£181,316:$284,711). 16.V.95
From the Collection of Joseph R. Ritman

This rearing horse bears the arms of the influential Colff, Van
Grootveld, Van Neercassel and Vervoorn families and was probably
commissioned in commemoration of their association with the Civic
Guard Guild of St George of Gorcum. It has a detachable head
decorated with a floral head-dress, bridle and reins. (ABOVE)

A coconut cup of an owl, with Belgian parcel-gilt mounts
MAKER'S MARK A PELICAN IN SHIELD, ANTWERP, 1548–49, height 17.5cm (6⅞in)
Geneva SF454,500 (£239,211:$375,620). 16.V.95
From the Collection of Joseph R. Ritman

This unusual piece consists of a realistically carved coconut with
a detachable head and silver rim mounts decorated with feathers.
The owl stands on an engraved rim and has a bell attached to
one leg. (ABOVE)

A George II silver seal salver

JOHN WHITE, ENGRAVED BY CHARLES GARDNER AND
SIGNED *C GARDNER SCULPT*, LONDON, 1728,
diameter 49cm (19¼in)
London £265,500 ($424,800). 8.VI.95
From the Silver of Lord Chancellor King
and the King Family

Peter King, 1st Lord King of Ockham in
Surrey, was born into relative obscurity but
favoured with a genius 'greatly superior to
his birth' he rose to high office, becoming
Lord Chancellor on 1 June 1725. The
superbly engraved roundel at the centre of
this salver bears the contemporary royal
arms, the seal of the Lord Chancellor, his
mace and the arms of King below a baron's
coronet. It is the only known piece of
signed engraving by Charles Gardner whose
contribution to this sphere was first
acknowledged in 1978. This documentary
piece provides a significant addition to the
art of engraved decoration on silver. (LEFT)

A set of four George II silver casters and a George II silver caddinet or plateau

ANNE TANQUERAY, LONDON, 1728, heights of casters 24.1cm and 19.7cm
(9½ and 7¾in), length of caddinet 62.3cm (24½in)
London casters £84,000 ($134,400), caddinet £194,000 ($310,400). 8.VI.95
From the Silver of Lord Chancellor King and the King Family

These unusual pieces may well have been used in
conjunction by the Lord Chancellor in his official capacity
and it is conceivable that, together with other components,
they may be part of the earliest known example of an
English *surtout de table* pre-dating by three years the
Kirkleatham Centrepiece, now at Temple Newsam. (RIGHT)

A set of four George II Rococo silver table candlesticks
PAUL DE LAMERIE, LONDON, 1744,
height 23.5cm (9¼in)
New York $211,500 (£133,245). 19.X.94
From the Estate of Pauline E. Woolworth

The conspicuous use of bees and beehives on the stems and domed bases of these magnificent candlesticks suggest a heraldic allusion. Of the few English families who incorporate these elements in their arms, perhaps the most likely candidate is the Huguenot family of Leheup. A coat of arms which included flying bees and beehives was granted to Isaac, Michael and Peter Leheup in 1744, the year in which the candlesticks were made. (RIGHT)

An Austrian silver soup tureen
JOSEPH IGNAZ WÜRTH, VIENNA, 1779–82,
width 67cm (26⅜in)
Geneva SF443,500 (£233,421:$336,529). 15.V.95

This tureen forms part of what was known as The Polish Service at the court of the Duke of Sachsen-Teschen. Made between 1779 and 1782 by the Imperial Court Goldsmith, Joseph Ignaz Würth, the service is one of the most important examples of Viennese eighteenth-century silver to have escaped the ravages of the Napoleonic wars. (BELOW)

An American silver spout cup and cover

SAMUEL VERNON, NEWPORT, RI, c.1730–35, MARKED *SV* ABOVE A *FLEUR DE LIS* IN HEART,
ENGRAVED WITH INITIALS *M*B* AND *A* ABOVE *C*B* ON BASE, height 15.9cm (6¼in)
New York $78,400 (£48,608). 22.VI.95

This silver spout cup, descended through the Nichols family of Newport,
Rhode Island, seems to be the only covered spout cup from the area to have
appeared publicly. (LEFT)

One of a pair of German silver-gilt ewers and dishes

CONRAD HÖLLING, HANOVER, 1707–08, ALSO
STRUCK *DD* BELOW A CROWN, height of ewers
29.5cm (11½in), diameter of dishes 61.5cm (24½in)
London £639,500 ($1,004,015). 25.V.95
From the Collection of the Late Sir Harold
Wernher, Luton Hoo

This pair of ewers and dishes was made
for George Louis, Elector of Hanover,
later King George I of Great Britain.
The electoral cap or bonnet and plain
inescutcheon of the armorials date the
silver to between 1692, when George
Louis' father was created Elector of
Hanover, and 1708 when George Louis
himself was introduced into the College
of Electors and the plain inescutcheon
was replaced by *gules, the crown of
Charlemagne proper*. The pieces are
struck with a crowned *DD* which is
as yet unidentified and has only been
found on silver by the same maker and
with the same provenance. It has been
suggested that this mark relates to the
Celle Court Goldsmith Lewin Dedeke
who is known to have collaborated
with Hölling on various court
commissions. (LEFT)

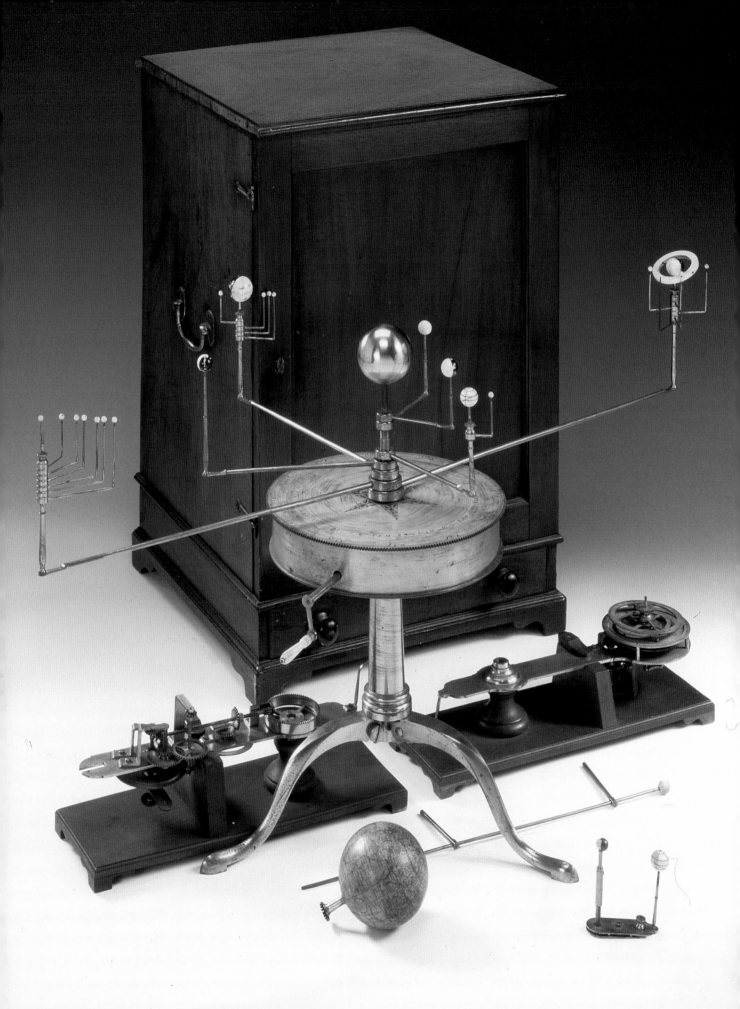

COLLECTORS' CATEGORIES *by Hilary Kay*

A Robert Bate brass planetarium, tellurium and lunarium
ENGLAND, EARLY NINETEENTH CENTURY, height: instrument 43cm (17in), case 58cm (23in)
London £36,700 ($59,821).
3.III.95 (LEFT)

A close helmet
INNSBRUCK COURT WORKSHOP, IN THE MANNER OF HANS SEUSENHOFER, c.1515–30, height 28cm (11in)
Billingshurst
£26,450 ($42,320).
24.VII.95 (BELOW)

From Antonio Stradivari and Château Pétrus to John Lennon and Ferrari, the Collectors' Division is one of the fastest growing and most diverse within Sotheby's. The 1994–95 season has seen the market for collectibles continue to strengthen. For those areas unaffected by the recent worldwide recession this environment has enabled new heights to be scaled, whilst in other fields it has been a time to re-establish the strong sales of three or four years ago.

The musical instrument department welcomed the return of instruments by Antonio Stradivari to their sales this season and with them the recovery of the market from the doldrums of the early 1990s. A 1711 violin by Stradivari sold in March for £386,500 whilst the ex-Tom Jenkins Stradivari violin of 1667 realized £375,500 in June. The Early Music sale in 1994 contained important keyboard instruments, the most noteworthy being a piano from about 1785 by the Irish maker William Southwell, which sold for £32,200.

The international wine department achieved a 150 per cent rise in sales over the previous season. This spectacular increase was both a reflection of a rising market and of Sotheby's dynamic entry on to the New York and Zürich wine auction scenes. Over $5 million of wine was sold in New York's first season and two world record prices were achieved at the inaugural auction in October 1994. In Europe the market has been dramatized by a perceived shortage of fine wine which has galvanized collectors and wine lovers into buying.

Philately is another international interest and the season was marked by a significant growth in sales. In Hong Kong, a fine sale of postage stamps of the Far East included the magnificent Collection of Imperial China formed by Charles Goodwyn. Highlights from the two philatelic sales held in New York included the Erich Koenig Collection of Mexican stamps and covers which realized $565,782.

The solid results of recent years have been sustained in sales of coins and historical medals. In New York a recently rediscovered specimen of the Ultra-High relief 1907 Double Eagle reached $242,000 while a proof of the 1875

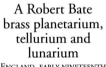

RENÉ LALIQUE
A 'vitesse' glass
mascot
EMBOSSED *R LALIQUE FRANCE*,
1929–30s, height 18.3cm (7⅛in)
Birmingham £5,850
($9,435). 8.V.95 (ABOVE)

US gold twenty-dollar piece attained $110,000. The London season culminated in July with the auction of a connoisseur's selection of ancient Greek and Roman coins of outstanding quality which totalled over £2 million. Included were a Cretan silver stater of 280 BC (£66,000) and an aureus of Mexentius (£71,500).

Sustained growth was seen in the market for gallantry medals, orders and decorations together with a number of outstanding prices, not least the £111,500 paid for Air Commodore West's World War I Victoria Cross collection. The market for European orders and decorations has witnessed several new developments including substantial growth in interest for Imperial Russian insignia; a notable price was the SF43,000 achieved for a superb St Andrew collar of 1864.

The market for sporting guns has been very buoyant with a great demand for the best quality guns which retain their original finish, now hard to find. Condition is more important than ever with buyers increasingly conversant with barrel specifications, types of action and overall condition.

Entering its thirtieth year in March 1995, Sotheby's motor car department is the oldest car auctioneer in Europe. This season, pre-war racing and sports cars attracted international interest. A 1927 Bentley 3-litre team car achieved £199,500 and a 1934 Maserati 4 CS 1½-litre supercharged sports two-seater was sold for £122,500. American sales included the Collection of the late Willet H. Brown in which some of the finest marques from the pre-World War I to post-World War II European exotics came under the hammer. Realizing $3.9 million and with 99 per cent sold, it was welcomed as a further sign of renewed confidence in the collectors' car market.

The fifth sale of comic books and comic art held by Sotheby's totalled over $2 million, with the best performers from 'golden age' comics such as Detective Comics No. 27 (in which Batman first appeared) which achieved $68,500. Continuing the theme, original artwork by Bob Kane for the Batman Daily, 1943 achieved a remarkable $29,900. Hollywood memorabilia has continued to thrive this season with an Oscar award from 1928 realizing £41,400 and the ventriloquist's dummy, Charlie McCarthy, achieving $112,500.

Animation art remains extremely popular in America with examples of 'Vintage Art' (1920–50) remaining the most sought-after lots. The sale of artwork from the Disney blockbuster The Lion King set a world record for animation art at auction, achieving nearly $2 million and attracting many new buyers.

In 1994, the largest sale of rock 'n' roll memorabilia ever held in London totalled £917,600. Included were icons such as the painted bass drumskin from the album sleeve of The Beatles' Sgt. Pepper's Lonely Hearts Club Band (£52,100) and the historic 1957 recording of John Lennon with his first group, The Quarrymen (£78,500). There has been exciting growth in the market for memorabilia relating to more recent bands such as Nirvana and Pearl Jam with auction prices now rivalling the supergroups of the 1960s and 70s.

Having seen dramatic growth during the recession years, this season saw little movement in the market for teddy bears, toys and automata. Interest in dolls fresh to the market and in original condition remained strong as did that for German character dolls, good clothing and dolls' accessories. The bear market is bullish with Steiff bears remaining the most popular. Rare tinplate toys attracted competition on both sides of the Atlantic. In New York toys from the FORBES Collection were the focus whilst in London Lehmann toys have become increasingly sought-after. The tinplate clockwork passenger liner Prinses Juliana by Märklin achieved £36,700. In the same vein, the Scheer Collection of biscuit and decorative tins included one in the form of a motorcycle combination by Gray, Dunn & Co which sold for £5,750.

Mechanical music sales were buoyant this season, helped by the return of private buyers from the Far East. A Philharmonic orchestrion organ by Welte & Son made £100,500.

Sotheby's annual sale of golfing memorabilia was held in St Andrews, birthplace of golf and venue for the 1995 Open Championship. The highlight was a group of eighteen outstanding watercolours by Michael Brown painted between 1892–1916 which reached £521,325. In July, Sotheby's first sale devoted to cricket included equipment, books, prints, photographs and ceramics. Tossing for Innings, an oil on canvas by Robert James, sold for £45,500.

The market for scientific and technological instruments has remained steady with highlights including the Robert Bate orrery (£36,700) and a Jonathan Sisson theodolite (£23,000). In October, Sotheby's offered the Collection of Harriet Wynter and in March optical toys, magic lanterns and cinema ephemera from the Ron Morris Collection were sold. The Maritime Sale saw the market stable but with notable achievements being the £28,750 for a carved oak figurehead of Ajax and £54,300 realized by an Admiralty model of a seventy-gun ship-of-the-line, formerly in the Royal Collection at Windsor Castle.

The collectibles area is renowned for breaking new ground and this season was no exception. The array of manuscripts, ceramics, pictures and opera performance costumes from the Collection of Dame Joan Sutherland, O.M. and Richard Bonynge, C.B.E., attracted enormous interest, while the first sale of fabric swatch books and designs in March included woven silks from the French company Bianchini-Ferier which were used by many of the leading pre-war Paris couturiers including Jeanne Lanvin and Jean Patou. We look forward to further developments within the broadening and strengthening market for collectibles in the forthcoming season.

A King Kong poster
1933, RKO, STYLE A, three-sheet, 206 x 104cm (81 x 41in) New York $112,500 (£72,000). 10.XII.94 (ABOVE)

A KW lithographed tin motorcyclist with sidecar
GERMANY, 1920s, length 22.9cm (9in) New York $7,762 (£4,968). 19.XII.94 From the FORBES Magazine Collection (BELOW)

STAMPS

NETHERLANDS

Hindenburg crash cover
1 May 1937
New York $9,200 (£5,796). 11.X.94

This remarkably well preserved cover survived the Hindenburg airship disaster of 1937. Although the envelope was burnt round its edges when the airship exploded into flames, the adhesive, cachet, address and airmail label were, miraculously, left untouched. (LEFT)

GREAT BRITAIN

Illustrated soldier's letter
12 February 1841
London £4,025 ($6,279). 16.XII.94

Franked with an 1840 1d black, this unusual letter was sent to Phoebe Collins in Thame from her brother in Chatham whilst he was serving with the 96th Regiment. The letter commences, 'My Dearest Sister I have sent you another picture to match my last that I sent you' and is illustrated with his portrait, 'In full uniform for Chatham fairs'. (LEFT)

MEXICO
1921 10c blue and brown, centre inverted
New York $25,300 (£15,686). 31.V.95
From the Erich Koenig Collection

This is the finest of only two recorded examples of the rarest stamp of Mexico in which the central image has been printed the wrong way up. Never before offered at auction, this lot attained a world record price for a twentieth-century Mexican stamp. (LEFT)

CEYLON
1857–59 4d dull rose
London £14,950 ($23,920). 20.VII.95

This 4d dull rose is used together with a 5d chestnut on a folded outer wrapper dated 17 January 1860 and addressed to William Poole King, an 'African Merchant', of Bristol. The cover is endorsed 'Via Marseilles P Steamer Bentinck'. The 4d stamp is extremely rare and this appears to be a previously unrecorded example. (RIGHT)

CHINA
The Dowager Empress 'Missing Bat'
Hong Kong HK$230,000 (£18,400:$29,716). 4.V.95

This stamp is a very fine example of perhaps the most romantic and mystical error of all the Dowager issues. The 1 candarin value has a design which takes the form of a round archaic form of 'Shou' (longevity) surrounded by five bats 'Wu-Fu'. The bats have come to signify the 'five happinesses' of Chinese lore, namely long life, health, wealth, virtuosity and a natural death. Towards the end of the life of the printing stone it is believed that a piece disintegrated with the result that one of the bats had 'flown clean away', leaving four bats signifying ill-fortune instead of good. (LEFT)

COINS AND MEDALS

Tetradrachm from Naxos, Sicily
*c.*460 BC
London £132,000 ($209,880). 5.VII.95

This coin is arguably one of the masterpieces of Greek art. The head of the god Dionysus is engraved in the severe style of the early Classical period. (LEFT)

Stater from Gortyna, Crete
*c.*280 BC
London £66,000 ($104,940). 5.VII.95

The rape of Europa has been a popular theme in art since ancient times. Here Europa is depicted sitting in a tree. This beautiful coin is extremely unusual as it preserves so many of the fine details of the original design. It is rare to find Cretan coins in such an excellent state of preservation, as they were often only roughly struck over earlier coins. (RIGHT)

Roman aureus depicting Septimius Severus and his family
AD 209
London £35,200 ($55,968). 5.VII.95

This aureus bears the portraits of Septimius Severus and his wife Julia Domna on the obverse with the legend FELICITAS PVBLICA ('public prosperity'). Apart from a specimen recorded in the Bibliothèque Nationale and stolen in the 1830s, this is the only known example. (LEFT)

Ultra-High relief Double Eagle
UNITED STATES OF AMERICA, 1907, ROMAN NUMERALS,
DESIGNED BY AUGUSTUS SAINT-GAUDENS
New York $242,000 (£150,040). 21.VI.95

Commissioned by President Theodore Roosevelt who referred to it as his 'pet baby', this supremely sculptural coin proved impossible to mass-produce in view of the inordinately high striking pressures required to make it. Currency versions, produced until the 1930s in much lower relief, represented a pale reflection of the original concept. (LEFT)

Proof three dollars
UNITED STATES OF AMERICA, 1875
New York $90,200 (£57,728). 13.XII.94

The 1875 three dollar gold piece is one of the great rarities of the United States series as only twenty pieces were struck in that year.
(RIGHT)

Bank Portugaloser
HAMBURG, GERMANY, 1726
London £11,550 ($18,365). 6.X.94

The obverse of the coin, illustrated here, depicts a desk supporting an open ledger and covered by a cloth displaying the Hamburg city arms. To one side is a coffer and moneybags; to the other is a table with scales, coins for weighing and a chequer board. (LEFT)

ARMS AND ARMOUR

A detached wheel-lock mechanism for a pistol

FRANCE, c.1620–30, UNSIGNED, BUT ALMOST CERTAINLY BY
JEAN HENEQUIN, METZ, the plate 12cm (4¾in)
New York $17,250 (£10,695). 31.V.95

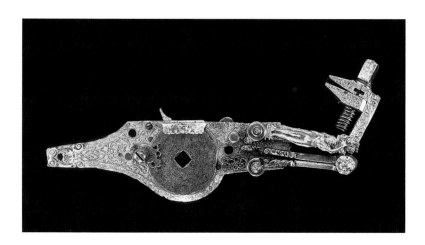

The chiselled ornament on this extremely rare wheel-lock mechanism is strongly characteristic of that of the School of Fontainebleau. A leading exponent of this school, Etienne Delaune (1518–83), published in Strasbourg and Augsburg many small-scale engravings intended for use by goldsmiths and metalworkers. His designs typically featured densely packed scroll and strapwork in the Mannerist style, with trophies and elongated female nude figures, all of which are incorporated in this fine example. (RIGHT)

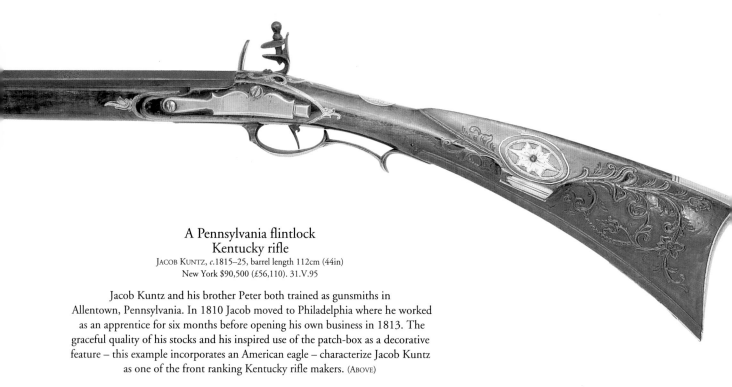

A Pennsylvania flintlock Kentucky rifle

JACOB KUNTZ, c.1815–25, barrel length 112cm (44in)
New York $90,500 (£56,110). 31.V.95

Jacob Kuntz and his brother Peter both trained as gunsmiths in Allentown, Pennsylvania. In 1810 Jacob moved to Philadelphia where he worked as an apprentice for six months before opening his own business in 1813. The graceful quality of his stocks and his inspired use of the patch-box as a decorative feature – this example incorporates an American eagle – characterize Jacob Kuntz as one of the front ranking Kentucky rifle makers. (ABOVE)

SPORTING GUNS

A .22 (Hornet) 'Hercules' model boxlock ejector rifle
BY E.J. CHURCHILL
Gleneagles £15,525 ($23,909). 29.VIII.94

Very few rifles of this calibre were built by the gunmaker E.J. Churchill. This rare example was made in 1938 and appears virtually unused. The scroll-backed frame is engraved with fine foliate scrolls and the rifle is fitted with a *Carl Zeiss, Jena* telescopic sight. (LEFT)

A 12-bore assisted opening round action ejector 'Pike' gun
BY DAVID MCKAY BROWN
FOR THE ENGRAVER MALCOLM APPLEBY
Gleneagles £16,100 ($24,794). 29.VIII.94

Malcolm Appleby trained at the Royal College of Art and is a Freeman of the Worshipful Company of Goldsmiths. He specializes in designing new styles of engraving, most of which are based on a particular theme. In this example the gun's features are used to portray those of a pike and the engraving represents scales of varying size and texture according to the anatomy of the fish. (RIGHT)

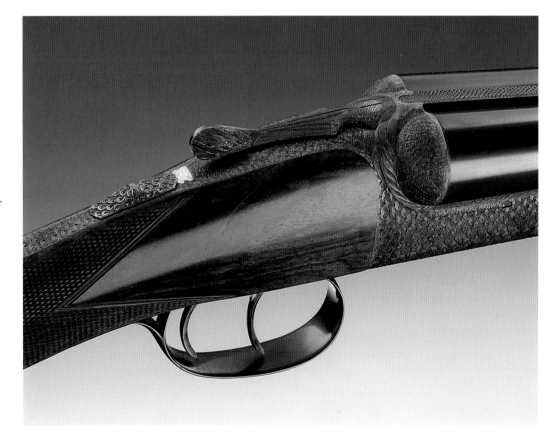

WAR MEDALS

A Great War V.C., M.C. group awarded to Air Commodore F.M.F. 'Freddie' West, Royal Flying Corps and Royal Air Force, late Royal Munster Fusiliers
Billingshurst £111,500 ($177,285). 24.III.95

On 10 August 1918, 'Freddie' West flew his Armstrong-Whitworth FK8 far over the enemy lines in France and, from a low altitude, fired at a huge concentration of German transport and troops. Attacked by ground fire, he was also surprised by two enemy aircraft. At the outset of the fight his left leg was severed by an explosive bullet and fell onto the controls. Although wounded in the other leg and suffering massive blood loss, he managed to level out the aeroplane enabling his Observer to get several bursts into the enemy machines, and then by sheer grit and determination safely landed over the Allied lines. Before undergoing surgery, West insisted on communicating his valuable information regarding the German reserves to his Squadron adjutant. (LEFT)

Orders, Medals and Decorations, formerly included in the Personal Collections of Wilhelm II, late King of Prussia and Emperor of Germany
Geneva SF218,500 (£115,571:$180,579). 16.V.95

Following his abdication in 1918, Wilhelm II spent the remainder of his life in Doorn, Holland. On his death in 1941 many of his possessions were removed to Berlin and were lost in the turbulent summer of 1945. However, in 1950, the 'Great Group' of 21 orders and medals (mounted for breast wear) and 67 other pieces resurfaced and a selection was bought by Major E.A. Jeffries. In due course, the collection was dispersed only to be almost completely reassembled by collector Michael Forman with the addition of complementary items from other sources, such as the fine Scottish brooch given by Queen Victoria to her grandson on his eighteenth birthday in 1877. (LEFT)

MUSICAL INSTRUMENTS

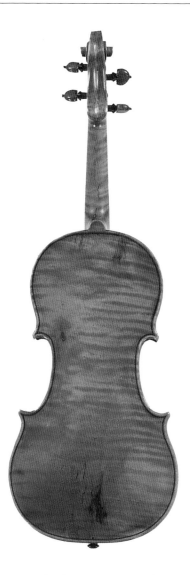

A violin by Antonio Stradivari
CREMONA, 1667, length of back 35cm (13¾in)
London £375,500 ($604,555). 20.VI.95

One of the recorded owners of this early Stradivarius is the celebrated English violinist Tom Jenkins (1920–57). Jenkins gained tremendous popularity as a violinist and orchestra leader during the heyday of the BBC's light music broadcasts between the 1930s and 1950s. The great demand for light music in the post-war years meant that the audience for his Sunday evening broadcasts grew to an estimated ten million people. Jenkins was also in demand for classical recitals and in 1948 decided to buy a Stradivarius to replace the Gagliano he had been using up until that time. Formerly sold at Sotheby's in London on 12 November 1987, it is now in the possession of the ten-year-old virtuoso musician, Christine Thompson. (ABOVE)

A violin by Antonio Stradivari
CREMONA, 1711, length of back 35.4cm (13¹⁵⁄₁₆in)
London £386,500 ($610,670). 21.III.95
Ex-Vogelweith

Constructed in the golden period of Stradivari's output as an instrument maker, this violin has a one-piece back. (ABOVE)

VETERAN, VINTAGE AND CLASSIC CARS

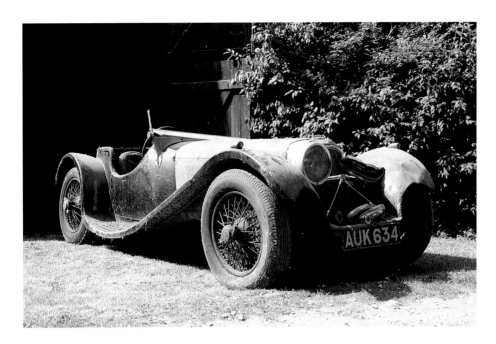

1937 SS Jaguar 100 2½-litre sports two-seater
Hendon £62,000 ($96,100). 5.IX.94

This recent 'barn discovery' has a well recorded history and is an original car in all respects. Factory publicity described the new SS 100 as 'primarily intended for competition work and sufficiently tractable to use as a fast tourer without modification'. Although in its earlier years it participated in a number of Welsh and Scottish rallies, the car was last used in 1965, and subsequently laid up until its discovery in July 1994. (LEFT)

1927 Bentley 3-litre Le Mans no. 2 works team car sports tourer
Hendon £199,500 ($311,220). 5.XII.94

Built in the Bentley Motors Racing Shop as a Works entry for the 1927 Le Mans, this 3-litre Bentley was constructed with a full racing specification engine and carried the relatively newly-developed integral sump and lower-geared steering, both of which became standard on the 4½-litre model. Although the car crashed during the course of the race, it was quickly repaired and subsequently appeared at a victory ascent of the Shelsley Walsh Hill Climb driven by Sammy Davis. (RIGHT)

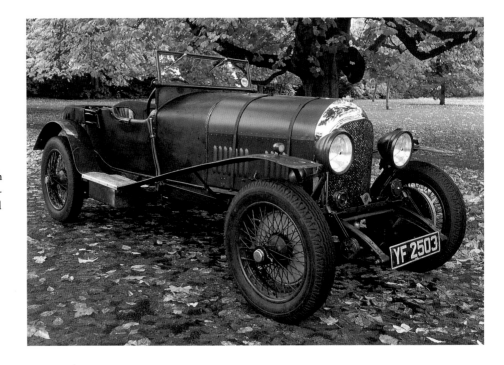

1913 Isotta-Fraschini Tipo 1M Racing Runabout

Los Angeles $365,500 (£229,874). 17.VI.95
From the Willett H. Brown Collection

The Tipo 1M Isotta-Fraschinis were purpose-built machines constructed at the behest of the American importer of the marque to compete in the Indianapolis 500 race. Only six 1M cars were ever built and this one, according to an Isotta-Fraschini authority, is the third made and a member of the trio which ran in the Indianapolis 500. Discovered many years ago in a derelict state, it was restored to its current excellent condition by a prominent Pennsylvania collector and is one of two 1M models still in existence. (ABOVE)

1912 Mercer Type 35c Raceabout

Los Angeles $228,000 (£143,396). 17.VI.95
From the Willett H. Brown Collection

Financed by the Roebling family of Brooklyn Bridge fame and carrying the name of the New Jersey county where it was built, the Mercer blazed an enviable record of victories on race tracks and roads in the hands of amateur and professional drivers of the day. Mercers were the sports cars Americans really loved first; they carried a factory-guaranteed minimum top speed of 70 miles per hour in stock form in an era when most cars struggled to reach 40 mph. (LEFT)

WINE

A bottle of Château d'Yquem 1847
New York (with Sherry-Lehmann) $18,400 (£11,592). 4.II.95

1847 was a legendary year for Sauternes, making
this bottle one of the greatest wines to come up in
any recent sale. It is thought there are very few left
anywhere, and this example had the additional
assurance of having been recorked and relabelled
at the Château in 1993. (ABOVE)

A bottle of Château Mouton Rothschild
1945 'Année de la Victoire'
London £2,640 ($4,145). 17.V.95

Many consider this to be one of the finest of all
wines. It has extraordinary opulence with what
seems like everlasting power. This example has
benefited from its excellent storage conditions.

(ABOVE)

COLLECTORS' SALES

A Welte & Son Philharmonic orchestrion organ
GERMANY, *c.*1910, height 335cm (132in)
London £100,500 ($157,785). 24.XI.94

This model is known as the *Titanic* since it is purported that a similar organ was built for the
famous liner but had not been installed when the ship sank in April 1912. According to
current records, there are believed to be only five of this style still extant. It contains 270
wood and metal pipes and its percussion includes bass and snare drums, a cymbal, triangle
and timpani. (ABOVE)

Charlie McCarthy
1936, BASS WOOD PERFORMER MADE BY HERB BARBER
New York $112,500 (£70,875). 10.VI.95

Edgar Bergen's celebrated dummy, Charlie McCarthy, ignited humour and laughter
in America for more than fifty years. The appeal of the duo embraced generations
of fans, from vaudeville, through their routines on radio and in film, to their
appearances on television. Originally modelled after an Irish newsboy in a sweater
and cap, McCarthy evolved into the world's best-dressed dummy, wearing full
evening dress, top hat and monocle. This particular dummy was Bergen's principal
partner in film and radio performances; the first Charlie McCarthy, commissioned
towards the end of Bergen's college career, was used during
their years in vaudeville. (ABOVE)

The painted bass drumskin from the album sleeve of
The Beatles' *Sgt. Pepper's Lonely Hearts Club Band*
1967, diameter 76cm (30in)
London £52,100 ($81,276). 15.IX.94

Nothing is known of the whereabouts of this piece between March
1967 and its discovery in the late seventies during the renovation of a
property in the Chelsea/Fulham area of London. Peter Blake, who
was responsible for the sleeve's design and the commissioning of
fairground artist Joe Ephgrave to paint the drumskin, has confirmed
this as the original that appears on the album cover. (RIGHT)

Madonna's personal
1969 Mercedes-
Benz 280SE
New York $56,350 (£35,501).
10.VI.95

In 1968 Daimler-Benz
introduced the new
280S/SE series to replace
the 250SE and 300SE,
setting a new standard
in luxury and comfort.
Featured in Madonna's
1992 video *Deeper and
Deeper*, this sleek
automobile exemplifies
the cosmopolitan style of
the 'mod' decade. (LEFT)

Celluloid from *Cinderella*
1950, WALT DISNEY, 29.2 x 34.3cm (11½ x 13½in)
New York $29,900 (£18,837). 9.VI.95

Cinderella throws her hands up in surprise as her
Fairy Godmother magically dresses her in the
ballgown of her dreams. This trimmed cel on
a watercolour production background is signed
by Walt Disney. (LEFT)

The Circle of Life Continues
1995, WALT DISNEY, SPECIALLY CREATED
FOR THE CATALOGUE COVER
New York $37,375 (£23,920). 10.II.95
Proceeds donated to the National
Audubon Society

The Lion King is the thirty-
second feature-length animated
film produced by the Walt
Disney Studios and is the first to
be based on original source
material and set in a natural
environment populated entirely
by animals, untouched by man.
This specially created artwork
depicts the wise sage Rafiki as he
presents Simba and Nala's cub to
the Pride Lands, while Pumbaa,
Timon and Zazu look on. (RIGHT)

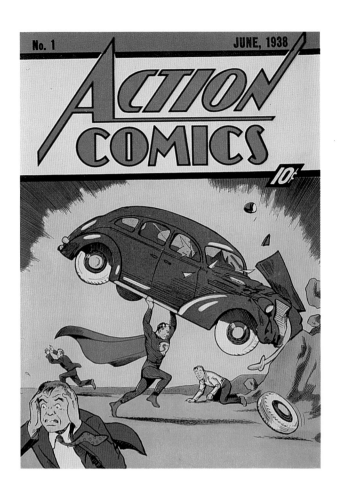

Action Comics No. 1
JUNE 1938, D.C. COMICS
New York $75,100 (£47,313). 17.VI.95

The inaugural edition of *Action Comics* featured the very first appearance of Jerry Siegel and Joe Shuster's legendary creation, Superman. From his 'birth' in 1938 to the present day, Superman has become arguably the most popular fictional character of all time. (LEFT)

The *Gone With The Wind* poster
1939, MGM, 165.1 x 109.8cm (65 x 43in)
New York $71,250 (£45,600). 10.XII.94

In 1939 MGM introduced seven-colour printing for the poster of their greatest epic film, *Gone With The Wind*. This seven-colour version is rare not only for its highly unusual presentation of the leading characters but also because it is the only one of its size known to exist. (RIGHT)

A Huntley & Palmers clockwork double decker biscuit tin
*c.*1929, length 24cm (9½in)
London £4,370 ($6,992). 8.VI.95
From the Scheer Collection

Huntley & Palmers produced a variety of novelty biscuit tins including a cannon, a tug boat, pillar and sentry boxes, a windmill, an Egyptian vase and a crocodile handbag. This version of the 11E bus to Liverpool Street carries Huntley & Palmers advertising throughout and is full of passengers, some conversing, others reading the paper or smoking a pipe. (BELOW)

Beverly Machine Company 1 cent 'Standard Grip Testing Machine' wrist strength tester
*c.*1897, height 145cm (57in)
New York $107,000 (£68,480). 16.IX.94
From the Smith Collection

In the days before radio or television, coin-operated arcade machines provided hours of entertainment. This balancing figure measures the user's strength by extending his brass tongue according to the force applied to the side handles. (ABOVE)

A Märklin *Prinses Juliana* clockwork tinplate liner
GERMANY, *c.*1909, length 73cm (28¾in)
London £36,700 ($58,750). 8.VI.95

Manufactured for the Dutch market this liner is steered by the ship's wheel and has a keywind to a massive spring motor which turns the propellor. Its accessories include twenty-nine passengers at leisure, a waiter bearing a tray and sailors going about their business. (RIGHT)

A carved figural chess set

PROBABLY PARIS, NINETEENTH CENTURY IN SIXTEENTH-CENTURY STYLE, height: the kings 13cm (5⅛in), the pawns 9cm (3½in)
London £29,900 ($47,840). 8.VI.95

European chess sets of this size and quality of carving rarely come onto the auction market. Notable here are the bishops in the form of jesters, one dancing with a fan and the other holding a cup and ball toy, and the kings and queens, carved to represent Henri II and Mary Queen of Scots, Philip II of Spain and Catherine de' Medici. This set appeared in the 1936 French film *La kermesse heroïque*. (LEFT)

J. MICHAEL BROWN
Original artwork for the Life Association of Scotland calendar 1915: Prestwick, the Himalaya Hole 1914

St Andrews £48,800 ($78,080). 15.VII.95

Brown's watercolours for the Life Association calendars portray a host of golfing personalities including Harry Vardon, James Braid, J.H. Taylor and George Duncan, shown here. Historically, these pictures are important since they illustrate that the iron putter was used earlier and more widely than previously thought. (LEFT)

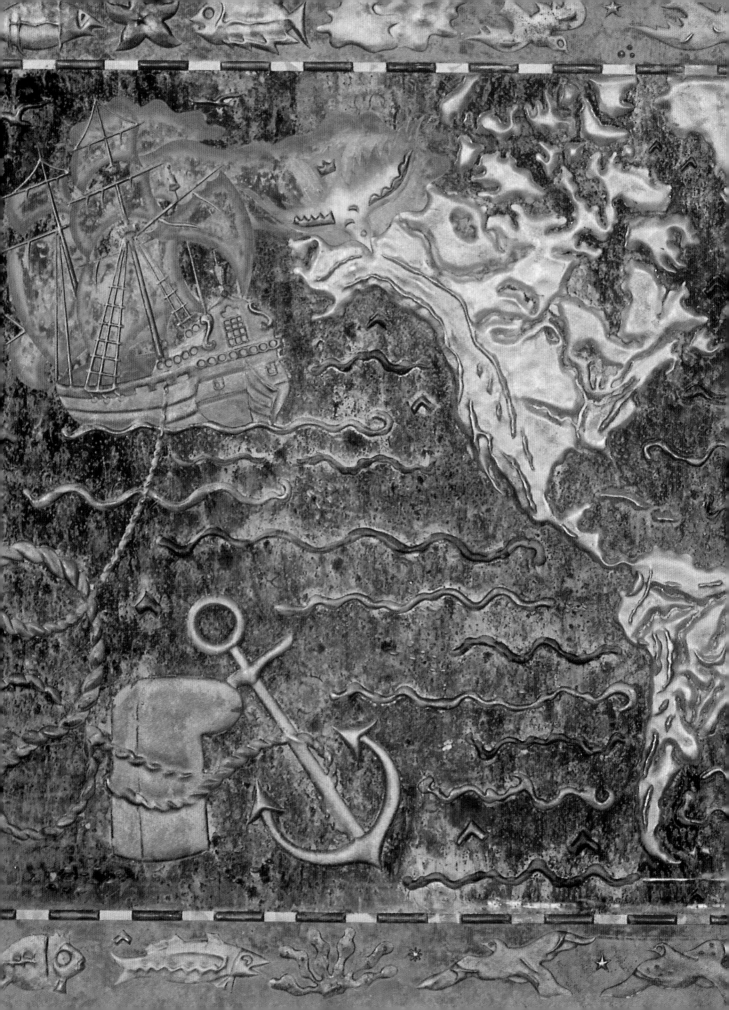

III
Art
at
Large

COLLECTIONS OF THE YEAR *by Ronald Varney*

As the sale events of an auction season whirr past week after week from September to July, unfolding like the chapters of a tightly-plotted suspense novel, the appearance of a collection on the scene is always an occasion of particular fascination. Of course, the sheer variety of collections passing through the saleroom in a typical season is riveting enough, with occasional moments of truly inspired connoisseurship. To prove the point one has only to cite the auction in March of the Haydon-Baillie Collection of Concorde memorabilia, an amazing group comprising artefacts connected with every stage of the fabled aircraft's development since its inception in the 1960s. Highlighted by 110 original technical design drawings, the sale also included such exotica as the fully-working

nose cone of an actual Concorde, surely one of the more surreal items to be knocked down in the London salerooms in recent years.

Apart from this variety in the collections that appear on the market, one is struck also by the style and character of the collectors themselves. Many of these individuals, regrettably, are glimpsed only through a brief biographical preface in the sale catalogue before their collections, often representing a lifelong passion, are dispersed and pass into memory. However, these brief essays tell much. They echo with tales not simply of conquest and acquisition, but also of great tragedy and sacrifice.

In the catalogue for the November sale in Edinburgh of the Iris Fox Collection of Ceramics, for example, one reads that the collector,

A test specimen droop nose section
COMPLETE WITH VISOR AND INTERNAL HYDRAULIC RAMS FOR ITS OPERATION, length 74.7m (24½ft) London £36,700 ($58,720). 16.III.95 From the Concorde Archive, the Haydon-Baillie Naval and Aircraft Museum (LEFT)

born into poverty in the Welsh Valleys, later married Stanley Fox and 'together they endured the pain of losing their only child in an accident'. Later, Iris and her husband moved to Edinburgh and set up a boarding house for students. Although barely able to read or write, Iris nonetheless built up a successful business letting out rooms and flats, and also opened an antique shop. 'How did she acquire her superb collection?' the catalogue essayist asks, answering, 'Primarily by starting to buy Wemyss, Dunmore and other Scottish pottery, long before anyone else recognized its true worth and, secondly, because she was prepared to sacrifice all creature comforts to have funds to pay for acquisitions.'

The Fox sale exceeded all expectations, bringing £458,296, and the proceeds went to local charities.

Though from an altogether different background, Alfred Richet was an equally ardent collector. Born into an affluent Paris family, Richet was the son of a Nobel prizewinner for science and was raised in an environment of enlightenment and sophistication. At home the family entertained such luminaries as Marie Curie, Henri Bergson and Sarah Bernhardt. An early passion for Modern art set Richet on the path to collecting, and in the 1920s he established the Galerie Percier in Paris to promote the work of young contemporary artists. A man of elegance and taste, Richet became enamoured

FERNAND LÉGER
Contrastes de formes
SIGNED WITH INITIALS AND DATED *13*, GOUACHE AND BRUSH AND INDIAN INK ON PAPER, 49.5 x 63cm (19½ x 24¾in)
London £441,500 ($688,740). 29.XI.94
From the Alfred Richet Collection (ABOVE LEFT)

Alfred Richet in his office in Paris, *circa* 1930 (ABOVE RIGHT)

A view of the Bay
Bedroom at Luton Hoo,
Bedfordshire, showing
part of the Holland
suite (ABOVE)

Robert Adam in the eighteenth century and one of England's most famous stately homes. The Luton Hoo Sale, as it came to be known, encompassed superlatives in abundance. As the preface to the lavish catalogue stated, 'The art collection formed by the late Sir Harold Wernher and his father Sir Julius Wernher is among the greatest of its kind assembled in England, remarkable for its range, breadth and quality, and for the fascinating events and personalities which form the background to its genesis and development.' As certain treasures had from time to time passed into other collections, including those of the National Gallery in London and the Kaiser Friedrich Museum in Berlin, a further selection was now being offered, including many works from the private apartments never before seen by the public.

Through its haunting, grainy black and white period photographs of the family and the house, with glorious colour illustrations of the property being sold and extensive story-like notes on each piece, the Luton Hoo catalogue gave one the sensation of a sweeping historical tale like *Buddenbrooks*, in which a great family is examined, only in this case through its possessions rather than its mores. One notable section of this catalogue told the story of the Holland suite, a group of Adam Revival furniture by the royal cabinetmakers Holland & Sons, exhibited at the Universal Exhibition in Paris in 1878 and originally belonging to Sir Richard Wallace. Covering an impressive twenty-three pages, the Holland suite was delightfully illustrated through archival pictures from the original ledgers of Holland & Sons and described in a narrative on its construction and eventual purchase by Sir Julius and Lady Wernher in 1896, who were then 'engaged in furnishing their London residence, Bath House, Piccadilly'.

The Luton Hoo Sale was a triumph, and no doubt the unusual quality and rarity of the items offered, especially those with royal provenance, helped push the sale total above expectations to £4.5 million. Museums battled with collectors and dealers for possession of some of the finest works. The Ulster Museum, for example, succeeded in acquiring the Kildare Toilet

of Cubist painting and sculpture, and with the aid of eminent dealer Daniel-Henry Kahnweiler began forming a collection of works by Picasso, Léger, Gris, Miro and other modern masters.

Richet died in 1992 at the age of 99. While many of the original paintings in the collection had passed into other hands, the remaining core, a radiant group of twenty paintings, drawings and sculpture by several of the artists Richet most admired, were offered at Sotheby's London in November. One of these works, *Contrastes de formes*, 1913, is from a revolutionary series executed by Léger and now acknowledged as his most important contribution to Modern art. Brought together for the last time in the single-owner catalogue, prefaced by an enchanting black and white photograph of Richet on the telephone in his Paris office *circa* 1930, the Richet Collection summoned briefly some of the avante-garde romance of decades past.

In terms of historical resonance, perhaps no other collection sale of the year brought more press attention or stirred more excitement than that in May of property from the Collection of the late Sir Harold Wernher which was housed at Luton Hoo in Bedfordshire, originally built by

Service, a dazzling 28-piece silver-gilt toilet service produced in 1720–22 for the 19th Earl of Kildare, for which they paid £452,528.

On reflection, May 1995 was an extraordinary month for the sale of single-owner collections. In addition to the Luton Hoo Sale in London, three others of note took place in America, each commanding wide attention.

While Sotheby's has offered many corporate collections in its long history, the IBM Collection must be one of the most intriguing in terms of its evolution. In 1937 the Chairman and founder of IBM, Thomas Watson, Sr., hoping to engender goodwill between artists and commerce, began a series of art contests in each of the 79 countries in which IBM conducted business. The best works were exhibited with IBM's most advanced products in the company's Gallery of Science and Art at the 1939 World's Fair in New York. Having thus established a standard of corporate art patronage, IBM continued to acquire works and refine its collection in succeeding decades, expanding its range to include nineteenth- and twentieth-century American art, European art, twentieth-century Mexican art as well as Contemporary art. While the legendary Thomas Watson originally inspired this art patronage (he was particularly fond of the paintings of Grandma Moses), it was the remarkable taste and foresight of the firm's curators and advisers that enabled IBM to build such a formidable collection.

Amid a packed saleroom buzzing with anticipation, the American paintings, drawings and watercolours from the IBM Collection sold for $19.1 million, with many works soaring beyond the high estimates and several artists' records being broken. Frank Benson's luminous portrait of his young daughters, *The Sisters*, brought $4.2 million, while another masterpiece, George Bellows' landscape, *Easter Snow*, sold for $2.9 million, a new record. In the separate auction of Latin American paintings, the results were also stunning, with Frida Kahlo's *Autorretrato con chango y loro* setting a new record for any Latin American work of art of $3.2 million.

While the works in the IBM Collection had been exhibited from time to time over the past fifty years, especially in the company's own

The Arabian bedstead
FROM THE HOLLAND SUITE,
length 216cm (7ft 1in)
London £56,500 ($88,705).
25.V.95
From the Collection of the
Late Sir Harold Wernher,
Luton Hoo (ABOVE)

gallery in New York, that gallery has now closed, the paintings have been dispersed, and so an odyssey of heroic corporate collecting ends.

'Within a period of less than five years,' stated the catalogue introduction to the Donald and Jean Stralem Collection, 'they purchased the works that remained as the core of the collection for the next five decades.' This memorable sale brought an astonishing $65.2 million, the highest total for any single-owner sale in five years and one of the highest of all time.

Angel Fernandez de Soto by Pablo Picasso, one of the last works from the artist's Blue Period which will ever be available for sale, brought $29,152,500, the highest price paid for any painting at auction since 1990, and *La pose Hindoue*, one of the many odalisques Matisse executed in Nice in the 1920s, brought $14,852,500, setting a record for any painting by the artist at auction. Another work by Matisse, *Jeune femme au piano*, dated 1925, fetched $5,502,500, a further dramatic sign of the powerful aura the Stralem Collection cast over its bidders.

As for the collectors themselves, Jean Stralem was born into a family of prominent art patrons. Her grandfather was Philip Lehman, whose

EDWARD BEYER

Churches,
Blacksmith Shop
and College: A
View of Salem of
Virginia in 1855
DATED 1855, OIL ON CANVAS,
72.4 x 121.9cm (28½ x 48in)
Charlottesville, Virginia
$118,000 (£73,160). 26.V.95
From the Collection of Dr and
Mrs Henry P. Deyerle (ABOVE)

collection of early Italian pictures formed the basis of the renowned collection given to the Metropolitan Museum of Art by his son Robert. With her husband Donald, a banker, Mrs Stralem formed a collection of great breadth and quality, represented by such Impressionist and Modern masters as Renoir, Redon, Rouault, Maillol, Matisse, Bonnard and Vuillard. The latter was represented by a group of eight lyrical oil paintings, including the boldly colourful composition *La soirée musicale*, which sold for $1,597,500, double its high estimate.

Discriminating and reserved, the Stralems were of a generation of post-war American collectors actively buying serious pictures, and the appearance of such collections on the market these days raises the highest expectations.

Of the same generation as the Stralems was Dr Henry P. Deyerle, whose distinguished collection of Americana was sold under a tent at the Boar's Head Inn, Charlottesville, Virginia in

late May. As described in the catalogue preface, Dr Deyerle was 'a physician and a surgeon of informed intellect and rare skills, but he also had a prodigious knowledge of objects of everyday life made and used in early America'. In restless pursuit of these objects, and often with his children in tow, Dr Deyerle scoured the state of Virginia, particularly the Shenandoah Valley, in search of the finest examples of spatterware, frakturs, redware, wrought-iron household utensils and firearms, silver and other examples of early Americana. Tenacious as he was at collecting, Dr Deyerle was also, in words of high praise, 'a Virginia gentleman'.

The Deyerle Collection sale established a new auction record of $4.2 million for a sale of Americana. With many new buyers actively competing, the bidding was at times frenzied – perhaps because of the extreme heat of the day – and many works sold for multiples of their estimates. This success was perhaps as much a tribute to the quality, rarity and condition of the works as to the Deyerle provenance, which proved irresistible. For example, the top lot, a paint-decorated pine dower chest, *circa* 1800, that had been estimated at $40,000–60,000, sold for a record $343,500 to the Colonial Williamsburg Foundation.

Easily the most festive and imaginative auction of the year was the Man Ray sale, which took place in March in London and offered from the Estate of Juliet Man Ray works remaining in the artist's studio at 2 bis, rue Férou in Paris, where Juliet and Man Ray lived from 1951 until the artist's death in 1976. Like Man Ray's work – examples that come to mind are the blue painted French baguette on a weighing scale, the palette-shaped wooden table, the ready made flat iron with carrying case and the sensational chess sets – the sale itself was entertaining and fun.

Man Ray's bizarre but fertile imagination was vividly evident in the breathtaking range of paintings, objects, photographs, drawings and lithographs offered, comprising nearly 600 works. Since his work is so widely dispersed in public and private collections throughout the world, and thus not easily studied *en suite*, the sale – and specifically the catalogue – present-ed an extraordinary opportunity for collectors to view works in every medium spanning the artist's entire career.

After a reception and dinner held in the spirit of Surrealism, the sale was an occasion for pitched bidding battles as work after work sold for prices well beyond their pre-sale estimates. Of particular note was *Le beau temps*, a very large and complex allegorical work painted on the eve of World War II which, in Man Ray's words, 'constituted the climax of my Surrealist period'. The painting, which Man Ray kept with him until his death, brought £529,500, a record for the artist. The final result of the sale, with 594 lots sold, delighted everyone.

No other sale this century has offered such a panoramic statement of a single artist's work. Perhaps for this very reason, the Man Ray catalogue, a stylish and treasure-packed encyclopedia, was received as a work of art itself. And quickly vanished.

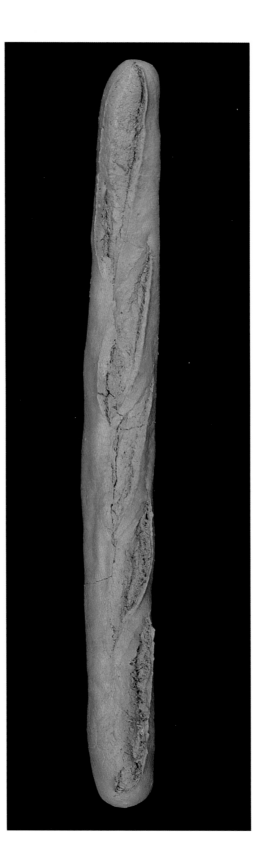

MAN RAY

Pain peint – Blue Bred: Favorite Food for Blue Birds (detail)

BLUE PAINTED FRENCH BAGUETTE PRESENTED ON AN IRON WEIGHING SCALE, length: baguette 73cm (28¾in), scales 47cm (18½in)
London £27,600 ($43,884). 23.III.95
From the Estate of Juliet Man Ray, the Man Ray Trust and the Family of Juliet Man Ray
(LEFT)

A TENDENCY TO SELF-DESTRUCTION

THE PRESERVATION OF TAPESTRIES *by Mette de Hamel*

From the Middle Ages, tapestries have played a significant role in the domestic interiors of people of property and wealth. Initially serving the very real purpose of providing insulation and warmth in what must have been draughty and cold halls and castles, they soon became status symbols, displaying images of victories and possessions which echoed the powerful positions or aspirations of their owners. Their value and visual impact made tapestries appropriate diplomatic gifts, and for centuries they have been used not only as magnificent decoration but also as symbols of state, power and wealth.

Tapestries are, by their very nature, especially vulnerable to damage. A most unusual disaster occurred to Charles V of France in 1352 when one of his tapestries hanging in the Hôtel St Paul was torn by an escaped bear. More usual was the damage caused by frequent moving and rehanging as medieval kings and princes kept peripatetic courts, endlessly on the move from castle to castle, and needing the instantaneous comfort bestowed by their decorative wall hangings.

Sections of tapestries woven in silk are often the first to deteriorate; here many hands point to such an area at the Chevalier workshop in France. (LEFT)

After initial tests to prove that it is safe to wet-clean, a tapestry is immersed in softened water in a custom-built tank at the Textile Conservation Centre, Hampton Court Palace. Once cleaned, it is then rinsed in de-ionized water and left to dry on a mesh support which allows air to pass all around it. (BELOW)

One of the conservators at the Textile Conservation Centre, Hampton Court Palace, carrying out extremely skilled and time consuming warp couching. A linen support fabric is placed beneath the areas of damage, then couching threads in matching colours are stitched over the original warps. (RIGHT)

This detail illustrates the visual improvement achieved by replacing crude and stretched slit-stitching. The new stitches to the left of the line are virtually invisible. (FAR RIGHT)

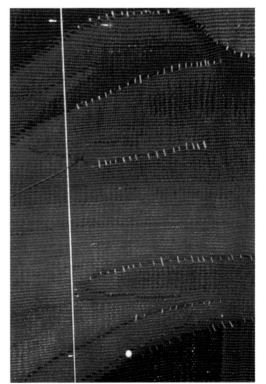

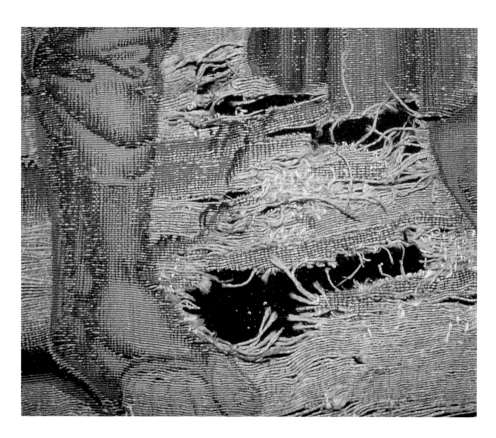

A severely damaged area, shown before and after restoration, from *The History of Moses*, a tapestry series woven in Brussels around 1535–40. The light-coloured uneven stitching visible near the holes (ABOVE) demonstrates how even temporary mending has helped to save, at least for a while, part of an old tapestry.

The same area after careful restoration (ABOVE RIGHT). This work was carried out by the Belgian conservation firm of Gaspard De Wit.

Sometimes the tapestries had to be folded or cut to fit new spaces. They were hung on bars with rings or hooks or were attached by nails or by whatever means available, and this constant use and adaptation took its toll. Light – especially sunlight – can cause severe damage, not only in the fading of the colours but in the actual breakdown of the fibres.

A little knowledge of the means of making tapestries will explain this tendency to self-destruction. A tapestry is woven on a loom. The loom is usually strung vertically with threads generally of wool or cotton known as warps. At right angles to these threads the design is woven across the warp in wool and silk known as the weft. Because tapestries tend to be oblong in shape, it is simplest to turn the whole design around so that the narrower side forms the width and then to weave the weft horizontally across it, row by row, longer and longer, until the tapestry reaches its final extent. When the design is complete and turned the right way up to be hung, it is actually supported by the weft rather than the warp. As a result a tapestry tends to hang from the weaker wool and silk threads rather than from the much stronger wool threads. As tapestries can be very heavy, this presents a constant risk.

A second in-built problem for any tapestry is created by the dyes which were used for colouring the wools and silks. Many early dyes, such as the dark brown, were fixed to the wools by an iron-based mordant used in the dyeing process. Inevitably, the metallic elements tend to oxidize and the fibres themselves break down. In later tapestries especially, it is all too common to find that the areas woven in silk have simply fallen out as pale-coloured dust.

For the owner of an ancient tapestry today, the fraught question of safe-keeping and preservation is a crucial one. There are many contrasting approaches to the whole business of preserving tapestries, and conservators (in the same way as dentists, plumbers and hairdressers) often vigorously disagree with each other's techniques and

fundamental ethics. Frequently the differences come down to a question of deciding between conservation, which simply arrests further damage or decay, and restoration, which helps recreate the original appearance of the tapestry before it became damaged.

At the risk of over-simplification, the European tradition has generally been for restoration whereas the English and American (and Swiss) approach has preferred conservation. Tapestries need constant maintenance and repair from the moment they are made. In the past this was usually carried out by the tapestry manufacturers themselves. The great European tapestry centres such as Arras, Tournai, Brussels and others, have been in business since at least the fourteenth century and from the seventeenth century onwards tapestry-making in France was taken under royal patronage at Gobelins and Beauvais. Therefore it has always been quite natural to return a tapestry to a weaving workshop when it has become damaged, and one can often detect areas which have

been completely removed and reconstructed using the original weaving techniques, with the insertion of new warps. Results can be very skilfully achieved. If a weaving workshop was not easily accessible, continental owners of tapestries would sometimes have the repairs stitched by hand, but always with the aim of recreating the original design. Frequently, the only obvious sign of re-weaving of patches of a tapestry is a difference of dye batches used for the silk, and this may become increasingly obvious with the passage of time, since the old and new colours will probably not fade at precisely the same rate.

In England, however, tapestry production was historically very different. Although England was the major wool supplier in the Middle Ages, very little actual tapestry weaving took place before the establishment of the Mortlake factory in 1619, and very little after the closure of that workshop by agreement of Queen Anne in 1703. Repairs to tapestries have often been a much more amateur and ad hoc business of salvage rather than restoration. A good example occured in a tapestry from an English collection recently worked on by the Textile Restoration Studio in Cheshire: on the back could be seen patches of early seventeenth-century damask, eighteenth-century mattress ticking, nineteenth-century William Morris fabric and early twentieth-century cotton lining. The whole history of English textile manufacture is here, and although it bears no relation to tapestry technique, it has saved the tapestry from utter ruin.

Even the modern and entirely international world of conservation reflects the differences between these two styles. Art conservation, as a professional post-graduate academic subject, has mostly evolved since the Second World War. In England, the Victoria & Albert Museum led the way in addressing questions of the safe-keeping and display of their own very important holdings of historical textiles, and textile conservation has been studied at the Museum since the 1950s. In 1975 the Textile Conservation Centre was established at Hampton Court Palace, a pleasing coincidence of site since the builder of the palace, Cardinal Wolsey, owned what was then the largest collection of tapestries in England. The Textile Conservation Centre has become one of

The shelves behind the conservators at the Gaspard De Wit studios contain wools and silks in the multitude of shades necessary to find a perfect colour match.
(ABOVE)

the world's leading locations for teaching, research and practice in its subject, and offers a three-year post-graduate course, affiliated to the Courtauld Institute at London University. It also undertakes private commissions to conserve textiles including tapestries. As the Centre receives financial support from cultural foundations, it is able to pursue research independently from exclusively commercial motives, and its work is consistently of the highest quality.

Similar research is undertaken at the Abbegg Stiftung, established in 1967 near Bern, Switzerland, to house what was at that time the private collection of textiles and tapestries assembled by

Werner Abbegg. The studios of the Abbegg Stiftung are now among the most advanced and sophisticated and they have exerted a great influence regarding approaches to conservation.

In North America, too, tapestry conservation follows a pattern first established in Britain. The University of Delaware and the Winterthur Museum, for example, offer a three-year Master of Science degree course in textile conservation taught by Linda Eaton who herself trained at the Textile Conservation Centre, Hampton Court Palace. Some museums in America adopt a policy of major re-weaving of damaged areas – even in the Metropolitan Museum of Art, New York, there are examples where such work has been judged appropriate – whilst others prefer to follow a rigorous policy of purist conservation.

The difference is partly a matter of ethics and partly of practical commonsense. While the old tapestry-weaving centres of France and the Netherlands have regarded traditional restoration as a living art, like, perhaps, house restoration or car maintenance, the newer approaches pioneered in England and Switzerland in the 1960s and 1970s have adopted the policy of minimum interference. Instead of reconstructing lost pieces, the intention would be not to re-create or to re-weave, but simply to make safe whatever remains of the original. The aim has become one of slowing down the inevitable process of deterioration; this is indeed conservation. Recent research into the nature of ancient dyes allows us to reproduce almost exactly the colour tones of the original yarns, but in fact modern synthetic dyes are more stable and can be matched to the shade of the original, even to its state of fading. If a substantial part of an old tapestry is missing, a conservator would prefer to create a detachable patch behind the hole, blended to the exact colours, without actual re-weaving. A conserved tapestry therefore gives a complete effect without attempting to deceive or to interfere with the structure of the original. This technique has had a universal influence on the conservation of tapestries.

Today, the whole range of techniques and styles of conservation are available to owners and collectors of tapestries. Neither full restoration nor minimal conservation is necessarily correct in every case. The size and location of the tapestry, its historical and indeed commercial value, and plans for display, if any, will all influence the final decision. Conservation can be considerably less expensive than full restoration, and an owner can delight in knowing that the tapestry has been saved with integrity. But other owners, like the princes of the Middle Ages, may prefer to spend more to have a tapestry totally restored to the glowing splendour with which it once overlooked the courts of Europe. A careful middle path will often be the wisest course, but art collecting has never been motivated only by wisdom, and let taste and the pleasure of ownership guide us, too.

The labour-intensive work of conservation and restoration (shown here at the Chevalier workshop) is inevitably expensive. Whether a tapestry is more or less valuable, the number of hours involved in its preservation will be the same. (ABOVE)

The ad hoc business of patching is demonstrated by this ill-matching kelim patch found on a tapestry worked on at the Textile Restoration Studio, Cheshire. (LEFT)

WINNING THE LOTTERY *by Philip Hook*

PABLO PICASSO
Le repas frugal
ETCHING, 1905, FROM AN
EDITION OF 250 PUBLISHED BY
VOLLARD, 1913, 63.1 x 49.4cm
(24¾ x 19½in)
London £67,500 ($107,325)
2.XII.94 (BELOW)

The front counter at Sotheby's is a place where dreams are dreamed. It is the playground and, more frequently, the final resting place of the most extravagant fantasies of owners of works of art. People arrive clutching plastic bags the contents of which have already been earmarked for paying off the mortgage, endowing a pension fund, or financing a month's holiday in the Bahamas. In most cases, the verdict – broken gently, with consummate tact,

by the expert concerned – will permit only the purchase of a cheap day return to Brighton. But just occasionally the visit to Sotheby's is as good as the winning lottery ticket.

Take the case of the two sisters who early in 1994 went to a car boot sale in the London area. In amongst the second-hand hairdriers and the cracked pots, one of them noticed a print that quite appealed to her. She was told the price was £5, which struck her as a bit steep. She offered £3 and was turned down. Just before they left, the other sister went back and bought the print for the full asking price. It depicted a man and a woman sitting at a table in front of the remains of a threadbare meal. 'I liked it,' she said. 'It didn't have a frame, but I stuck it up in my kitchen with Blu-tack. After a while, I began to find it a bit depressing,' added the buyer. 'Their faces looked sad.' So one day she took it down and, just to check, she brought it into Sotheby's. Now the dream came true: the £5 print was swiftly identified as a good impression of Picasso's 1905 etching *Le repas frugal*. On 2 December 1994 it was included in the major Modern Prints sale and fetched £67,500. The reaction of the sister who had offered only £3 for it is not recorded.

Prints constitute an area in which connoisseurship and specialist knowledge are all-important. Distinguishing between early and late impressions, and knowing what to look for on plate marks are skills which can only be acquired after many years' experience. This is therefore a particularly fertile field for discoveries. A wonderful example was the cache of Old Master prints, forgotten for many years in a trunk among nesting mice, which were found by a Thames Valley man while clearing his outhouse. He took them to Clive Stewart-Lockhart of Newbury auctioneers Drewatt Neate who immediately recognized their importance and, as Old Master prints are such a specialized field, decided to contact Richard

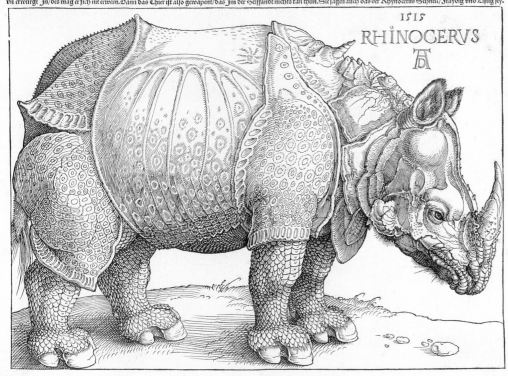

Nach Chriſtus gepurt.1513. Jar.Adi.j.May. Hat man dem groſmechtigen Kunig von Portugall Emanuell gen Lyſabona pracht auß India/ein ſollich lebendig Thier. Das nennen ſie Rhinocerus.Das iſt hye mit aller ſeiner geſtalt Abconderfet.Es hat ein farb wie ein geſprecklete Schildtkrot.Vnd iſt võ dicken Schalen vberlegt faſt feſt.Vnd iſt in der gröſ als der Helffandt Aber nyderdrechtiger von paynen/vnd faſt weerhafftig.Es hat ein ſcharff ſtarck Horn voin auff der naſen/Das begyndt es albeg zu werzen wo es bey ſtaynen iſt.Das doſig Thier iſt des Helffants todt feyndt.Der Helffandt furcht es faſt vbel/dann wo es Jn ankumbt/ſo laufft Jm das Thier mit dem kopff zwiſchen dye fordern payn/vnd reyſt den Helffandt vnden am pauch auff vñ erwürgt Jn/des mag er ſich nit erweren.Dann das Thier iſt alſo gewapent/das Jn der Helffandt nichts kan thun.Sie ſagen auch das der Rhynocerus Schnell/ Fraydig vnd Liſtig ſey.

1515
RHINOCERVS

Godfrey, Sotheby's Old Master prints expert in London, for advice. Richard Godfrey was highly impressed: the prints were the finest woodcuts he had seen for very many years. He explained, 'In an age when so many prints have been cleaned and spoiled, the "benign neglect" suffered by these prints in the trunk has preserved them in an almost perfect condition.'

Two of the prints were by Albrecht Dürer, *The Rhinoceros* and *Samson Rending the Lion*. Both were comparable in quality and in even better condition than the best examples of the same images in the British Museum. A third was a fine impression of a scarce print of *The Alphabet: Letter E*, by the artist known simply as The Master E.S. They had been stored in one of a dozen old wooden trunks left over from the clearance of a relative's house twenty years ago. According to the owner, its contents had been undisturbed for 100 years or more. He described what happened

JOSEPH MALLORD
WILLIAM TURNER
Sisteron, France
PEN, INK, WATERCOLOUR AND
BODYCOLOUR OVER PENCIL
ON BUFF PAPER,
14 x 19cm (5½ x 7½in)
London £29,900 ($47,840).
10.XI.94 (ABOVE)

when he first opened the trunk: 'Low value books had been chucked about on top and mice had chewed an album of airs from Mozart operas into two beautiful cup-shaped nests. The occupants had vanished but I had the feeling they weren't far away. The prints were wrapped in some rather high-class greaseproof paper inside old marbled folders. I decided to take them to the local auctioneers for advice.'

Mr Stewart-Lockhart said, 'I was thankful that the mice who had started on Mozart had not had Dürer for pudding!' In the end, *The Alphabet: Letter E* fetched £98,300, *The Rhinoceros*

£111,500, and *Samson Rending the Lion* a glorious £199,500. If the mice had got to them, it would have been an expensive meal.

Many people fantasize that the unidentified watercolour on their drawing-room wall will turn out to be a Turner. Last year the dream came true for a Yorkshire couple when John Phillips of Sotheby's Harrogate office visited their home on the outskirts of Sheffield to value their collection. One of the pictures he looked at was a tiny watercolour of a view in the Rhone Valley in France measuring 14 x 19cm (5½ x 7½in). 'They were almost rather embarrassed when they took me

DIEGO RIVERA
Couteau et fruit
devant la fenêtre
Signed and dated *Octe 1917*,
OIL ON CANVAS,
91.8 x 92.4cm (36⅛ x 36⅜in)
New York $2,202,500
(£1,387,575). 15.XI.94
(Left)

into their sitting-room to show me the picture,'
said John Phillips. 'The mount claimed it was by
Turner but they always thought it was a copy, in
fact it had become a family joke and was always
referred to as "the Turner"! They were extremely
surprised when I said it could very well be by the
artist and I sent photographs to my colleagues in
London to have the watercolour investigated.'

Research by Henry Wemyss, head of Sotheby's
British watercolour department, led him to
an article written about a nineteenth-century collection of Turner watercolours belonging to the
Victorian artist Myles Birket Foster. The article
was illustrated with sepia photographs taken
in the 1860s, one of which showed the Turner
owned by the Yorkshire couple. The watercolour
had last been seen in 1894 when it was included
in an auction. The view was identified as Sisteron
in France and dated from Turner's tour of
the area in 1836. In the end the 'Turner' that
really was a Turner, estimated at £12–18,000,
came up for auction on 10 November 1994
and fetched £29,900.

The case of the still life by Diego Rivera sold
in Sotheby's New York the same month was a
different sort of discovery. Rivera is the most

TOMMASO DI CRISTOFANO DI FINO, CALLED MASOLINO DA PANICALE
A Prophet or Evangelist
SHAPED TOP, GOLD GROUND, TEMPERA ON PANEL, 21.9 x 15.6cm (8⅝ x 6⅛in)
New York $299,500 (£191,680). 19.V.95 (ABOVE)

famous Mexican painter of this century, and was working in Paris with other major masters of the Modern Movement when *Couteau et fruit devant la fenêtre* was painted in 1917.

Dr Ramón Favela, the expert on Rivera who is preparing the artist's *catalogue raisonné*, had been aware of the existence of this crucial work for a long time, but had no idea of its whereabouts. In Dr Favela's words, 'The significance of this transitional painting for Rivera and for his *oeuvre* is that it is one of the earliest recorded works from the period when he "left Cubism" and entered into a thorough and rigorous study of his adopted French mentor, Cézanne, and post-Cubist Curvilinear Perspective. The still life was set up and painted from his studio window on the rue du Départ looking out on the decidedly Delaunay-like rooftops of Paris. On a more personal and even sentimental note, this transitional and experimental painting was completed in Rivera's Parisian studio, signed and dated on Wednesday 31 October 1917, three days after his first and only son (from his relationship with the Russian artist Angelina Beloff) had died from consumption in wartime Paris. That in itself makes this painting something of a rare human and psychological testament as well as a visual record of a key moment in an artist's career.'

Sotheby's Latin American department had traced the picture to a Sotheby's sale in New York on 1 November 1946, but there were no clues as to what had happened to it since. Then, out of the blue, it was consigned for auction at Sotheby's. It transpired that the seller was the same buyer of 48 years earlier, who had been quietly enjoying the painting on his wall for the best part of half a century. The conclusion to the story was that the re-emerged picture attracted enormous interest and against an estimate of $400–600,000 fetched $2.2 million.

From a twentieth-century Mexican to an early fifteenth-century Italian. In January 1995 a Connecticut woman sent slides of her painting of a prophet to the New York Old Master department. She imagined that the tiny 21.9 x 15.6cm (8⅝ x 6⅛in) panel might be Italian, and was aware that it had been in her family for generations, but beyond that she knew nothing more about it. The department were very excited, and when the owner brought the original in, they were able to identify it as an extraordinarily rare early work by Masolino da Panicale (*c.*1383–1436). Masolino was an associate of Masaccio, which links him to the very dawn of Italian Renaissance painting. Discoveries like all those mentioned so far tend to strike buyers as especially desirable: their years of 'neglect' endow them with a freshness which the market finds highly appealing. After considerable competition the Masolino, estimated at $50–70,000, fetched $299,500.

Some art discoveries in Britain are witnessed by millions. I am thinking of those made on the very successful BBC TV programme *The Antiques Roadshow.* I have been appearing on this programme for a number of years, and can vouch for the fact that discoveries – the more dramatic the better – are the lifeblood of the show. In the ideal scenario an innocent owner is amazed when the battered picture which he or she has just pulled out of a supermarket carrier bag is identified by the expert as a masterpiece. For the best television, the owner should then proceed to faint or burst into tears of joy. Unfortunately, the British are notoriously reluctant to reveal their emotions publicly and this national restraint is a constant source of frustration to the producer. It is no coincidence that the best reaction I have ever had on camera was from an American. I had just told him that his picture should be insured for £50,000. Having thought that it might be worth a few hundred, he turned exultantly to a little old lady standing in the crowd behind him and exclaimed: 'Want to marry me now?'

The couple who brought their Edwardian genre painting into the Colchester *Antiques Roadshow* in May 1994 had similarly modest expectations. Painted by Arthur Elsley, it depicted two children and a dog playing in a manner calculated to pluck at the sentimental spectator's heartstrings. My colleague and I felt it was extremely commercial. When the news was broken that it might be worth £25–40,000, they were suitably flabbergasted (although, being British, no random proposals of marriage ensued).

Subsequently, the happy owners decided to sell their Elsley. Very properly, *The Antiques Roadshow* has a policy of offering no guidance to

its participants as to selling procedure. Therefore it was entirely the owners' independent decision when they brought the painting into Sotheby's for inclusion in the November 1994 Victorian Pictures auction. It is inevitably an anxious moment when a valuation which has been beamed into millions of homes round the country is finally put to the test of the market. Thus there was enormous relief all round when the picture fetched £48,800. A happy ending: and it is one of the pleasures of the art market that there will doubtless be many more of them for Sotheby's to report next year, too.

ARTHUR JOHN ELSLEY
You Daresn't
SIGNED AND DATED *ARTHUR J. ELSLEY/1905*, OIL ON CANVAS, 90 x 64.5cm (35½ x 25¼in)
London £48,800 ($80,032).
2.XI.94 (ABOVE)

SAN SIMEON: THE DIVERSE COLLECTION OF

WILLIAM RANDOLPH HEARST *by Jana Seely*

William Randolph
Hearst. (ABOVE)

On arches spanning the room that was once William Randolph Hearst's private study, painted characters enact scenes from folk tales and the Bible. A collection of Gothic and Renaissance sculptures and religious objects is displayed on a ledge below the clerestory windows: the Spanish polychrome reliquary bust of a saint occupies the space adjacent to a stone Madonna and Child from France, which in turn stands next to one of a pair of fifteenth-century Italian rooster-shaped iron brackets. Bookcases filled with volumes, many signed by their authors, line the walls. Display cabinets contain vessels made from silver, ivory, and maiolica: monstrance, tankard, cup, drinking horn. A sixteenth-century French mantelpiece

flanked by Gothic limestone arches covers the greater part of a wall. Examples of the decorative arts are evident everywhere: an elaborate Augsburg clock, brass candlesticks, iron lecterns, Persian carpets. And on a table in the centre of the room rests a newspaper.

The key location given to this otherwise unremarkable object is fitting, for the room in which this newspaper is to be found, the Gothic study, was the hub of William Randolph Hearst's publishing empire when he was at the San Simeon estate he called 'the ranch', in the Santa Lucia Mountains of California's Central Coast. Construction of Hearst Castle, as it is known, began in 1919 on the 'Camp Hill' site of Hearst's childhood family camping trips. The family fortune, amassed by father George Hearst through silver mining and subsequent investments, was inherited by William Randolph Hearst from his mother Phoebe Apperson Hearst on her death in the influenza epidemic of 1919, and provided the financial backing for the venture. The continually-evolving design of the estate was the result of a collaborative effort between Hearst and École des Beaux-Arts-trained architect Julia Morgan until work finally ceased in 1947.

Almost three decades of building, with innumerable changes along the way, produced an imposing main house and three smaller guest houses in the Mediterranean Revival style of architecture, combining both Spanish and Italian elements. Set among plants and trees also in the Mediterranean vernacular, the remarkable hilltop estate resembles a European village with the towered main house positioned as the central cathedral and the three surrounding guest houses as the other village buildings.

Julia Morgan had encountered the structures that inspired her designs for the San Simeon estate in the course of her travels, especially through Spain and Italy. Another source for the

estate's overall tone can perhaps be found in the international expositions that took place in the United States around the turn of the century. The popularity of these World's Fairs demonstrated a growing American interest in all things cultural and international. In particular, The Panama Pacific International Exposition in San Francisco in 1915, which Hearst helped finance, may have influenced his plan for San Simeon. There was, at this celebration of the opening of the Panama Canal, a preponderance of Spanish-Moorish architecture.

The same style comes through clearly in the architecture and the art of Hearst Castle. The buildings' exteriors and interiors were made up from different antique elements, mostly Spanish and Italian, augmented with work by Hearst craftsmen. This integration of antique and modern produced a unique result. Although used in a new way, these historically-rich artefacts of art and architecture formed a tangible link with the past traditions of Europe.

Striving for such a link was a common theme among newly wealthy American connoisseurs in the late nineteenth and early twentieth centuries. The prestige associated with the acquisition of art has been an established fact since ancient times. Turn-of-the-century millionaires built mansions which housed and enhanced the status of their possessions. J.P. Morgan, Isabella Stewart Gardner and Andrew Mellon acquired works of art that were destined to become the core of the

William Randolph Hearst's Gothic study.
(ABOVE)

The façade of the main house at San Simeon is embellished with antique
elements supplemented by the work of Hearst's craftsmen. (ABOVE)

major art museums in the USA. Many pieces
were probably acquired with an eye to eventual
incorporation into a museum environment, with
more than a passing consideration for long-term
preservation, protection and ultimate public display.

Although William Randolph Hearst also provided a considerable amount of art for museums
in the United States, through donation or sale,
the San Simeon collection as a whole is intact, *in
situ*, as it was at the time of Hearst's residence.
There is a vast quantity of fine and decorative art,
representing numerous cultures and spanning
centuries and continents. Everything was purchased with the intention that it was to be used
and enjoyed. Hearst was a voracious collector
with diverse interests and areas of acquisition. He
bought from the same dealers and auction houses
as the other great contemporary collectors, but he
bought more. There was frequently fierce competition for the same pieces of art, but Hearst
bought eclectically and in quantity. A contribut-
ing factor in the expansiveness of his buying
strategy may have been that he had so many residences to furnish. Different Hearst properties
exhibited different characters and called for a
wide variety of furnishings: Wyntoon, a village of
Bavarian chalets in northern California, received
much of the Germanic collection; silver was often
destined for St Donat's, Hearst's fourteenth-
century castle in Wales, and at San Simeon the
focus was on Spanish and Italian works.

William Randolph Hearst's penchant for collecting began at the age of ten on a European visit
with his mother Phoebe Apperson Hearst in
1873. On this journey, he bought many small
items such as coins, stamps, beer steins and
porcelains. It was during this same trip that
young Hearst asked his mother to purchase the
Louvre. Phoebe Hearst was also a collector and
connoisseur of art and undoubtedly influenced
her son who, in his thirties, began collecting in
earnest, poring over auction catalogues, taking
extended trips abroad and spending lavish sums
of money. He collected not only fine and decorative arts, but also gathered manuscripts, rare
books and autographs into his possession.
Hearst's connection to the printed word was earlier
demonstrated when, at the age of twenty-three,

he became both publisher and editor of the San Francisco *Examiner*, owned by his father George Hearst. William Randolph Hearst turned the faltering newspaper around and went on to purchase other papers in major American cities. He also bought or founded numerous magazines. And again Hearst went on to expand his communications empire by embarking on the production of newsreels and, ultimately, feature films.

This Hollywood connection further highlights the fact that the San Simeon estate was a weekend Mecca not only for members of the movie-making community, but also for other visitors who included assorted celebrities, politicians, writers and athletes. All the guests at San Simeon occupied rooms furnished with the works of art accumulated by Hearst. They slept in sixteenth-century beds, kept their clothes in seventeenth-century chests-of-drawers and watched fires burning beneath five-hundred-year-old mantels. In a *Newsweek* interview of 6 May 1946, when asked if his pleasure in the art treasures he had acquired equalled the amount of money he had spent on them, Hearst replied that the enjoyment he received was only second in importance to the enjoyment others obtained from them.

The dining hall. Choirstalls and tapestries cover the walls, banners hang overhead and silver candlesticks and serving dishes decorate long refectory tables. (ABOVE)

The Sekhmet fountain, designed by architect Julia Morgan, incorporates four Egyptian sculptures of the lion-faced goddess dating from between the sixteenth and thirteenth centuries BC. (ABOVE)

One of the ways William Randolph Hearst ensured others' enjoyment of art was by enlivening mundane domestic items with antique components; Hearst residences were furnished not only with fine antique mantels, but also with antique fireplace equipment such as andirons, pokers and grates. Wrought-iron candlestands were transformed into floor lamps, marble columns were used as sculpture pedestals, iron grilles protected windows and architectural elements such as ceilings were frequently incorporated into the very fabric of the building, often augmented, sometimes altered, by the work of Hearst craftsmen.

This intense interest in a wide range of objects not traditionally sought by the other great collectors is one of the factors that sets William Randolph Hearst apart and contributes to his reputation as something of a maverick. His purchases included doorknockers, warming pans, tile stoves, musical instruments, pipes and lanterns in addition to mainstream art such as paintings, sculpture, tapestries and silver.

Many of these more traditional art forms are very fine indeed. A collection of 155 Greek pots encircles the room on the cornice of the Hearst Castle library. Classical sarcophagi border the esplanade that curves its way through the gardens. Four Egyptian sculptures of the lion-faced goddess Sekhmet comprise an exterior fountain designed by Julia Morgan. Limestone, marble, granite and bronze sculptures dating from the sixteenth century BC to the twentieth century AD embellish the gardens and building exteriors.

Inside, these same materials, with the addition of wood which is sometimes polychromed or gilded, are the media that constitute the sculpture in the collection. Bronze river gods recline on tables while marble lions crouch on shelves and stairways. Various saints inhabit the rooms of Hearst Castle along with figure groups depicting the Madonna and Child and the Holy Family.

Religious themes abound at San Simeon in paintings as well as sculpture. This is attributable not to any special piety, but is simply because the majority of Spanish and Italian Renaissance art, which forms the bulk of the collection, has a devotional theme. The Madonna and Child *motif* is the most prevalent, the earliest example being a fourteenth-century work attributed to the School of Duccio di Buoninsegna. Diptychs and altarpieces from northern and southern Europe decorate several rooms.

Non-devotional themes are also important components of the collection. Later paintings include a number of royal portraits by Franz Xaver Winterhalter and Napoleonic scenes by Jean Léon Gérôme, and elaborately painted ceilings add interest and diversity.

The high quality of the fine art at San Simeon is echoed by the magnificent collection of textiles. Oriental carpets, many inherited from Hearst's mother, cover floors and are used as decorative hangings. Renaissance vestments – copes and chasubles – adorn the walls. Altar frontals are displayed hanging above fireplaces, beds and other large pieces of furniture.

It is perhaps in the furniture collection, mostly sixteenth- and seventeenth-century Spanish and Italian, that the extent of William Randolph Hearst's buying fervour is most apparent. The size of the estate necessitated the purchase of large numbers of objects to furnish all the rooms: chairs, tables, beds, chests, chests-of-drawers, armoires. As a result there are numerous examples of many types of objects. Instead of the four or five seventeenth-century Spanish tables which might be found in many museums, at San Simeon there are forty-five, along with comparable numbers of chairs and chests. This multiplicity has proved an invaluable resource for research into manufacturing techniques and design.

Almost as notable as the Hearst collection that remains at San Simeon are the possessions from various Hearst sources which were dispersed through auctions and private sales beginning in 1937 as a result of Hearst's financial crisis amplified by the Depression. Remarkably, many of these items were put on sale to the general public through the Gimbel Brothers department store in New York and by the end of the first year at least $11 million had been generated. The 1941 catalogue for this sale graphically illustrates the enormous diversity and the eclectic nature of Hearst's collecting habits. An incredible array of about 20,000 objects was on offer: paintings by van Dyck, croziers, chalices, Charles Dickens' sideboard, pulpits, stained glass, arms and armour, mirrors, firescreens, George Washington's waistcoat and Thomas Jefferson's Bible.

Diversity is still the hallmark of Hearst Castle. A Lalique frosted glass bottle shares a room in the Doge's suite with a sixteenth-century Italian maiolica inkwell in the shape of St George, and a black granite Egyptian sculpture dating from between the fourth and the first century BC. But high quality examples of fine and decorative arts can be encountered in every room, clearly demonstrating Hearst's philosophy that art should be used and enjoyed.

In 1958, Hearst Castle was given to the State of California by the Hearst Corporation. It is today administered by California State Parks as an historic house museum, fulfilling the estate's potential envisioned by William Randolph Hearst when, as early as 1927, he made the statement: 'I see no reason why the ranch should not be a museum of the best things that I can secure.'

The Lucanian Panathenaic amphora in the library dates from the early fourth century BC and was decorated by the Amykos Painter. It was purchased by William Randolph Hearst through Sotheby's in 1920.
(ABOVE)

THE NEW GRAND TOUR: VENICE

by Dr Bruna Caruso Cherubini

Arriving in Venice remains a uniquely compelling experience. (ABOVE)

For every young gentleman in the late eighteenth century, the journey across the lagoon to Venice was an obligatory part of the Grand Tour. This long pilgrimage of instruction was meant to complete a young man's education, giving him the opportunity to experience a variety of different countries and their cultures. In a boat laden with luggage and servants, young men, accompanied by their tutor, would cross the lagoon, transfixed. Rising out of the sea and silhouetted against the sky, Venice was uniquely alluring – a city shrouded in myth and exuding an atmosphere of sophistication.

Despite declining political and military power, the unrivalled artistic and architectural treasures of *la Serenissima* bore witness to a thousand years of history. Though the very survival of the republic was under threat, the Venetians were proud of their independence and cultural heritage. Life for most of them, and for the many foreigners living in the city, was one of unrestrained pleasure.

Indeed, Venice had gained the reputation of being the most lively and frivolous capital city in Europe: parties were thrown in aristocratic mansions where ladies would parade their latest suitors and men indulge an uncontrollable passion for gambling, elegant receptions were held in convent parlours and the numerous cafés became meeting places for artists and courtesans alike. Magnificent public festivities took place regularly throughout the year. These lavish ceremonies and colourful regattas were intended to honour the republic's former glory and create an atmosphere of permanent celebration. On 26 December, the long Carnival began and with it the opportunity to appear publicly in costume. This was the most extravagant celebration of the year, highlighting the Venetians' free-spirited nature and their love of games and pretence.

Venice, however, was not known solely for its sophisticated and hedonistic lifestyle. The city's identity was also deeply rooted in an overwhelming passion for the arts, the influence of which spread throughout Europe. The many theatres were filled to capacity with enthusiastic audiences who noisily showed their appreciation for, or disapproval of, the operas staged with marvellous sets and costumes, the revived comedies of Carlo Goldoni or Carlo Gozzi's fantastical allegories. Exceptional musical conservatories were established in the foundling homes of the *Mendicanti*, *Derelitti* and the *Zitelle*, where the most famous Venetian maestros, such as Marcello, Galuppi, Albinoni and Vivaldi, instructed the girls in singing and playing instruments. This led to the foundation of numerous musical centres which gained huge popularity and international renown.

The eighteenth century also witnessed a remarkable period in Venetian painting. The sensuous and imaginative work of the city's figurative painters (such as Sebastiano Ricci or Giambattista Tiepolo), the harmonious rationality of the *vedutisti* (Canaletto and Francesco Guardi) and the unsettling and evocative intensity of Giovanni Battista Piazzetta's portraits, were evidence of tremendous vitality in the visual arts. Venetian art continued to be one of the driving forces of European culture.

Today, Venice finds itself once more approaching the turn of the century beset by crises and worries. Tourism has been transformed from the preserve of the very rich to a mass phenomenon. The city is still a Mecca for travellers from all over the world. Five million people visit the Piazza San Marco every year and the city is increasingly treated as a consumer item, quickly digested and superficially appreciated.

One way of solving this problem, of experiencing the true Venice, is to exploit the very fabric of the city. Many hotels can be found in old and wonderfully evocative buildings. The Dandolo on the Riva degli Schiavoni (now called Hotel Danieli), the Gritti on the Grand Canal (Gritti Palace Hotel) and the Gritti in the Campo della Bragora (La Residenza) are well-known examples of Gothic *palazzi* which immediately spring to mind. The charm of their surroundings is accentuated by the memory of illustrious former guests – Dickens, Wagner, Proust, Debussy, George Sand, Alfred de Musset, Ruskin and Hemingway.

A pleasant way of passing the time is to relax in one of the cafés, such as the Florian or the Quadri, which stand under the Procuratie arcades in the Piazza San Marco. Here you can experience the same atmosphere and elegant surroundings that Goldoni, Gozzi, Antonio Canova and Balzac would have enjoyed. Visit the church of Santa Maria della Pietà and listen to a Vivaldi concert and you will feel an even closer link with the past. This is the church where the 'red priest' himself composed and performed his music for an audience of exacting and enthusiastic aristocrats.

Some of the traditional festivals are still celebrated, evoking the hedonistic spirit of days gone by. Sit in a gondola in the historic regatta and become part of the long procession of richly decorated boats passing along the Grand Canal, recalling the welcome given by Venice to Catherine Cornaro, Queen of Cyprus. Or celebrate Carnival at a fancy-dress ball held in the sumptuous reception rooms of the Gothic Pisani-Moretta *palazzo*.

Designed by Giannantonio Selva in 1790–92, the interior of the Fenice Theatre was substantially altered in 1836 after a major fire. (BELOW)

The sumptuous reception hall of the Danieli Hotel. (ABOVE)

The Manfrediniana Gallery in the Seminario Patriarcale, the Querini-Stampalia Gallery, the Franchetti Gallery in the Ca' d'Oro and the Museum of Oriental Art in the Ca' Pesaro are equally important testaments to the Venetians' passion for collecting art. In some ways, the Peggy Guggenheim collection of Modern and Contemporary art in Venice can be regarded as a more recent example of the same tradition.

Two other important museums had very different beginnings. The Accademia Galleries were established in Napoleonic times partly for the education of pupils at the Academy of Fine Arts, but mainly to house paintings from the numerous secular and religious institutions abolished in Venice at the time. The original collection of the Museum of Modern Art dates from the end of the nineteenth century. It is made up of a selection of works from the early Biennales and demonstrates the prevailing feeling of the time that the cultural debate unfolding in Venice needed to reach an international level.

The difficulty faced by visitors in choosing between the many, often ill-defined, museums is one of the reasons why the municipality of Venice is currently undertaking the ambitious task of reorganizing its museum system. Tourists will be able to choose between four groups of museums, each run as a single unit: Contemporary art, Old Masters and Ancient art, eighteenth-century art and history, and Venice and its traditions. Each of these groups is to be equipped with an information service and booking offices located in four key points in the city – the Biennale pavilion in the Giardini di Castello, the Piazza San Marco, the Ca' Rezzonico and the Fóndaco dei Turchi. At present, the concentration of tourists around the Piazza San Marco, St Mark's Basilica and the Palazzo Ducale (which has over a million visitors each year) is too great. The new system should create a more even flow of tourists along the various cultural routes, especially as temporary exhibitions are gradually moved away from the overcrowded central area.

This complex scheme has two important aims. The first is to offer a well-thought-out, lively cultural itinerary which covers all the main museums so that the visitor can reconstruct the city's history

A second way of interpreting the past is to visit the many art collections in the state, municipal and private museums. Every rich and powerful patrician family in Venice regarded it almost as a duty to glorify the family name by owning as many works of art as possible, thereby creating a whole series of largely similar collections. After the fall of the republic in the nineteenth century, the interest in collecting art remained very much alive. Collections were built up, often eclectically, perhaps in part to preserve the memory of the city's former glory. So it was that in 1830, Teodoro Correr left to Venice a collection of thousands of objects housed in the family estate. Today, this forms the substantial core of exhibits at the municipal museums. Over the years, the collection has been enlarged with donations and acquisitions, and it has now been subdivided into various buildings.

and culture, and also to stimulate a desire to discover the contexts in which specific types of art evolved – particularly in the areas which lie between the museums. Venice is fortunate in that a very large number of masterpieces can still be seen in their original locations: churches, schools and public and private *palazzi*.

The second aim is to establish a permanent centre for contemporary visual art, architecture, cinema, theatre and music to supplement the prestigious programme of the Biennale and re-establish Venice as an international centre for artistic research and creation. Such an ambitious project represents an enormous challenge and the next few years should see the city transformed into a hub of ideas and activity.

As part of this process of regeneration Venice will need to find new, spacious exhibition areas (for example the Arsenal Corderie, the Procuratie in the Piazza San Marco or the Punta della Dogana), unearth some of the works of art currently lying in storerooms and reorganize the museums' collections along much more coherent and systematic lines. The management of each of the four groups of museums will be entrusted to a number of independent private foundations – though the city council will retain a supervisory role and a power of veto over possible initiatives which they consider to be against the interests of the city. It will also be necessary to co-ordinate the programmes of the municipal museums with those of other Venetian institutions, such as the Soprintendenza ai Beni Artistici e Culturali, the Biennale and other private foundations. Finally, Venice will have to co-operate with other international cultural centres, such as the Guggenheim Museum in New York and the Réunion des Musées Nationaux, in order to organize loans and exchange of collections and to co-curate temporary exhibitions.

Signs of this revival are already visible. The palace of Ca' Rezzonico, home to the Museum of Eighteenth-Century Venice, has recently been renovated along modern, functional lines. A more dynamic administration of the municipal museums has led to a reduction in their deficit from 7 billion to 3 billion lire in two years and they should soon be back in credit.

Venice is approaching the turn of the century at the centre of a close-knit network of local, national and international projects. Among a number of international initiatives, the role of the many private committees who work under the administrative umbrella of UNESCO's 'International Campaign for the Safeguarding of Venice' has become increasingly important over the past thirty years. As a result of their efforts, dozens of secular and religious buildings, monuments and individual works of art have been restored to their former glory. Save Venice, one of the most important private committees and one in which Sotheby's is actively involved, recently completed the restoration of the façade of Santa Maria dei Miracoli which overlooks the canal and is one of the earliest and finest examples of Venetian Renaissance architecture.

It is hoped that the setting up of four cultural itineraries will help to ease overcrowding in the most popular sites and will introduce visitors to other aspects of Venice. (ABOVE)

PRINCIPAL OFFICERS AND SPECIALISTS

Diana D. Brooks
President and
Chief Executive Officer

Simon de Pury
Chairman, Sotheby's Europe

Henry Wyndham
Chairman, Sotheby's
United Kingdom

John L. Marion
Honorary Chairman, Sotheby's
North and South America

Richard Oldenburg
Chairman, Sotheby's
North and South America

Julian Thompson
Chairman, Sotheby's Asia

George Bailey
Managing Director,
Sotheby's Europe

William F. Ruprecht
Managing Director, Sotheby's
North and South America

C. Hugh Hildesley
Executive Vice President,
Sotheby's North and South America

American Decorative Arts
and Furniture
Wendell Garrett
New York (212) 606 7137
Leslie B. Keno
New York (212) 606 7130
William W. Stahl, Jr.
New York (212) 606 7110

American Folk Art
Nancy Druckman
New York (212) 606 7225

American Indian Art
Ellen Napiura Taubman
New York (212) 606 7540

American Paintings, Drawings
and Sculpture
Dara Mitchell
New York (212) 606 7280
Peter B. Rathbone
New York (212) 606 7280

Animation and Comic Art
Jon Baddeley
London (0171) 408 5205
Dana Hawkes
New York (212) 606 7424

Antiquities and Indian Art
Richard M. Keresey (antiquities)
New York (212) 606 7328
Brendan Lynch (Indian)
London (0171) 408 5154
Felicity Nicholson (antiquities)
London (0171) 408 5111
Carlton Rochell (Indian)
New York (212) 606 7328

Applied Arts from 1850
Barbara E. Deisroth
New York (212) 606 7170
Philippe Garner
London (0171) 408 5138

Arms, Armour and Medals
David Erskine-Hill (medals)
London (0171) 408 5315 or
Sussex (01403) 783933
Nicholas McCullough (consultant)
New York (212) 606 7260

Books and Manuscripts
Paul Needham
New York (212) 606 7385
David N. Redden
New York (212) 606 7386
Stephen Roe
London (0171) 408 5286

British Paintings 1500–1850
David Moore-Gwyn
London (0171) 408 5406
Henry Wemyss (watercolours)
London (0171) 408 5409

British Paintings from 1850
Martin Gallon (Victorian)
London (0171) 408 5386
Susannah Pollen
(twentieth-century)
London (0171) 408 5388
Simon Taylor (Victorian)
London (0171) 408 5385

Ceramics
Peter Arney
London (0171) 408 5134
Letitia Roberts
New York (212) 606 7180

Chinese Art
Carol Conover
New York (212) 606 7332
Gong Jisui (paintings)
New York (212) 606 7334
Mee Seen Loong
Hong Kong (852) 2524 8121
Colin Mackay
London (0171) 408 5145
Julian Thompson
London (0171) 408 5371

Clocks and Watches
Tina Millar (watches)
London (0171) 408 5328
Daryn Schnipper
New York (212) 606 7162
Michael Turner (clocks)
London (0171) 408 5329

Coins
Tom Eden (ancient and Islamic)
London (0171) 408 5313
James Morton (English and
paper money)
London (0171) 408 5314
Paul Song
New York (212) 606 7391

Collectors' Department
Dana Hawkes
New York (212) 606 7424
Hilary Kay
London (0171) 408 5020

Contemporary Art
Elena Geuna
London (0171) 408 5401
Tobias Meyer
London (0171) 408 5400
Robert Monk
New York (212) 606 7254

European Works of Art
Margaret Schwartz
New York (212) 606 7250
Elizabeth Wilson
London (0171) 408 5321

English Furniture and
Decorations
Graham Child
London (0171) 408 5347
Larry J. Sirolli
New York (212) 606 7577
William W. Stahl, Jr.
New York (212) 606 7110

French and Continental
Furniture and Decorations
Phillips Hathaway
New York (212) 606 7213
Alexandre Pradère
Paris 33 (1) 4266 40 60
Mario Tavella
London (0171) 408 5052

Garden Statuary
James Rylands
Sussex (01403) 783933
Elaine Whitmire
New York (212) 606 7285

Glass and Paperweights
Simon Cottle
London (0171) 408 5133
Lauren K. Tarshis
New York (212) 606 7180

Impressionist and Modern
Paintings
Alexander Apsis
New York (212) 606 7360
Melanie Clore
London (0171) 408 5394

Philip Hook
London (0171) 408 5223
David J. Nash
New York (212) 606 7351
Andrew Strauss
Paris 33 (1) 42 66 40 60
Michel Strauss
London (0171) 408 5403
John L. Tancock
New York (212) 606 7360

Islamic Art and Carpets
Prof. John Carswell (works of art)
London (0171) 408 5153
Jacqueline Coulter (carpets)
London (0171) 408 5152
Richard M. Keresey (works of art)
New York (212) 606 7328
Brendan Lynch (works of art)
London (0171) 408 5154
Mary Jo Otsea (carpets)
New York (212) 606 7996

Japanese Art
Neil Davey
London (0171) 408 5141
Ryoichi Iida
New York (212) 606 7338
Suzanne Mitchell
New York (212) 606 7339

Jewellery
David Bennett
Geneva 41 (22) 732 85 85
John D. Block
New York (212) 606 7392
Alexandra Rhodes
London (0171) 408 5306

Judaica
David Breuer-Weil
Tel Aviv 972 (3) 22 38 22
Paul Needham (books)
New York (212) 606 7385
Camille Previté
London (0171) 408 5334
Jennifer Roth (paintings)
New York (212) 606 7518
Kevin Tierney (silver)
New York (212) 606 7160

Korean Works of Art
Henry Howard-Sneyd
London (0171) 408 5147
Ryoichi Iida
New York (212) 606 7268
Suzanne Mitchell
New York (212) 606 7339

Latin American Paintings
August Uribe
New York (212) 606 7290

Musical Instruments
Graham Wells
London (0171) 408 5341
New York (212) 606 7938

**Nineteenth-Century European
Furniture and Works of Art**
Jonathan Meyer
London (0171) 408 5350
Elaine Whitmire
New York (212) 606 7285

**Nineteenth-Century European
Paintings and Drawings**
Michael Bing
London (0171) 408 5380
Benjamin Doller
New York (212) 606 7140
Nancy Harrison
New York (212) 606 7140

Nineteenth-Century Sculpture
Christopher Gow
New York (212) 606 7140
Diana Keith Neal
London (0171) 408 5337

**Old Master Paintings and
Drawings**
Alexander Bell
London (0171) 408 5420
Frédéric Gourd
Paris 33 (1) 42 66 40 60
Gregory Rubinstein
(drawings)
London (0171) 408 5417
Scott Schaefer (drawings)
New York (212) 606 7222

Julien Stock
Rome 39 (6) 684 1791
George Wachter
New York (212) 606 7230

Oriental Manuscripts
Marcus Fraser
London (0171) 408 5332
Carlton Rochell
New York (212) 606 7328

Photographs
Denise Bethel
New York (212) 606 7240
Philippe Garner
London (0171) 408 5138
Beth Gates-Warren
New York (212) 606 7240

**Portrait Miniatures and
Objects of Vertu**
Heinrich Graf von Spreti
Munich 49 (89) 291 31 51
Gerard Hill
New York (212) 606 7150
Haydn Williams
London (0171) 408 5326

Postage Stamps
Richard Ashton
London (0171) 408 5224
Robert A.G.A. Scott
New York (212) 606 7288

Pre-Columbian Art
Stacy Goodman
New York (212) 606 7330
Fatma Turkkan-Wille
Zürich 41 (1) 422 30 45

Prints
Mary Bartow (19th & 20th C.)
New York (212) 606 7117
Nancy Bialler (Old Master)
New York (212) 606 7117
Nina del Rio (Contemporary)
New York (212) 606 7113
Jonathan Pratt
London (0171) 408 5212

Russian Paintings and Icons
Gerard Hill
New York (212) 606 7150
Ivan Samarine
London (0171) 408 5325
John Stuart
London (0171) 408 2173

Silver
Harold Charteris (Continental)
London (0171) 408 5106
Ian Irving
New York (212) 606 7160
Kevin L. Tierney
New York (212) 606 7160
Peter Waldron (English)
London (0171) 408 5104

Sporting Guns
Adrian Weller
Sussex (01403) 783933

Tribal Art
Jean G. Fritts
New York (212) 606 7325

Trusts and Estates
James Stourton
London (0171) 408 5435
Warren P. Weitman
New York (212) 606 7198

Veteran, Vintage and Classic Cars
Martin Chisholm
London (0171) 408 5320
David Patridge
Rumney NH (603) 786 2338

Western Manuscripts
Dr Christopher de Hamel, FSA
London (0171) 408 5330

Wine
Jamie Ritchie
New York (212) 606 7207
Serena Sutcliffe, MW
London (0171) 408 5045

INDEX

ACKNOWLEDGMENTS

PROJECT EDITOR Emma Lawson
ART EDITOR Ruth Prentice
COPY EDITOR Kate Bell
DESIGNER Claire Graham
PICTURE RESEARCH Helen Fickling
PRODUCTION Mano Mylvaganam

Pages 22–23: *A Tiffany favrile leaded glass landscape window (detail), c.1904–10, 148 x 130cm (4ft 10¼in x 4ft 3¼in) New York $118,000 (£75,520). 19.XI.94*

Pages 62–63: *Edouard Joseph Dantan,* Un coin du Salon, en 1880 (A view of the rooms at the Salon of 1880), *signed and dated 1880, oil on canvas, 97.2 x 130.2cm (38¼ x 51¼in) New York $211,500 (£135,360). 24.V.95*

Pages 276–277: *Paula Ingrand, Coffee table (detail), marked in the design P. Ingrand, 1930s, height 45.5cm (17⅞in) London £3,910 ($6,295). 31.III.95*

PUBLISHER'S ACKNOWLEDGMENTS
The publisher would like to thank Ronald Varney, William F. Ruprecht, Suzanne McMillan, Luke Rittner, Amanda Brookes, Lynn Stowell Pearson, Julie Liepold, Sandy Mallett, Alec Cobbe, Rebecca Hossack, Adrian Sassoon, Catherine Turner, Christopher Wood, David Lee and all the Sotheby's departments for their help with this book.

Thanks are also due to Julie Westbury for the illustrations to Wolf Mankowitz's 'Portrait of an Incorrigible Collector', which appear on pages 14, 16, 18–19 and 21. Julie Westbury is an artist and teacher living in London. Her work, which has appeared in numerous exhibitions, is researched in museums and collections throughout the world. She is currently a Senior Lecturer at Middlesex University.

Prices given throughout this book include the buyer's premium applicable in the saleroom concerned. These prices are shown in the currency in which they were realized. The sterling and dollar equivalent figures, shown in brackets, are based upon the rates of exchange on the day of the sale.

PHOTOGRAPHIC ACKNOWLEDGMENTS
The publisher would like to thank the following photographers and organizations for their kind permission to reproduce the photographs in this book:

24 Joshua White/Frank Gehry & Associates; 25 Richard Einzig/Arcaid; 26 Richard Bryant/Arcaid; 28 Richard Glover; 29 Hayes Davidson/The Tate Gallery, London; 30 Courtesy of Daniel Libeskind; 31 Herbert F. Johnson Museum of Art, Cornell University; 32 Richard Land *Mirror Images*/V-topia exhibition/Ikon Gallery, Birmingham, July 1995; 33 Courtesy of The Louvre, Paris; 35 Courtesy of The San Diego Museum of Art; 36–37 Kevin Atherton/Chelsea College of Art and Design; 38 Courtesy of The National Gallery, London; 40–41 Frank Thurston; 42 Stephen Archer/Courtesy of The Royal Bank of Scotland; 44 Peter Fotheringham/The Dean Centre/National Galleries of Scotland; 45 The Trustees of the Paolozzi Foundation/National Galleries of Scotland; 46 Frank Thurston; 48 Bill Batten/Hatchlands/The National Trust Photographic Library; 49 Alec Cobbe/Hatchlands; 50 *Country Homes & Interiors*/Robert Harding Syndication; 51 Ray Main/The Sunday Times Syndication; 52 Peter Aprahamian/Rebecca Hossack, private collection; 54 *above* Richard Bryant/Arcaid (architect Eva Jiricna); 54 *above right* and 55 Richard Glover/Adrian Sassoon, private collection; 56 The Hayward Gallery, London; 57 The Barbican Art Gallery, London; 59 The Tate Gallery, London, Presented by the National Art Collection Fund; 60 Harry Shunk/The Hayward Gallery, London; 61 *above* Centre Georges Pompidou, Paris; 61 *below* The Tate Gallery, London; 284 Chevalier Conservation; 285 The Textile Conservation Centre, Hampton Court Palace; 286–288 Gaspard de Wit; 289 *above* Chevalier Conservation; 289 *below* The Textile Restoration Studio, Cheshire; 296 Range/Bettmann; 297–301 Hearst San Simeon State Historical Monument; 302 Mike Newton; 303–304 Mark E. Smith/Arsenale Editrice, Venice, Italy (Arsenale Editrice and Mark E. Smith); 305 Mike Newton.

Sotheby's, Billingshurst: 198 *right*, 264 *above*.

Sotheby's, Geneva: 228, 232, 234 *above left*, 235 *above*, 236, 240, 241 *below*, 243 *left*, 245 *above*, 246 *below*, 250, 252 *below*, 264 *below*.

Sotheby's, Hong Kong: 170, 171 *below*, 172, 175, 259 *below*.

Sotheby's, London: 2 © Man Ray Trust, 6 *below*, 12 *above*, 67 *below*, 68–69, 74, 75 *below*, 77 *below*, 78–81, 82–84, 85 *above*, 86, 87 *above*, 89, 92, 94, 97, 99, 102–105, 108, 111–113, 128, 131–132, 135 *above* and *below* © Man Ray Trust, 137, 139 *above*, 140, 142–143, 145, 148–156, 158, 161 *above*, 162 *right*, 163–164, 165 *below*, 166, 168, 173, 178, 180 *above* and *below right*, 182, 189–190, 193 *below*, 196, 199–200, 201 *below*, 203 *below*, 204, 208 *right*, 209, 210 *right*, 215 *above*, 220–222, 224, 226, 227 *above right* and *below*, 229, 231 *above*, 238–239, 243 *right*, 244, 245 *below*, 246 *above left* and *centre*, 248, 251, 253 *below*, 258 *below*, 259 *centre*, 260, 261 *below*, 263, 265, 266, 268 *right*, 269, 271 *above*, 274 *above right* and *below*, 275, 276–281, 283 © Man Ray Trust, 290 © 1995 DACS, London, 291–292, 295.

Sotheby's, Los Angeles: 267.

Sotheby's, Milan: 13, 136.

Sotheby's, Monaco: 72, 159, 205 *below*, 206, 231 *below*.

Sotheby's, New York: endpapers, 1, 4–5, 6 *above* and *centre*, 10 © Succession H. Matisse /1995, DACS, London, 11, 12 *below*, 22–23, 62–63, 64–66, 67 *above*, 70–71, 73, 75 *above*, 76, 77 *above*, 85 *below*, 87 *below*, 88, 90, 91 *above*, 93, 96, 98, 100–101, 106–107, 109–110, 114–125, 129–130, 133–134, 138, 139 *below*, 141, 144, 146–147, 157, 160, 161 *below*, 162 *left*, 165 *above*, 167, 169, 174, 176–177, 179, 180 *below left*, 181, 183–188, 191–192, 193 *above*, 194–195, 197, 198 *left*, 201 *above*, 202, 203 *above*, 205 *above*, 207, 208 *left*, 210 *left*, 211–214, 215 *below*, 216–219, 223, 225, 227 *above left*, 233, 234 *above right* and *below left* and *right*, 235 *centre* and *below*, 237 *below*, 241 *above*, 242, 246 *above right*, 247, 249, 252 *above*, 253 *above*, 258 *above*, 259 *above*, 261 *above* and *centre*, 262, 268 *left*, 270, 271 *below*, 272 *above* and *below* © The Walt Disney Company, 273, 274 *above left*, 282, 293–294.

Sotheby's, St Moritz: 230, 237 *above*.

Sotheby's, Sydney: 127.

Sotheby's, Taipei: 171 *above*.

Sotheby's, Tel Aviv: 95.

Sotheby's, Toronto: 126.

Sotheby's, Zurich: 91 *below*.

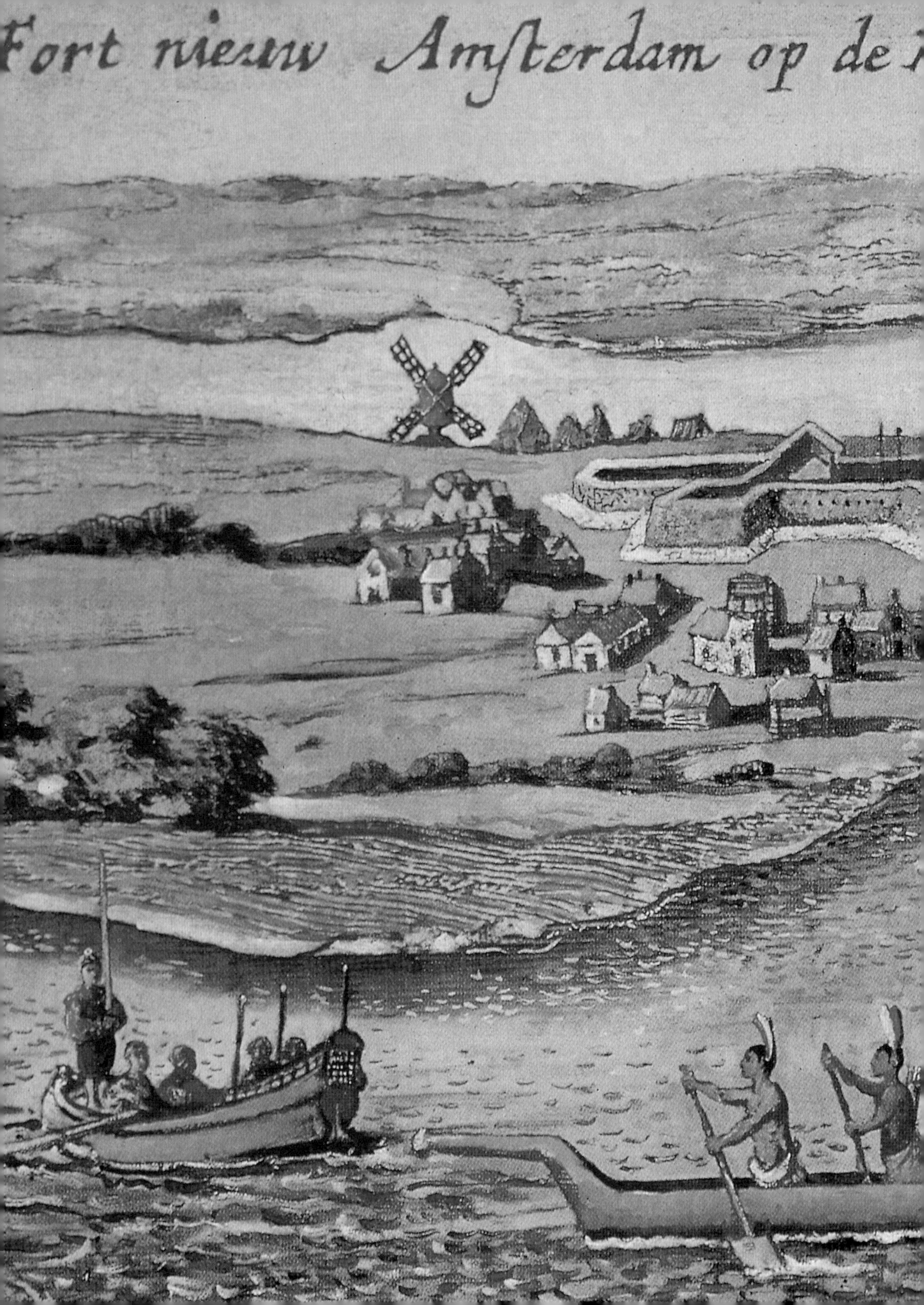
Fort nieuw Amsterdam op de